The Diesel Mechanics Student's Guide to Tractor-Trailer Operations
Second Edition

by

Mike Byrnes and Associates, Inc.
Publishers

Associate Member

Associate Member

3rd Printing

Other books by Mike Byrnes and Associates, Inc.:

BUMPER TO BUMPER®, The Complete Guide to Tractor-Trailer Operations, fourth edition
BUMPER TO BUMPER®, La guía completa para operaciones de autotransporte de carga (BUMPER TO BUMPER® in Spanish, published by Mike Byrnes and Associates, Inc.)
El Glosario, the BUMPER TO BUMPER® Spanish/English Glossary of Trucking Terms
Barron's How to Prepare for the Commercial Driver's License Truck Driver's Test (written by Mike Byrnes and Associates, Inc., published by Barron's Educational Series, Inc.)
Easy CDL apps for the iPhone and iPad (written by Mike Byrnes and Associates, Inc., published by Study By App, www.studybyapp.com)

TABLE OF CONTENTS

ACKNOWLEDGMENTS

Mike Byrnes and Associates, Inc. is a professional group, a network of resources that includes writers, editors, educators, artists and subject specialists experienced in truck driving and related occupations and concerns. Since 1987 we have developed and produced publications that address all skill levels: pre-employment or entry-level, on-the-job trainee and refresher. We specialize in materials that are easy to read. Our publications are written with the goal of meeting industry standards set by the Department of Transportation and other professional associations.

Mike Byrnes and Associates, Inc. has produced self-guided study programs for some of the country's largest combination home study/in-residence training schools. BUMPER TO BUMPER®, The Complete Guide to Tractor-Trailer Operations, is our original text on truck driving and related activities. It was first published in 1988 and has gone through numerous updates ever since.

We are grateful to Floyd Wyatt, Arizona Teamsters Apprenticeship and Training System and Bob Klauer, Metro Tech, Vocational Institute of Phoenix for the assistance that we received with the first edition of this mechanics student's guide to tractor-trailer operations. We also wish to thank PACCAR for the use of their illustrations. Thanks also to those who helped us with this second edition: Ron Brockman of Roadmasters Drivers School, Frank Baxter of North American Trade School and Gene Breeden of A-1 Truck Driving School.

PREFACE

Those in trucking like to explain how important the industry is to the American economy and way of life by saying, "If you have it, a truck probably brought it." Look around you now, right where you sit, and you'll begin to see the truth of that statement. There are few industries in America today that touch so many people in so many ways, every day. There are few industries that keep the nation's life blood pumping as much as trucking does.

And who keeps those trucks running? You—the diesel mechanic. Your job brings with it a lot of responsibility.

You must maintain the equipment and make sure it is safe. The health and safety of this nation's drivers and the motoring public may depend on the quality of your work.

You must keep those trucks running if the cargo transport industry is going to be cost effective or profitable. Trucks are not cheap. Neither is the maintenance on those trucks. It is your responsibility to help the truck owner get as many safe and economical miles as possible out of every piece of equipment. You do this by being a good diesel mechanic and by doing thorough, efficient work. That work will often require you to wear many hats. You'll wear an advisor's hat as you work with owners and drivers. You'll wear a troubleshooter's hat as you look for the seemingly impossible-to-find problem with the equipment. One of those hats will often put you behind the wheel of the rig you're working on. Thus being a topnotch diesel mechanic also means being a good truck driver. And that is why we have written this book.

We've been involved in training drivers of heavy trucks for decades, preparing them for a long, profitable and satisfying career. In the course of writing about the trucking industry, we've become more aware of the important role played by diesel mechanics. We wanted to write a book that would help mechanics have safe and successful careers contributing to the growth and safety of the trucking industry. That book would help make the workplace safe, protecting workers and employers from accidents. We also wanted a book that would help diesel mechanics become aware of the environmental impact of their work. Our goal was to offer a manual that was complete in giving a driver's, as well as a mechanic's, perspective of the equipment on a truck. Last, we wanted to help give mechanics a better appreciation for tractor-trailers and their drivers.

The book would have to be well illustrated. It had to have crisp, clear and accurate technical drawings as well as examples of the forms and reports that you will use in your work.

We wanted this book to be thorough. We wanted you to get more out of it than just a good knowledge of equipment or how to fill out an inspection report form. We wanted you to be able to communicate with the driver so the two of you could quickly identify problems and reach solutions.

To be successful, you must know more, do more and have a broader view of your responsibilities than ever before. You have to be able to read between the lines so you can relate a driver's vague complaint about a strange noise, smell or vibration to a mechanical problem in the truck.

If you feel the equipment is being abused, you'll want to be able to relay that information in a diplomatic way. If you notice a pattern of problems with a certain tractor or trailer, you'll want to recommend what can be done to keep the equipment out of the shop and on the road. All of this requires not only good mechanical skills but good communication skills as well.

Maintenance performed on equipment will never be a source of income to a trucking company. It will always be an expense. You, the mechanic, can do much to keep those expenses down. That makes you all the more valuable to your employer. We hope this book will help.

We also hope BUMPER TO BUMPER®, The Diesel Mechanics Student's Guide to Tractor-Trailer Operations, makes your training easy and enjoyable. If you have comments about the book, we'd love to hear them, be they criticisms or complaints. Just write us at BUMPER TO BUMPER,® The Diesel Mechanics Student's Guide to Tractor-Trailer Operations, Mike Byrnes and Associates, P. O. Box 8866, Corpus Christi, Texas, 78468-8866. Or, e-mail us at mbapub@aol.com. If you have a question or would like a reply, please say so in your letter and be sure to give us your address.

How This Book Is Organized

We know you are eager to start this book and get into learning about the total operation of tractors and trailers. Before you do, though, we hope you will read just a few more pages of introduction. We organized the book and put certain features in it to make reading easy. If you know about them, you should get more out of your reading.

FINDING YOUR WAY AROUND
The Table of Contents in BUMPER TO BUMPER,® The Mechanics Student's Guide to Tractor-Trailer Operations tells you the page number on which each chapter begins. Use the Table of Contents to go right to that part of the book you want to read or review. We've also indexed it for your convenience. The Index guides you to the location of material that deals with a particular subject. Say you want to find what the book has to say about the engine. Look up "engine" in the Index. Then go to the page or pages that are listed. Each one of those pages will have some material on the engine.

THE STRUCTURE OF THE CHAPTERS
You'll find that essential topics, words and key phrases are highlighted using **bold** type. So are the topic headings. Along with the lists of words with "bullets," these form a visible outline of the chapter. Use this outline to help focus your reading.

Scan the chapter by reading just the highlighted words before you read all the way through. This will give you an overview of what the chapter covers.

Then form mental questions about the subject matter you're about to read. Write these questions down. As you go through the chapter, read with an eye toward finding the answers. When you're done, look at your list of questions again. You should be able to answer all of them easily. If not, again scan the highlighted words for just that material which will answer the question.

Using this method, the material will fall into place more easily and stick with you longer. This "outline" will also help you when you return to the chapter for review. Scanning the words in bold may be all you need to do to recall the material.

Often, a picture can say it better than words, so BUMPER TO BUMPER® includes many technical illustrations and tables. They're numbered by chapter. For instance, the first illustration in Chapter 4 is numbered 4-1, "4" for Chapter 4 and "1" for first illustration, and so on.

ABOUT THE QUIZZES

You'll notice there are quizzes at the end of each chapter. They are designed to test your knowledge of the material presented in BUMPER TO BUMPER®, The Mechanics Student's Guide to Tractor-Trailer Operations. Your instructor may have you take these quizzes and turn them in for a grade. Even if you are not assigned the quizzes, you should take them anyway. They will help you measure your comprehension and progress.

If you're taking these quizzes on your own as open book tests, be sure to read the next section, Getting the Most in the Least Study Time. It includes valuable tips for answering the types of questions you'll find in this book. Then, to check your work, see your instructor for the answer key.

GETTING THE MOST IN THE LEAST STUDY TIME

Well, here you are, hitting the books — again. If you've been out of school for some time, you may be less than crazy about the idea. We want to assure you that this time around, things will be different. You'll probably enjoy and do better in your studies more now than you did in grade school. As an adult learner, your strong desire to succeed and your interest in the subject will help. Plus, BUMPER TO BUMPER, The Mechanics Student's Guide to Tractor-Trailer Operations is written in a practical, economical way so you don't have to read anything you won't use in your chosen career.

Still, if you don't have all the time in the world to study, you might appreciate some tips that will help you get the most in the least amount of time.

HAVE A PLAN OF ACTION

Your first step is to have a plan of action. When and where are you going to work on your studies? You'll have the easiest time of it if you work when you are alert, relaxed and free of distraction. Try to study at the same time every day or week. That helps make studying a habit.

Set yourself a goal, say, so many pages a session. Make this a reasonable goal. If you set your goal too high, you'll just feel bad when you fail to meet it. Instead, commit yourself to something doable. Then keep track of your progress. You'll feel an extra measure of accomplishment when you see how you are coming along. If you fall behind, you'll know to step up the pace so you don't have to cram it all in under pressure. Cramming is not a good learning method.

Find a good place in which to read, one where the noises of television, stereo and radio, not to mention other people, will not distract you. Read at a steady, even pace, with few interruptions. Have drinks, snacks or supplies you'll need in place before you sit down.

Work for about 45 minutes at a time. Then stop, stretch or walk around the room. This will give you the little mental break you need to keep from getting tired. Then go for another 45 minutes. Alternate good focused study with short breaks and in no time you will have met your goal for the session.

TEST FOR SUCCESS

The end of chapter test is also a type of learning aid. You may not have thought of a test this way before, but that's what it is. Answering questions helps you measure how well you understood what you read. If you can't answer some of the questions, you know just what parts you should review.

Here are some tips for answering questions you'll find in BUMPER TO BUMPER,® The Mechanics Student's Guide to Tractor-Trailer Operations.

TRUE/FALSE. Read the statement. Is the whole statement true? If so, select answer choice A, True. If any part of the statement is false, select answer choice B, False.

FILL IN THE BLANK. You're given a statement with some words missing. Fill in the blank with the word or words that will complete the statement and make it true.

MULTIPLE CHOICE. This is similar to fill-in-the-blank, except that some answers have been suggested. Only one of the choices is true. Here's how to go about finding which one.

Read the statement, filling in the blank with the material in the first answer choice, A. Does it make a true statement? If so, answer choice A is the correct choice. If not, ask yourself "why not?" Your response might lead you to the right answer choice. If this doesn't work, try the statement again, this time with the material in the next answer choice, B. Keep working through all the answer choices until you find the one that makes a true statement out of the question.

MATCHING. In these questions, you're asked to match items in one group with items in another group. Each item from one group will match one and only one other item from the other group.

YOUR ROLE IN THE TRUCKING INDUSTRY

As a diesel mechanic working on heavy trucks, **you are part of** an important industry, **an industry that employs more people than any other private industry in the United States.** The recent US Census reported over three million Americans worked as drivers in the trucking industry; nearly a quarter million workers served as heavy vehicle service technicians and mechanics.

The demands from within the trucking industry for good diesel mechanics are high but there are plenty of challenges diesel mechanics face before they become really good at what they do. Not only must you become good at working on those tractor-trailers, now you must be just as good at operating them.

Opportunities for Diesel Mechanics in the Trucking Industry

Mechanics who work on diesel trucks can be found in a variety of businesses. Each of those businesses has its own personality and working environment. Part of your role in the trucking industry will be determined by what type of business for which you want to work.

CARRIERS

Large trucking companies, or **carriers,** might **have a variety of trucks** on which you, along with a number of other mechanics, would be working. Other trucking companies might need only one mechanic or drive one type of truck. **Diesel mechanics who work for carriers have the added knowledge and responsibility of knowing the operating history of the trucks they repair.**

TRUCK STOPS

Truck stops hire diesel mechanics to work on trucks that might need maintenance while on the road. Professional drivers are always grateful for expert help, and the **reputations of the really good diesel mechanics** they find on the road **spread fast** and wide.

fig. 1-1
The trucking industry employs far more people than just drivers and mechanics.

INDEPENDENT GARAGES

Independent repair shops and garages inside and outside the city hire diesel mechanics to work on tractors brought in for repair by companies who do not have their own shop or drivers who find themselves stranded on a run. **Diesel mechanics working in garages** face the challenge and **benefit from the experience of constantly servicing a variety of truck makes and types.**

TRUCK DEALERSHIPS

Truck dealerships hire diesel mechanics to do warranty and other repair work, often on the trucks the dealership sells. This is **a great opportunity for diesel mechanics to get to know and become specialists with certain types of trucks.**

SCHOOLS

Truck driver training schools might hire a mechanic to keep their tractors and trailers road worthy. **Diesel mechanics schools are always looking for instructors with an excellent diesel mechanics background and good communication skills.** If you enjoy sharing what you know with others, this may be something to look into down the road.

LOCAL AND STATE GOVERNMENT

Highway departments employ mechanics to keep their vehicles and equipment operating safely and efficiently. **Cities and towns have fleets with all kinds of trucks and equipment** in a variety of numbers. Here you'll see not only tractor-trailers but light and medium duty trucks, machinery and possibly even boats.

fig. 1-2
This carrier's
organizational chart
shows how the different
jobs in trucking are
related.

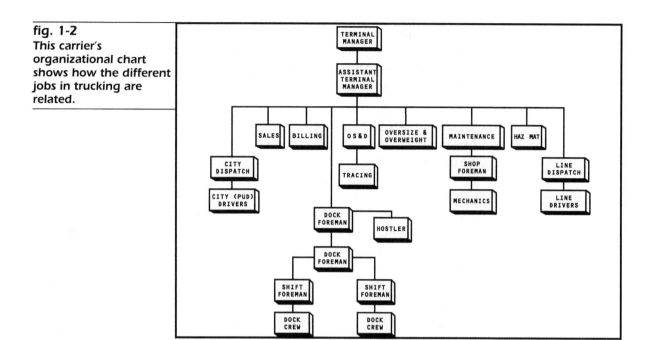

Getting Your CDL

As we mentioned earlier, a key ingredient to your success as a diesel mechanic will depend upon your ability to operate a commercial motor vehicle. This means **you'll need a Commercial Driver's License** (CDL).

WHAT THE CDL IS AND WHO NEEDS IT

Since the Motor Carrier Act of 1980, when trucking was deregulated, many new truck operators entered the industry. Trucking accidents went up almost 20 percent.

Most of the increase was tied to the truck driver. Unethical drivers carried several states' driver's licenses in hopes that bad driving records would get lost in the shuffle. Truck drivers used legal and illegal drugs and alcohol to battle fatigue and stress. Some truck drivers carried two or more log books and drove as much as 100 hours a week. Others cut corners by driving unsafe vehicles.

These are just some of the reasons the public began calling their elected officials for help. They demanded action to take the bad driver off the road. They wanted to feel safe again when they drove alongside an 18-wheeler. They wanted to bring back the super driver, the competent, honest professional who would stop and help a motorist in trouble.

The Commercial Motor Vehicle Safety Act (CMVSA) was passed in 1986 partly in response to this demand. The goal of the CMVSA is expressed in the Federal Motor Carrier Safety Regulations (FMCSR) Subpart A, Section 383, item 1. This states " The purpose of this part is

to help reduce or prevent truck and bus accidents, fatalities, and injuries by requiring drivers to have a single commercial motor vehicle driver's license and by disqualifying drivers who operate commercial motor vehicles in an unsafe manner."

WHEN A DIESEL MECHANIC NEEDS A CDL

So what does all of this have to do with you? You're the mechanic, not the driver, right? Wrong!

The regulations in FMCSR section 383 contain the guidelines for the Commercial Driver's License (CDL)program. **These regulations require everyone who operates a commercial motor vehicle to have certain knowledge and skills.** As a diesel mechanic, you will sometimes find yourself on public roads behind the wheel of a truck or tractor. Every time you are on these roads, you will have to have a valid CDL in your possession. **Even if your time behind the wheel is limited to taking a test drive** down the road or transporting an out-of-service vehicle just a mile or so into the shop, **you must have a Commercial Driver's License.**

A FEW CDL REQUIREMENTS

Just like full time drivers, you will have to show you have the required knowledge and skill to drive a tractor-trailer. **You will have to pass** the same **written and skills tests** that full time drivers must pass. These are given under the direction of your state's Department of Motor Vehicles. Then you will receive a CDL and be able to drive a heavy truck on public roads.

Even though you will be driving a truck only irregularly, **your driving and employment records must be** as **clean** as those of full time drivers. **Employers are required to check the employment records of driver applicants as far back as 10 years. Employed drivers must notify their employer and home state in writing when they receive a violation or suspension.** There are federal penalties involved for persons convicted of criminal acts and traffic violations, such as driving under the influence of drugs or alcohol (DUI). It is a serious offense to conceal or hide the truth about past records.

If you are seeking to enter the industry, you must understand just how serious the problem has become. To keep your record clean, you must say no to drugs and no to alcohol. Value and preserve the quality of work you do whether you plan to be a diesel mechanic, dispatcher or driver.

Advances in the Trucking Industry

What will the future bring to diesel mechanics and the trucking industry? Which way is the industry leaning? What are the trends?

Recent advances in the trucking industry that are **directly related to diesel mechanics include:**

- improved and longer-lasting equipment
- faster and more accurate communications
- new technologies in the truck and in the shop
- greater efficiency and more economy
- improved highway designs
- more emphasis on safety and environmental concerns

IMPROVED EQUIPMENT

As technology in the trucking industry moves forward, so does equipment. Computers now aid nearly every system in the truck. Hybrid metals, fuels, materials and designs for engines, brakes, suspensions, cooling systems and other parts of the truck help to keep it going as the demands on the truck increase.

COMMUNICATIONS

Advances in communications are bringing more efficient service. Mechanics and dispatchers are in constant contact with drivers. They can use two-way radios, mobile telephones, fax machines, toll-free numbers and even the Internet to reach any driver at any given time and place. Mobile phones allow the mechanic to offer troubleshooting tips to the driver over the phone without the driver ever leaving the truck.

A device placed in a truck can send signals to a satellite. The satellite can then return these signals to a computer at the company's terminal. In this way, the computer can track the truck and show on a screen where the truck is at any time. The dispatcher and driver can communicate instantly, by voice or electronically.

But in order to have all this modern technology work for a company, that **company must have mechanics who are skilled troubleshooters.** They must **also be able to communicate well with drivers.**

NEW TECHNOLOGIES ON THE TRUCK AND IN THE SHOP

Other electronic advances are playing a large part in the make-up of the truck itself. Some cabs have less wiring because sensors transmit signals to the dashboard instruments. A truck's onboard computer can transmit a printout of a trip sheet within minutes of arrival — even in route — showing fuel use, idling time and other important information. The same computer can pinpoint problems that affect economy or wear and tear on the truck.

The **advances in technology** haven't been limited to just the truck. Shops now have the technology to isolate nearly every problem with an engine. Improvements in electronic analysis equipment help every mechanic to diagnose problems better and make repairs more confidently.

fig. 1-2
Trucks on the road can now be tracked by satellites.

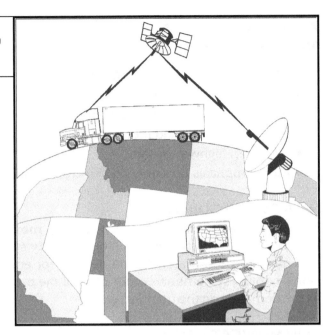

This means, however, that diesel mechanics must have the **math and reading skills** to be able to comprehend and calculate this information and come to the correct maintenance conclusions.

GREATER EFFICIENCY AND MORE ECONOMY

Because of the stiff competition in trucking industry, **carriers are doing everything they can to be efficient and operate economically.** New designs in trucks have been developed to reduce wind drag. Electronic fuel injection meters fuel into the engine better than older systems. Extra wide and extra long trailers were authorized for use on the interstate a few years ago which means trucks are hauling heavier loads.

IMPROVED ROADS

The roads themselves have improved right along with the trucks. Highway designs have hit new highs. New stretches of highways are designed to keep the driver alert and awake. Special surfaces allow rain to run off and make for better traction. Many on- and off-ramps are now lighted with nonglare lamps. Safety rules have been rewritten. Hazardous material handling has been tightened up. The result has been **greater safety for all** those using the public roads, truck drivers and motorists alike.

SAFETY CONCERNS

Mechanics who work on trucks and the drivers who drive them face increasingly stiff safety regulations. Governmental agencies such as **The Federal Highway Administration (FHWA), Occupational Safety and Health Administration (OSHA), National Institute for Occupational Safety and Health (NIOSH) and Mine Safety and Health Administration (MSHA) provide standards and regulations** that directly affect everyone in the shop and on the road. Mechanics must keep pace with technology and changes in the industry. As companies in the industry become more specialized, so must the mechanic. Trucks must pass strict inspections. Drivers and mechanics must meet physical, knowledge and skill requirements to drive on the road legally.

In fact, your role in promoting commercial vehicle safety is protected by the federal government. If you become aware of an actual or potential health or safety hazard at the workplace, you should report it. In most cases of working for a private company, "whistleblower" protection laws provide that your employer may not penalize you for doing this. Some states provide this protection for government employees, also. Your employer may not discharge, discipline or discriminate against you regarding your pay, terms or privileges of employment if, in **report**ing a violation of a **workplace health or safety regulation** you:

- filed a complaint
- began a proceeding
- testified in a proceeding
- will testify in a proceeding

You may call the toll free number 1-888-DOT-SAFT to make complaints about such violations or make them online using a secure system at http://www.1-888-DOT-SAFT.com.

ENVIRONMENTAL ISSUES
With the help of the Environmental Protection Agency (EPA), more companies are taking the environment seriously. **As a mechanic, a big part of your job will be working to meet or exceed EPA standards.** Trucks must pass rigid emissions tests. Used oil and hazardous waste collected on-site must be disposed of properly.

Your Future as a Diesel Mechanic

Highways are always being upgraded and the CDL testing program is putting better commercial drivers behind the wheel. As for the trucks themselves, if there is any **trend in** the area of **diesel mechanics**, it's **toward government regulations demanding efficient rigs that create less pollution. And that requires a better understanding between diesel mechanics who work on tractor-trailers and the drivers who drive them.** The more drivers put themselves in the shoes of the mechanic, the better care they will give their rig. By the same token, the more mechanics see through the eyes of the driver, the more they can appreciate the normal wear and tear a tractor receives. That makes the mechanic better able to service that tractor.

Chapter 1 Quiz

1. The trucking industry employs more people than any other private industry in the United States.
   A. True
   B. False

2. The FHWA and OSHA are two private associations that provide insurance and medical benefits to mechanics.
   A. True
   B. False

3. Which of the following is NOT an advance in the trucking industry?
   A. improved and longer-lasting equipment
   B. smaller load capacity
   C. greater efficiency and more economy
   D. faster and more accurate communications

4. Employers are required to check employment records as far back as 10 years for new hires.
   A. True
   B. False

5. Advances in technology make math and reading skills less important to a diesel mechanic.
   A. True
   B. False

6. One of the goals of the CMVSA is to prevent truck accidents.
   A. True
   B. False

7. _____ is not a government agency.
   A. MSHA
   B. FMCSR
   C. NIOSH
   D. FHWA

8. Diesel mechanics working in independent garages benefit from the experience of constantly servicing the same type of truck makes.
   A. True
   B. False

9. A good diesel mechanic must also be a good _____ .
   A. communicator
   B. troubleshooter
   C. driver
   D. all of the above

10. Diesel mechanics need a CDL to test drive a rig on public roads.
    A. True
    B. False

CHAPTER 2
DASHBOARD AND GAUGES

Getting into the Truck

The previous chapter gave you a good general knowledge of the trucking industry. It got you into the industry. In this chapter, we're going to get you into the truck. You'll begin to learn more of the specifics you'll need to know in order to maintain and drive a tractor-trailer. We'll go inside the tractor to take a look at the dashboard. You'll get a basic introduction to the components of the dashboard and to the systems those components monitor or control.

The first thing you will notice when you actually get into the truck and sit behind the wheel is **the dashboard.** The dashboard is also called a dash or instrument panel. Figure 2-1 on the next page shows you an example of the gauges, switches, lights and controls you'll find on a modern dashboard.

The dash houses a variety of **gauges and warning lights.** Some of these **monitor** the operating condition of **the engine.** Others **monitor** the operating condition of the engine's **auxiliary systems.** Each gauge and warning light has its own function.

Besides gauges and warning lights, there are also switches and controls on the dash. The **switches and controls** are used to **operate the vehicle.** An example of these is the parking light switch. When you activate this switch, you turn on the parking lights.

On the modern dash, gauges, lights, switches and controls are grouped together in clusters. These clusters are called **instrument clusters.** Figure 2-1 illustrates this.

Be aware, though, that all dashboards are not the same. They all have very nearly the same gauges, switches, lights and controls. They all tend to cluster these components, though not necessarily in the same way. They all tend to place the components used most often closer to the driver. However, you should note that the **arrangement of the clusters differs from truck to truck,** too. That is why you must become familiar with the dash of a truck before you drive it or do any work on it.

fig. 2-1
On a modern dashboard, you'll find components clustered according to their function.

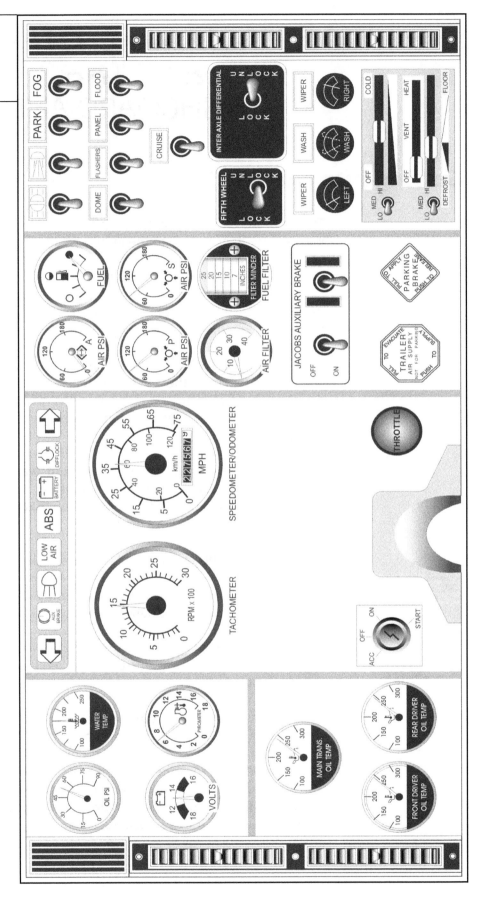

Using Figure 2-1 as a guide, let's take a quick look at the instrument panel to find out what's there and exactly where it is. Then, we'll look at each component more closely and you'll learn what each one does.

Dashboard Components

Let's start at the far left of the illustration. The first thing you'll see is an **air conditioning vent.** Next to the vent you'll notice four gauges. These four gauges make up **the engine cluster.** From left to right, the two on top are the oil pressure gauge and the engine coolant temperature gauge. The two on the bottom from left to right are the voltmeter and the pyrometer. You'll learn what a pyrometer is later in this chapter.

Below the engine cluster is a small cluster that we'll call **the unit cluster.** It includes gauges that tell you the temperature of various parts of the tractor. Most often, there will be a transmission temperature gauge and two rear axle gauges, one for the forward rear axle and one for the rear rear axle.

Next we have **the warning lights cluster.** Sometimes these lights are accompanied by buzzers to make sure you know there is a problem you must attend to immediately.

We'll call the gauges and controls behind the steering wheel **the steering wheel cluster.** Here you'll find the ignition switch, the tachometer, the speedometer/odometer and the throttle.

Next, moving from left to right, is another series of gauges. Those on top are **the brake application gauge and the fuel gauge.**

Under this cluster is **the air supply pressure gauge.** The left gauge shows the air pressure in the primary system. The right gauge shows the air pressure in the secondary system. The large cluster below the air gauges is made up of.

- the air pressure gauge
- the brake pressure gauge
- the air filter gauge
- the system parking brake knob
- the auxiliary brake controls
- the trailer air supply knob
- the parking brake knob

On the top right side of the dash is **the lights cluster.** It includes all the light switches except the dimmer switch, which may be on the turn signal stalk. You'll learn more about this switch later in this chapter.

Below the lights cluster is **the controls cluster.** We call it that because it consists of the controls that haven't fit into any other cluster. Here you'll find the fifth wheel slide control, the inter-axle differential control, the windshield wipers controls and the heater and air conditioning controls.

Next to the lights cluster and the control cluster is another air conditioning vent.

That ends our get-acquainted tour of the dashboard. Now we'll focus on each cluster and tell you what each gauge shows and what each control and switch does. Then we'll take a quick look at the controls in the rest of the cab, including the pedals on the floor of the cab, the trailer brake hand control valve and the transmission control lever.

The Engine Cluster

THE ENGINE OIL PRESSURE GAUGE

This gauge **tells you the oil pressure in the engine.** When the oil is cold, the gauge will show a high reading. After the engine has warmed up, the reading should return to normal. Measurements are displayed in pounds per square inch gauge (psig) which most people refer to simply as pounds per square inch or psi.

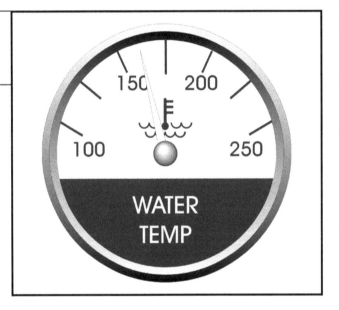

fig. 2-2
The water temperature gauge tells you the temperature of the engine coolant.

Always check this instrument after starting the engine. Oil pressure should come up in a few seconds. **If no pressure shows, stop the engine at once.** You can ruin the engine by running it with no oil pressure.

When the engine is running at normal temperatures and the oil is hot, the normal idle pressure runs from 10 to 20 psi and the **normal operating pressure runs from 30 to 75 psi.** The oil pressure gauge in Figure 2-1 is at 55 psi. That means our truck is running in the normal range. Refer to the manual provided for the equipment showing specific gauges.

THE WATER TEMPERATURE GAUGE

This gauge is usually marked "Temp" or "Water Temp." **It shows the engine cooling system temperature.** The gauge displays measurements in degrees. A typical gauge will have a range of 100 to 250 degrees Fahrenheit.

In **normal** operation, the gauge may read between 165 and **210 degrees Fahrenheit.** The gauge may read higher when the truck is pulling a heavy load upgrade or operating in hot weather. If the temperature goes above the safe limit, the high engine temperature warning light will come on. In some cabs, a warning buzzer will sound, too.

THE VOLTMETER

This gauge **shows the charge condition of the battery.** The voltmeter is identified by the word "Volts" shown on the lower portion of the gauge. There is often a diagram of a battery as well as the word "Volts."

The voltmeter has a colored band divided into three segments. Each of these segments indicates a different battery condition. The left-hand red segment indicates an undercharged battery. The middle green segment indicates normal battery condition. The right-hand red segment indicates an overcharge condition. The gauge pointer indicates in which condition the battery is. If the voltmeter indicates a continuous undercharging or overcharging condition, there is probably a malfunction in the charging system. The voltmeter in Figure 2-1 is in the normal range.

THE PYROMETER

The pyrometer **tells you the engine exhaust temperature.** Because it shows changes in the exhaust temperatures almost as soon as they occur, this gauge is a very good indicator of how hard the engine is working. The safe temperature range will be shown on the dashboard next to the gauge or on the gauge. Stay within that range. High exhaust temperature indicates inefficient engine operation. It can damage the turbocharger and other engine parts.

The Unit Temperature Cluster

Unit temperature gauges monitor temperature in the various components of the truck. Some of these parts are in **the transmission** and the rear axle differentials. Some trucks have a gauge for **the forward rear axle differentials** and a gauge for **the rear rear axle differentials.** These gauges are usually clearly marked for the component they monitor.

Like the engine temperature gauge, the unit temperature gauges display measurement in degrees. A high temperature reading will alert you to problems in that particular part. If the temperature is high, you should stop the truck before damage occurs.

Oil temperatures in transmissions normally range from 180 to 250 degrees Fahrenheit. The normal range for axles is from 160 to 250 degrees Fahrenheit. Use these ranges as guidelines only. Your best source of information is the operators manual and the driver's experience of what normal temperatures are for the vehicle. If the temperature goes higher, you need to do something.

The Warning Lights Cluster

As with all the gauges, controls and switches in this chapter, the **placement of the warning lights cluster varies from truck to truck.**

This cluster is often called the telltale panel. Each individual warning light will be clearly marked. Some of these warning lights tell you a control is working. Some tell you a control or gauge is not working. Some of them tell you there is a problem that demands immediate attention.

To get to know these lights, let's begin at the left and move toward the right. We've included the identifying symbols.

- the left hand turn signal (L.H.)
- the water temperature warning light (WATER)
- the high beam light (H.B.)
- the low air pressure warning light (AIR)
- anti-lock brake system (ABS)
- battery
- differential lock warning light (D.L.)
- the right hand turn signal (R.H.)

The **turn signal indicator lights** should come on whenever you use the right or left turn signal. If they don't come on, that's a warning something is wrong. It could be the warning light or the signal itself. Check it out. The turn signals are important safety tools for communicating with other drivers when the vehicle is in motion. Also, it's illegal to drive without them.

The water temperature, low oil pressure and low air pressure warning lights should not come on. If they do, that's a warning something is wrong. The **water temperature warning light** will come on if the water temperature in the cooling system gets too high. The **low oil pressure warning light** will come on when the oil pressure is too low. The **low air pressure warning light** will come on if the air pressure in the braking system drops **below 60 psi.** The **low water level warning light** will come on if—you guessed it—the **water level is low.** These warning lights often have buzzers that sound, too. As you can see, they are really back-up systems for the gauges.

The high beam and differential lock lights are **reminders.** The **high beam light** reminds you the high beam is on. The **differential lock light** reminds you the differential lock is in the locked position. You'll learn about the differential lock control later in this chapter.

When you start up the truck, the lights on the warning light cluster should come on for a few moments to show they are working, then go out. If you have a light that doesn't come on, check to see if it is in fact broken. If you have one light that stays on after the others go out, you should check for problems in that system.

The Steering Wheel Cluster

THE TACHOMETER

A tachometer (also called a tach) **shows engine crankshaft revolutions per minute** (rpm). A tachometer can be mechanical or electrical.

The tachometer **tells you when it's time to shift gears.** To determine the engine rpm, you multiply the number shown on the tachometer by 100. For example, 15 on the tach means 1,500 rpm.

The number of revolutions per minute an engine can turn differs from engine to engine. An average high horsepower diesel only turns up to 2,100 rpm. The range of the engine may go from 500 rpm (idle speed) to 2,100 rpm. The typical operating range is even shorter. Stay within the operating range for good engine performance.

Engine speeds in most engines are **governed.** This means that the number of rpm the engine will make in any gear is limited. If you want to see how many rpm the engine is turning, just look at the tach. This is called "driving by the tach."

THE SPEEDOMETER/ODOMETER

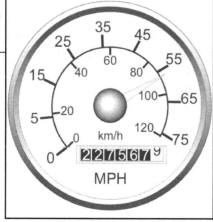

fig. 2-3
The speedometer gauge is combined with an odometer.

The speedometer **shows truck speed in miles per hour** (mph). It may be mechanical or electrical. Inside the speedometer is an odometer. The **odometer keeps track of the total miles** the truck is driven. Mileage is shown in miles and sometimes tenths of miles.

THE IGNITION SWITCH

The ignition switch **turns on the truck electrical systems and turns the engine over so it can**

start. A truck may have a starter button you push in, or the starter may take a key. When the key is straight up and down, the switch is off. When the key is turned to the left, the accessory circuits are on. By turning the key to the right (on) position, the accessory and ignition circuits are turned on. By turning the key to the far right (start position), the starter switch is engaged.

Release the key as soon as the engine turns over. After a false start, do not operate the starter again until the engine has stopped completely. Let the starter cool for 30 seconds before trying again.

THE HAND THROTTLE

The hand throttle is a kind of accelerator on the dash. It can be **pulled out to set a specific engine speed,** or rpm. You could use the throttle in extremely cold weather to keep the engine warm when idling. You might also use it to get engine speed up and deliver more power to operate a power take-off (PTO) device. You'll learn about PTOs later in this chapter.

CRUISE CONTROL

The **cruise control acts much like the hand throttle,** but as the name implies, you will use the cruise control after you reach highway speeds. A switch turns the cruise control on and a second switch or button is used to set the desired cruise speed.

The Fuel Cluster

THE FUEL GAUGE

The fuel gauge **indicates the fuel** level in the supply tanks. Most fuel gauges are electrically operated. The fuel gauge is connected to a sending unit in the supply tank. Some trucks use more than one fuel supply tank. If this is the case, be sure to check the fuel level in all tanks before assuming you're out of fuel. The fuel gauge in Figure 2-1 shows the tank is full.

THE FUEL FILTER GAUGE

This gauge **indicates the condition of the fuel filter.** It is marked "Fuel Filter." It has a colored band divided into two segments. The left segment is white. The middle and right segments are red. It also has numbered markings. The fuel filter is clogged if the needle reads in the red range.

The Brake Cluster

THE AIR PRESSURE GAUGE

This gauge is used on trucks equipped with air brakes and is identified by the word "Air" on the lower portion of its face. (Because the vehicle has a dual air braking system, there will be a gauge for each half of the system. Such a vehicle might have two gauges, or one gauge with two needles.) One gauge will be marked as the primary (P) or as (1). The other gauge will be marked as secondary (S) or (2). The air pressure gauge shows a reading in pounds per square inch (psi). It indicates **psi available in the reservoirs for braking power.**

Use the air pressure gauge to check the operation of the air compressor. It is an important safety indicator. The **normal** gauge reading **is 100 to 120 psi.** The pressure will vary in this range because of compressor operation and brake application.

Don't drive a truck with air brakes until the gauge reads **at least 100 psi.** Should the pressure drop below 90 pounds when you are driving the truck, stop immediately. If you don't, pressure may continue to drop and the emergency spring brakes may come on automatically.

THE LOW AIR PRESSURE WARNING DEVICE

We mentioned this device when we looked at the warning lights cluster. However, since it's part of the air brake system, we'll discuss it in greater detail here. All trucks with air brakes also have a **low air pressure warning device.** The device must be easily seen or heard, and it's usually a light or a buzzer. Sometimes it's both. It gives a continuous warning whenever the air pressure drops below a safe level, usually 60 psi. The warning won't stop until the air pressure exceeds 60 psi.

THE AIR BRAKE APPLICATION GAUGE

This gauge **shows the amount of pressure applied to the brakes.** Naturally, a heavy brake application will cause a higher reading than a light brake application. When the brakes are released, the gauge pointer should return to zero.

THE ENGINE AIR FILTER GAUGE

This gauge **indicates the condition of the air filter.** It's marked "Air Filter." If the gauge reads in the red area, you have a clogged air filter. A clogged air filter should be cleaned or changed right away. It's important to keep the air filter clean because a clogged air filter restricts air flow. Restricted air flow interferes with the operation of the engine.

THE AUXILIARY BRAKE OR ENGINE RETARDER

Some trucks use engine retarders **to help the service brakes slow the truck down.** The controls needed to operate the retarder are located on the dash. Our example in Figure 2-1 shows controls for the Jacobs auxiliary brake, also called the Jake Brake. Auxiliary brakes will be discussed in Chapter 16. You'll learn when and how they're used.

THE TRAILER AIR SUPPLY VALVE KNOB

The trailer air supply valve controls the tractor protection valve (TPV) which is usually under the left rear of the cab. The trailer air supply valve supplies air to the trailer. The TPV **prevents the loss of tractor air pressure in a trailer breakaway.** If the trailer air lines break, the TPV automatically shuts off the air supply to the trailer. This unit was designed to function automatically. However, it can be operated manually.

fig. 2-4
The trailer air supply controls the tractor protection valve which protects the tractor brake air supply in case of emergency .

The trailer air supply valve knob is labeled, colored red and eight-sided, like a stop sign. It has two positions, normal and emergency. When it's in the normal position, the service and emergency brakes of both the tractor and the trailer are functional. However, if there is a large air loss from the trailer, the TPV will close automatically and the knob will pop out to the emergency position. This closes the air lines leading to the trailer which automatically set the trailer brakes, and protects the air in the tractor from loss. If the air in the tractor is lost, the tractor service brakes cannot work and the emergency brakes will come on.

You should manually pull this control knob out to the emergency position whenever you couple or uncouple a trailer. You should also pull it out when you bobtail (drive the tractor without a trailer). Once a trailer is coupled to the tractor, return the trailer air supply valve knob to the normal position. The control should be in the normal position whenever a trailer is coupled to the tractor.

THE PARKING BRAKE VALVE

This control knob is labeled, colored yellow and diamond shaped. It should be applied when you park the rig. It **applies the parking brakes for both the tractor and the trailer.** To apply this brake, pull the knob out. To release, push the knob in.

THE TRACTOR PARKING BRAKE VALVE

On trucks equipped with this optional valve, this control knob is labeled, blue in color and round in shape. It **applies the tractor parking brakes only.** To apply the tractor parking brakes, pull the knob out.

To release the tractor parking brakes, push the knob in. You'll use these brakes when coupling or uncoupling.

The Lights Cluster

From left to right, the light switches listed below are in the lights cluster on the dashboard shown in Figure 2-1. Light control switches can be **toggle switches** (levers that pivot), **rocker (flip) switches or push/pull buttons.** Each switch will be clearly marked to indicate which lights it controls. Remember that dashboards differ from truck to truck. Nearly every truck will have a lights cluster. It may not have all the light switches in the following list, or it may have many more.

- headlights switch
- clearance lights switch
- parking lights switch
- fog lights switch

- dome light switch
- emergency flashers switch
- panel lights switch
- flood light switch

You'll often find the emergency flasher control (usually with the turn signal flasher), the dome light and the panel light switches closer to the steering wheel. In Figure 2-1, the headlights and clearance lights switches are labeled with a symbol or icon. These icons are used on many dashboards to designate the headlights and the clearance lights. You will learn how these lights, the parking, fog and emergency lights, must be used as you read the following chapters. The dome light lights the inside of the cab. The panel light lights up the dashboard. The flood light is used at night when a driver needs to check the load on the road or in an emergency.

The Controls Cluster

THE FIFTH WHEEL SLIDE CONTROL
This control is used **to lock the fifth wheel in position.** It allows you to slide the fifth wheel back and forth to distribute the weight better.

THE INTER-AXLE DIFFERENTIAL
If a rig has dual rear axles it may have an inter-axle differential and an inter-axle differential control. The inter-axle differential **allows the front axle to turn at a different speed than the rear axle.** When the control is set at the unlocked position, the inter-axle differential lets each axle shaft and wheel turn at a different speed than the others. The control should be set on the unlocked position unless the road surface is slippery and traction is poor. Then the control should be put in the locked position, locking the front and rear axles so power will go equally to both rear axles. Do not run on dry roads with the inter-axle

differential in the locked position. You could damage it. You'll learn more about inter-axle differentials in Chapter 7, on the drive train.

THE WINDSHIELD WIPERS

Truck windshield wipers are operated by air or electricity. Usually, **wipers** have **two controls, one for each wiper.** To turn the wiper on low speed, the knob is turned to the first position to the right. To operate the wiper on high speed, the knob is turned to the second position to the right. To turn the wiper off, the knob is turned all the way to the left.

Some air wiper systems use one control knob for both wipers. It's located on the dash. Others have one control knob for each wiper. To turn the wipers on, turn the knobs to the right. To turn the wipers off, turn the knobs to the left. Wiper speeds are controlled by the position of the knobs.

There is a **separate knob for the windshield washers.** In Figure 2-1, it's located between the wiper controls.

THE AIR CONDITIONING CONTROLS

Cab temperature is easily controlled in modern trucks. There may be up to nine air outlets in the cab and two in the sleeper. It may be hard to believe there is enough room in the cab for such a large dashboard and so many other cab controls. Fan speed controls include low, medium and high. Controls are included for cooling, heating and defrosting.

The Rest of the Cab

That finishes our tour of the dashboard. So, we'll leave the dashboard and tour the controls in the rest of the cab. Let's start with the pedals on the floor of the cab.

THE ACCELERATOR PEDAL

You'll find the accelerator on the floor of the cab under the steering wheel. You **use your right foot** to operate this pedal and **control engine speed.** When you depress the pedal, the speed of the vehicle increases. As you let your foot off the pedal, the speed decreases. If you take your foot off the pedal, the engine idles.

THE BRAKE PEDAL

You'll find the brake pedal just to the left of the accelerator. You **operate** this pedal **with your right foot.** When you depress the brake pedal, all the brakes are applied.

THE CLUTCH PEDAL

To the left of the brake pedal is the clutch pedal. You **use your left foot** to operate the clutch pedal. When you depress the clutch pedal, the

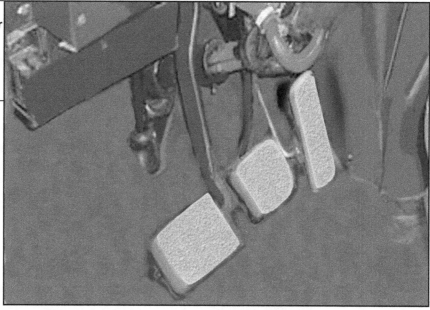

fig. 2-5
The controls on the floor under the steering wheel are, from right to left, the accelerator, the brake pedal and the clutch pedal.

clutch is disengaged. When you release the clutch pedal, the clutch is engaged. Depressing the clutch pedal all the way to the floor engages the clutch brake.

THE DIMMER SWITCH

The dimmer switch is combined with the turn signal which is mounted on the steering column below the steering wheel. It controls the high beams and the low beams on the trucks' headlights. Low beams should be used when driving in traffic. High beams should be used on open roads when there is not oncoming traffic and no traffice closer than 500 feet in front of you.

THE TRAILER BRAKE HAND CONTROL VALVE

This lever is usually located on the steering column. It **operates the trailer brakes only.** To engage the trailer brakes, you move the handle down.

THE TRANSMISSION SHIFT CONTROL LEVERS

Transmissions differ from truck to truck. However, the transmission shift control lever most often **extends through the cab floor.** It's always on the right-hand side of the driver.You'll learn more about transmission levers in the next chapter.

THE POWER TAKE-OFF (PTO) LEVER

The power take-off lever is really a knob, although it's often called a lever.And, there are two of them. You'll find them on trucks such as winch trucks, snow-blower trucks and dump trucks equipped with power take-off units (PTO). If a truck has a PTO, you will use the knob or switch to connect the PTO to the transmission. Then use the second knob or switch to control the mechanism being powered by the PTO.

Chapter 2 Quiz

1. Gauges and warning lights on the dash monitor only the operating condition of the engine.
    A. True
    B. False

2. As you look at different truck dashboards, you will find similar gauges, knobs and switches laid out in _____ patterns.
    A. identical
    B. confusing
    C. different
    D. unidentified

3. The needle on the water temperature gauge will point to _____ degrees when the engine has reached normal operating temperature.
    A. 225-250
    B. 200-225
    C. 165-210
    D. 100-150

4. You have started the engine. If the oil pressure does not come up within seconds, you should _____.
    A. not be too concerned. It's probably a faulty gauge.
    B. think that an extremely heavy grade of oil is taking a long time to thin out and register.
    C. go have breakfast and check again when you finish.
    D. shut off the engine at once.

5. The low air pressure warning light will come on if the air pressure in the system drops below _____ psi.
    A. 120
    B. 100
    C. 90
    D. 60

6. The term given to limiting the number of rpm your engine is able to turn is called _____.
    A. slack adjusting
    B. cruise control
    C. governed speed
    D. locking the differential

7.   To observe the amount of air pressure being sent to the service brakes when you depress the treadle valve, check the
     _____.
     A.   speedometer
     B.   application pressure gauge
     C.   tachometer
     D.   primary system pressure gauge

8.   The primary and secondary air pressure gauges show the psi available in the reservoirs for braking power.
     A.   True
     B.   False

9.   When in the out or emergency position, the red trailer air supply valve prevents the loss of tractor air pressure by closing
     _____.
     A.   off the wet tank reservoir
     B.   the tractor protection valve
     C.   the primary air system reservoir
     D.   the relay valves to the trailer's brake chambers

10. The dash-mounted parking brake valve knob is diamond shaped and red.
     A.   True
     B.   False

CHAPTER 3

TRANSMISSIONS

What Is a Transmission?

The truck engine is the component that produces the power to move the vehicle. The force of combustion causes pistons to move up and down. Then this movement of the pistons is changed to a circular motion by the crankshaft. We go into how and why in Chapter 6. The transmission gets this circular motion to the wheels. It's an **assembly** of gears and shafts that **transmits the power from the engine** through the driveline to the driving axles, **the wheels** and the tires.

The circular motion produced by the engine is measured in revolutions per minute (rpm). The wheels of the truck also rotate, of course, but you don't normally measure that in rpm. An engine can operate efficiently only within a rather small rpm range. Yet the wheels have to be able to travel through a broader range of speeds than that. This is another important function of the transmission. It expands the limited range of speeds the engine can turn at into the **wider range of speeds** needed by the wheels to move the truck down the road. This allows the engine to stay in the narrow speed range where it can operate efficiently and produce the most power (torque) while the truck's wheels can go from barely moving to highway speeds.

Transmitting Force

In the case of a vehicle transmission, the turning of the engine is what makes the vehicle's wheels turn. How does the transmission get the force from the engine to the wheels? We said the transmission was an assembly of gears and shafts. Let's explore how this assembly transmits power. We'll look at the gears first.

Take two gears, A and B, both the same size. They have the same number of teeth, and the same amount of space between the teeth. Now let's mesh them and apply a force to one gear, turning Gear A through one revolution. As the teeth of Gear A press on the teeth of Gear B, Gear B also moves. When Gear A completes one revolution, so has Gear B. What we have just done is to transmit a force acting on Gear A to Gear B.

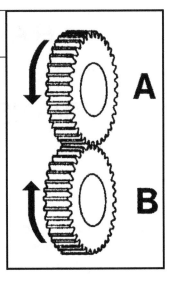

fig. 3-1
Simple transmission of force.

That was simple. Let's make it a little more interesting. We'll use gears of different sizes. A gear is sized by how many teeth it has. A gear with 12 teeth is larger than a gear with eight teeth (assuming, of course, that the space between the teeth is equal on both gears). Let's mesh those gears and apply a force to the smaller gear, A. When our smaller gear, A, has made one complete revolution, Gear B has only made two-thirds of a revolution. Only eight of its teeth have been contacted by the eight teeth of Gear A. To move Gear B all the way around, we have to move Gear A one-half turn more so four more of Gear A's teeth will move the last four of Gear B's.

Why is this important? To answer that question, we have to make two statements about force. One is that, to get a certain amount of work done with a small gear will take more time than with a larger gear. You've just seen a simple demonstration of this with our large and small gears. To make large gear B go all the way around, small gear A had to make more than one complete turn (took more time). If Gear A were the same size or larger than Gear B, it would have moved Gear B through one revolution in less time. So here's our second statement about force: **the least speed is produced when a small gear turns a larger gear.**

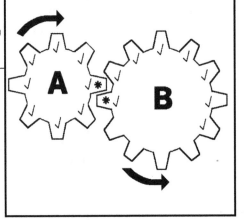

fig. 3-2
The small gear, A, will have to make more than one complete revolution to turn Gear B once.

This **difference in size between one gear and another** is called **gear ratio**. A gear ratio always describes the gear doing the driving acting upon the gear being driven. So, a gear ratio of 5:1 means a small gear is going through five revolutions to turn a larger gear once. If the larger gear were turning the smaller gear, the ratio would be 1:5.

Still don't see why this is important? Recall that at the start of this chapter, we said that the engine has a limited range of rpm compared to the wheels. We had to find some way to get the wheels to turn at more and different speeds than the engine is capable of doing. We use the principle of gear ratio to do this. You can see from our discussion that **different ratios** would **result in faster or slower speeds.** With the right combinations of small gears and large gears, an engine can drive the wheels at different rates of speed and operate very efficiently under many conditions. How much speed is produced depends on which gear is engaged, or turning the other gear.

You might see this better if we introduce some shafts to connect the engine and wheels. For the purposes of this demonstration, we're going to oversimplify, and leave out some very important components of a true transmission. We'll put them back in later in the chapter.

Look at Figure 3-3. We've got a shaft coming out of the engine. At the end of our engine shaft, we have a gear. At the other end of our assembly, we have a wheel, and it, too, is connected to a shaft with a gear on the end. If we turn on the engine, the speed of the turning engine will be transmitted to the engine shaft, and to the gear that's attached to it. If we mesh the two gears, the engine shaft gear will turn the wheel shaft gear, which will turn the wheel shaft, and finally, the wheel itself. In a very simple way, we have transmitted the turning of the engine to the wheel to make the wheel turn.

fig. 3-3
Using gears and shafts to transmit the turning of the engine to a wheel.

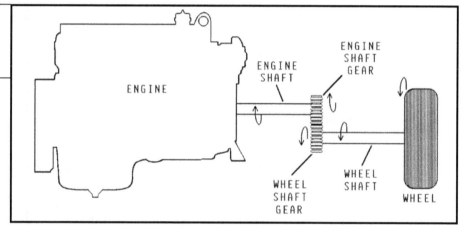

EXPANDING THE RANGE OF SPEED

Let's look at what different gear ratios (different combinations of gears) at the same engine speed will get us. Let's take a very small engine shaft gear turning a very much larger wheel shaft gear, say a 17:1 ratio. Here we have the least speed. Speed, if you think about it, is how far you can go in a given amount of time. If our wheel were going forward, as well as around and around, it would cover a distance. The longer it takes the wheel to make a revolution, the longer it takes to cover that distance. Our gear ratio tells us that large wheel shaft gear is only going to make one revolution for every 17 times the engine shaft gear turns. The wheel will be turning quite slowly, taking a long time to go a distance. In other words, it's moving at low speed.

Now let's take another gear ratio, 5:1. Remember, the engine speed hasn't changed. Now our wheel shaft gear turns once for every five revolutions of the engine shaft gear. The wheel's turning faster, so it covers the same distance in less time. We have more speed.

Last, let's look at a gear ratio of 1:1. The gears are the same size. As you've probably guessed by now, this gives us the most speed of our three combinations.

In a vehicle, these different combinations meet different needs. To get a vehicle going from a standstill, it takes a lot of power. At the same time, you want very little speed. If the wheels were turning very quickly, the vehicle would lurch into motion. You'd have a jackrabbit start. The 17:1 gear ratio will get the truck into motion, at the low speed desired.

At the other extreme, a 1:1 gear ratio is well suited for traveling at highway speeds. In order to go 50 miles per hour, the wheels must turn very fast. The 1:1 gear ratio yields the most speed of our three combinations.

If we had all three combinations in one vehicle, we would have three speeds: slow, medium and fast. Our engine, within its limited rpm range, would be able to drive the wheels through a wide range of speeds. Clearly, though, our basic transmission, pictured in Figure 3-3, will not work. We need a way to connect three different gear combinations to the engine and wheels in a way that lets us use just one at a time. Fortunately, this has already been invented.

Shifting Gears

The input shaft (sometimes called the clutch shaft) of the transmission is more or less what we've been calling the "engine shaft." It's connected to the engine through the clutch, which we'll discuss in more detail later in this chapter. The output shaft is roughly equivalent to what we've been calling the "wheel shaft." It's connected to the wheels through the drive shaft and drive axle. The input and output shafts can be in line with each other or parallel to each other and together are called the mainshaft.

Transmitting the power from the input shaft to the output shaft is the countershaft. It's called that because it turns in a direction opposite (or counter) to that of the engine. The input shaft has only one gear which drives the countershaft. Both the output shaft and countershaft have gears of various sizes on them.

SLIDING GEARS
There are basically two ways to achieve different gear combinations in today's truck transmissions. In the sliding gear transmission, different sized gears slide along the output shaft. The output shaft is grooved, or splined, along its length. The core of the output shaft gears has ridges that mesh with the output shaft grooves so that if an output shaft gear is turning, the output shaft turns with it. The output shaft gears can

slide along the length of the output shaft. On the other hand, the gears on the countershaft are fixed. They do not slide on the shaft. If a moving countershaft gear meshes with an output shaft gear, the countershaft gear will turn the output shaft gear and the output shaft it-self. Gears are changed by sliding one output shaft gear out of mesh with a countershaft gear, and sliding a different output shaft gear into mesh with another countershaft gear. That is to say, **only one pair of gears is in mesh at any given time.**

Look at Figure 3-4 (A), which pictures the in-line input shaft-output shaft type of assembly. Starting from the left, note the input shaft gear, rotating with the input shaft. It meshes with the countershaft drive gear, which gets the countershaft turning (remember, the countershaft gears are fixed on the shaft). The shifter yokes at the top of the picture have selected low gear, putting the low output shaft gear in mesh with the low countershaft gear. Note the very small countershaft gear in comparison with the larger output shaft gear. The low countershaft gear drives the low output shaft gear, and that turns the output shaft.

fig. 3-4
Shifting from low (A) to second gear (B) with sliding gears.

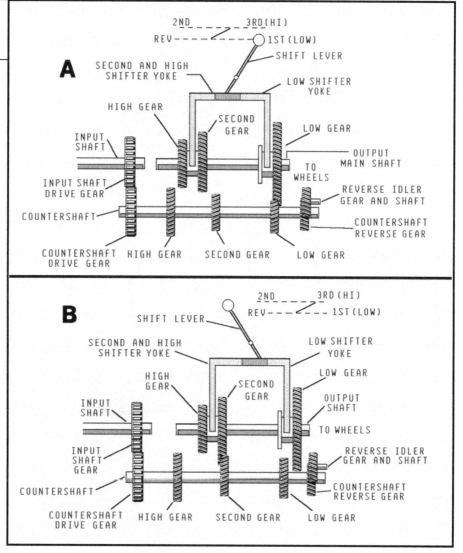

This will turn the drive shaft and wheels. Since we have such a high gear ratio, the wheels will turn slowly.

In Figure 3-4 (B), the shifter yokes have selected second, taking the countershaft and output shaft low gears out of mesh and putting the countershaft and output shaft second gears in mesh. Note the two gears are more equal in size. The gear ratio is smaller than in low gear, so we will get more speed.

SLIDING CLUTCH

In the sliding clutch type, the gears on the output shaft are floating. They are not fixed to the shaft. All combinations of gears are in mesh at the same time (so this is sometimes called constant mesh transmission). But if none of the output shaft gears is locked into place on the output shaft, no power is transmitted. A mechanism called a sliding clutch or shifter collar causes one output shaft gear to lock onto its shaft. Since this gear is in mesh with a countershaft gear, that gets the shaft turning. The effect is that although **all the gear sets are in mesh at the same time, only one is working.**

Look at Figure 3-5, which shows first gear engaged. From left to right, you see five sets of meshed gears: drive, third, second, first and reverse. Note the gear ratios. A large countershaft gear is driving a smaller output shaft gear in third, the second gears are fairly similar in size and in first, the small gear is driving a larger gear. All the gears are in mesh, as we said, but only one set, first gear, is engaged. Note the position of the shift collar. This collar can also engage the reverse gear, by moving the shift lever to the left. Moving the shift lever to the left causes the shifter yoke to move to the right.

fig. 3-5
First gear engaged by shifter collar in sliding clutch transmission.

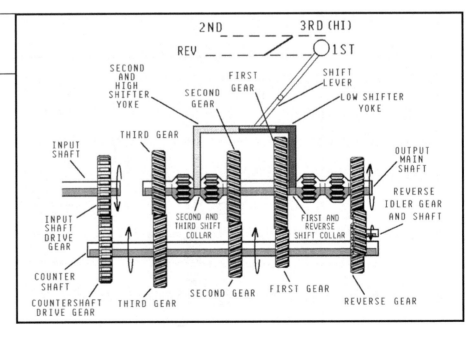

REVERSE

How do we get the wheels to turn in the opposite direction? A reverse idler shaft and gear serve this purpose. The reverse idler shaft gear does not slide on its shaft. The reverse idler gear and countershaft gear are always engaged, so they always turn together. When reverse is needed, the input shaft gear, in mesh with the countershaft gear, turns the countershaft. The countershaft gear, in mesh with the reverse idler shaft gear, turns the reverse idler gear. The reverse idler shaft gear turns the output shaft gear, and the output shaft turns. Putting in this extra gear, the **reverse idler shaft gear,** is what **reverses the motion.** Look at Figure 3-5, and trace this reversing in the constant mesh transmission. Figure 3-6 shows how reverse works in sliding gear transmissions.

In reverse, the reverse idler shaft turns counterclockwise, the countershaft turns clockwise, and the output shaft turns counterclockwise. This makes the wheels turn backwards, causing the truck to back up.

That's the basic idea behind the transmission of power and the right kind of speed from the engine to the wheels. In the trucks that you'll work on and drive, it's a little more complex than what we've described. We've described only three forward gear combinations and one reverse. But once you understand the three-speed, you can work out the principle behind whatever transmission the truck has.

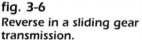

fig. 3-6
Reverse in a sliding gear transmission.

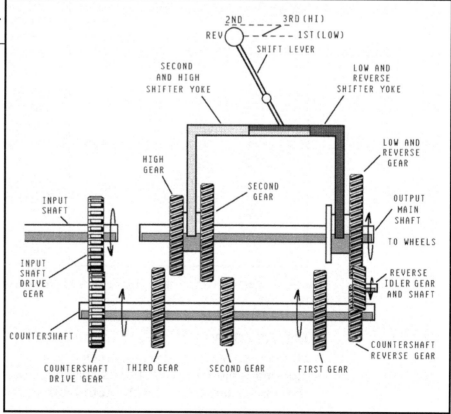

If a truck is going to be faced with many different challenges in terms of load weight, grade, road conditions and running speeds, it will probably have a wide choice of gear ratios to achieve a high degree of operating efficiency. If the work a truck will do is fairly simple, it might not need so many options.

Features of Heavy Truck Transmissions

Here are some other features of heavy truck transmissions that we should explore:

- multiple countershaft
- clutch brake
- ranges and splitters

fig. 3-7
(A) Single countershaft
(B) Twin countershaft
(C) Triple countershaft.

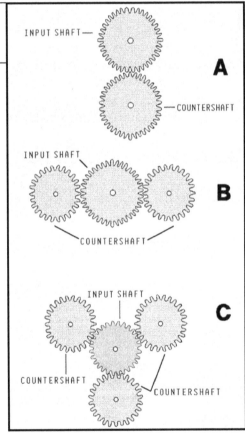

MULTIPLE COUNTERSHAFT

Truck transmissions have more than one countershaft. Figure 3-7 on the next page shows the different number of countershafts used and their locations in the transmission.

The operating principle of a multiple countershaft transmission is the same as a single countershaft unit. The main difference is **the multiple countershaft** unit **spreads out the force** that acts **on the countershaft.** Over time, it is this force, and the work it causes the countershaft to do, that causes the shaft to wear out. When the clutch is let out, the work load is taken up by more than one countershaft. Each countershaft has to do less work, bear less force. You can see that dividing this power would increase shaft and transmission life.

CLUTCH BRAKE

Sometimes, such as when the truck is standing still, the countershaft is stopped while the input shaft is still spinning. The clutch brake **stops the input shaft to match the countershaft.** When the clutch pedal is pushed all the way to the floor, the clutch brake stops the input shaft from turning.

You would use the clutch brake when starting the engine. After the engine starts, release the clutch, then let the engine idle to warm up. The clutch pedal is now out, the clutch is engaged and the input shaft turns. **To shift into LO gear** you have to stop the input shaft.

You'll also use the clutch brake at stop lights. When you have to wait for a long red light, you'll have to keep your foot on the brake and clutch with the truck in gear.

You'll also use the clutch brake when you have been out of the truck with the engine idling. After you reenter the truck, depress the clutch into the clutch brake area. Application of the clutch brake stops the rotation of the input shaft quickly. You don't have to wait for the shaft to lose momentum gradually and eventually come to a stop so that you can shift into a gear without grinding.

RANGES AND SPLITTERS

Truck transmissions differ from three-speed transmissions in that they use **compound transmissions.** That means they use more than one transmission. Compound transmissions **increase the number of gear ratios.** The more gear ratios there are in higher gears, the quicker the truck can be brought to highway speed. This **improves engine efficiency.** The first compound transmission was the **auxiliary transmission,** which is two transmissions, one behind the other. This combination of transmissions (sometimes called a twin stick or Brownie) is rarely used anymore, but it did lead to the development of modern range control and splitter transmissions. With both these types, there is one transmission box and one gear shift with a range control and/or splitter control.

Ranges

The **range control offers a high range and a low range** of the gears. You recall we said it might be good to have more than three gear ratio options. If you wanted nine gear ratios, you might assume you add six more combinations of gears. Range control on a transmission offers more gear ratio options with fewer than an equal number of gear combinations. Keeping the need to add hardware to a minimum keeps down the total weight of the vehicle. And, it keeps the transmission from becoming mechanically complicated.

The range control transmission comes in several speeds. For example, the seven-speed transmission has a four-speed main transmission with a high and low range. So, why doesn't the range control make this transmission into an eight-speed? You might think that if you start out with four gears, and add a second range, your total would be eight. Instead, when you use this model and go from low to high range, you do

fig. 3-8
The shift pattern for the nine-speed and 10-speed transmission.

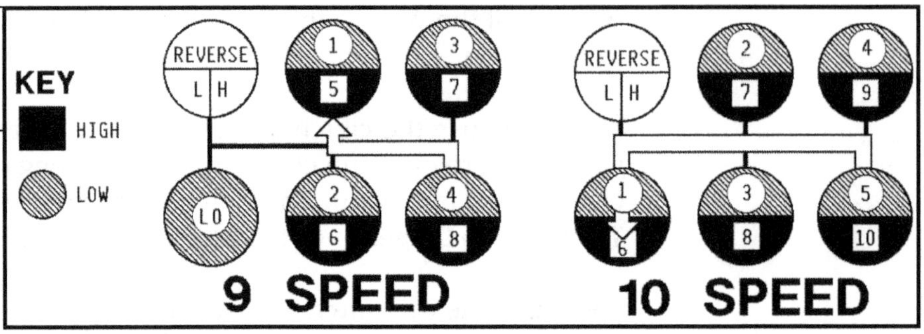

not shift from fourth low to first high. Rather, you shift from fourth low to second high. The seven-speed transmission is not pictured here but the same holds true for other transmissions with ranges. The **nine-speed range control** is a five-speed main transmission. The range control does not make it ten. When you shift from low range to high range, you go from fifth low to second high (see Figure 3-8).

However, with the **10-speed range control,** you do shift from fifth low to first high (see Figure 3-8). How will you know which is to be the case in the truck you're about to drive? Well, you could memorize all the different transmissions and ranges available. But that's not really necessary. Somewhere inside the truck, you should find a shift pattern for the transmission which will describe what to do. It may be on the dashboard, or on the sun visor.

Splitters

The **13-speed transmission** is a five-speed main transmission with high/low range and a splitter control. The splitter has the effect of putting another gear between each of the gear combinations in high range, thus doubling the available combinations in that range. Here's how it adds up. There are five gear ratios in low range plus four gear ratios in high range. The splitter makes eight gear ratios out of the four in high range. Eight plus five equals 13.

Automatic Transmissions

Most of today's trucks used for heavy duty applications have manual transmissions installed in them, so we've focused on that type. But automatic transmissions are available. In some respects, they're easier to drive. The disadvantages are, they can cost more to buy, they are more difficult to maintain and they don't offer quite the extensive range of gear selections that manuals offer.

Chapter 3 Quiz

1. The transmission is _____ that transmits the power from the engine through the driveline to the driving axles, the wheels and the tires.
   A. a set of levers
   B. a two-part device
   C. a range control
   D. an assembly of gears and shafts

2. In the sliding gear transmission, the _____ gears slide on their shaft.
   A. output shaft
   B. countershaft
   C. drive shaft
   D. reverse idler shaft

3. The _____ always turn together.
   A. countershaft gear and the reverse idler gear
   B. countershaft and the mainshaft
   C. input shaft and the output shaft
   D. reverse idler shaft gear and the input shaft

4. A gear ratio always describes the gear doing the driving acting upon the gear being driven.
   A. True
   B. False

5. The input shaft and the output shaft are never parallel to each other.
   A. True
   B. False

6. The most speed is produced with a _____ gear ratio.
   A. 17:1
   B. 5:1
   C. 1:1
   D. 0:17

7. A transmission with a range control will always have a splitter.
   A. True
   B. False

8. A five-speed main transmission with a range control and a splitter will have _____ speeds.
    A. 5
    B. 8
    C. 13
    D. 15

9. The main advantage of multiple countershafts is they _____ .
    A. help obtain highway speeds faster
    B. increase transmission life
    C. increase the number of available gear ratios
    D. increase the weight of the transmission

10. One use of the clutch brake is to put an idling turck into gear without grinding.
    A. True
    B. False

CHAPTER 4

AIR BRAKES

Good Brakes Save Lives

You learned in Chapter 3 that the transmission is the part of the truck that turns engine power into the torque that will make the wheels turn and move the vehicle down the road. Now that you understand what makes the truck go, you need to understand what makes it stop: the brakes.

You must be familiar with the parts of **the brake system** and how the system works **so you can use and inspect the brakes properly.** If you can do this, you can pass the CDL Air Brake knowledge and skills tests. (If you don't pass the tests, you'll have an air brake restriction on your license. With this restriction, you won't be allowed to drive a vehicle with air brakes.)

The ability to maintain and use brakes properly could save your life and the lives of others. A three-year study conducted by the Office of Motor Carriers (OMC) showed that **brake failures are the leading mechanical cause of accidents.** The ability to detect problems with the brakes during inspections will ensure that the brakes will be there when they're needed.

The Basics of Brakes

The most basic thing you can learn about any system is its purpose. **The purpose of the brake system is to** slow, stop and park the vehicle, of course. But you may not realize that it's not enough just to stop a heavy duty truck. If damage and injury occur during a braking procedure, it can hardly be called a successful stop. You must be able to **slow, stop and park in a predictable, controlled way.**

The **basic parts** of the brake system are **the service brake and the emergency or spring (parking) brake.** All heavy duty highway trucks and trailers manufactured after 1975 must have both.

You control the service brake system with the brake pedal. Chapter 2 introduced this tractor control. The emergency or spring brake system comes into play when you park or if the brake system air pressure drops below 45 pounds per square inch (psi). This would happen if an air line breaks. If it does happen, the spring brake becomes an emergency brake that automatically brings the truck to a stop.

The basic theory of braking includes four factors: friction, heat, weight and speed.

Friction between the brake linings on the brake shoes and the brake drums stops the truck. Varying the amount of air pressure applied to the brakes changes the amount of force the brake shoe applies to the brake drum, and the amount of friction that's created. Since the brake drum is bolted to the wheel, if the drum slows, so does the wheel. This is how you control the slowing and stopping of the truck.

fig. 4-1
Friction between the brake lining and the brake drums slows the wheels and stops the truck.

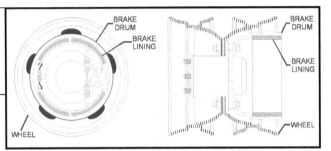

As you probably know, **where there's friction, there's heat.** Applying more air pressure means creating more friction, bringing the truck to a stop sooner. But it also means creating more heat. Repeatedly applying and releasing the brakes, known as pumping or fanning the brakes, also means creating more friction and more heat. If brakes are applied with a great deal of force or too often, **heat** can **build up.** This **can cause poor brake performance,** or what is known as brake fade.

Weight affects how much energy it takes to stop. **The more the truck weighs, the more energy it takes to stop.** If you double the weight, the energy needed to stop is also doubled. The more energy it takes, the more air pressure is needed. More air pressure means more friction which means more heat, and we're back again to causing brake fade.

To come to a safe stop, you must have more than good brakes. You must **have enough stopping distance.** The truck doesn't come to an immediate stop the minute you hit the brake pedal. The vehicle travels some distance before stopping. This is the stopping distance. Three things make up stopping distance: perception distance, reaction distance and braking distance.

Perception distance is how far the vehicle travels from the time the driver's eyes see a hazard until the driver's brain registers the need to stop. This takes about three-fourths of a second. At 55 mph perception distance is about 60 feet. **Reaction distance is how far the vehicle travels from when the driver's brain registers the need to stop until the driver's foot actually presses the brake pedal.** This usually takes another three-fourths of a second, or 60 feet at 55 mph.

Braking distance is **how far the vehicle travels until the brakes bring it to a complete stop.** At 55 mph on dry pavement with good brakes, this is about 170 feet. **Total stopping distance** at 55 mph under good conditions **is 290 feet.** Add to this **brake lag, the distance the vehicle travels before the brakes actually apply.** This could be as much as 32 feet from the time the driver presses the brake pedal until the brakes apply. There's little anyone can do to shorten this total stopping distance. A safe stop requires at least 290 feet. Often, you'll need more.

Speed affects how long it takes to stop the truck. If you double the speed from 20 to 40 mph, it takes four times the distance to stop. But the effect of speed is geometric. That means as speed increases, the relative time it takes to stop does not stay the same. It multiplies. For example, if you double the speed from 30 to 60 mph, it will take not twice as much, but six and one-half times the distance to stop.

The Air Brakes

Air brakes are **operated by compressed air.** So the parts of the system must be designed to maintain a supply of compressed air, plus direct and control its flow. These parts must also be designed to use the energy of compressed air to apply the brakes.

In this section, we're going to take a close look at the parts that perform these tasks. First let's list them to get an idea of the scope of the material we'll be covering.

- the compressor (1)
- the air governor (2)
- the air dryer (3)
- the alcohol evaporator (3)
- the air reservoir system (4)
- the system protection valves (5)
- the operational control valves (6)
- the warning devices
- the gauges
- the brake chambers (7)
- the slack adjusters (8)
- the brake drums
- the braking mechanism
- the glad hands (9)
- the stop lights

Many of these components have subparts. For instance, there are five system protection valves. You can see this is a complicated system. Once you know the parts, where they're located and what they do, you'll be on your way to being able to use and inspect the system properly. The numbers in the list match those in Figure 4-2.

THE COMPRESSOR
The compressor is a machine that draws in the air around it, **pumps** that **air** into a smaller space **to increase its pressure** and then pumps it into the air reservoir system where it is stored in air tanks until it is needed. The engine provides the power for the compressor, so it is

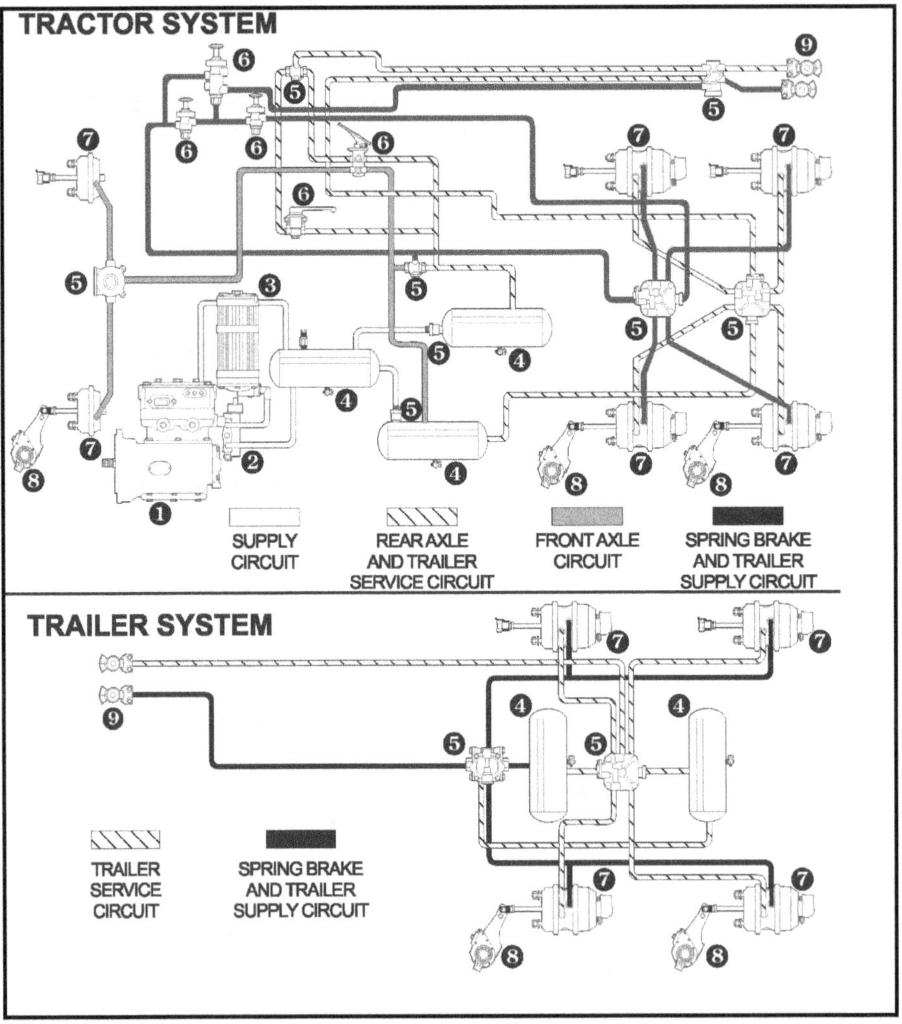

fig. 4-2
A typical air brake system for a tractor-trailer.

TRACTOR SYSTEM

| SUPPLY CIRCUIT | REAR AXLE AND TRAILER SERVICE CIRCUIT | FRONT AXLE CIRCUIT | SPRING BRAKE AND TRAILER SUPPLY CIRCUIT |

TRAILER SYSTEM

| TRAILER SERVICE CIRCUIT | SPRING BRAKE AND TRAILER SUPPLY CIRCUIT |

usually mounted on the side of the engine. Compressors can be gear- or belt-driven, and may have their own oil supply or be lubricated with engine oil.

THE AIR GOVERNOR

Located on the compressor, the air governor controls when the compressor will pump air into the reservoir system. It **regulates the amount of air pressure in the system.** When pressure reaches the cut-out level (around 120 or 125 psi), the governor stops the compressor from pumping air into the tanks. When the pressure in the tank falls to about 100 psi, the governor signals the compressor to cut in (begin pumping air into the tanks again).

THE AIR DRYER

When the air leaves the compressor, it flows through the air dryer. This **cleans and removes moisture and vaporized oil from the compressed air.** When you compress air, you also heat it. As it cools, any moisture in it condenses. Also, small amounts of oil from the compressor are vaporized and travel out of the compressor with the air. When the compressed air cools, this oil also condenses. The result will be a sludge that can clog and corrode valves if it's not removed from the system. In cold weather, this sludge can freeze in the lines and the valves. The air dryer does a pretty good job of removing this condensed moisture and oil. But the dryer doesn't get it all. You'll need to finish the job. We'll tell you how later.

THE ALCOHOL EVAPORATOR

Some vehicles have an alcohol evaporator. Putting alcohol in the air brake system keeps the moisture in the compressed air from freezing. Ice in the system could cause brake failure.

THE AIR RESERVOIR SYSTEM

From the air dryer, the compressed air goes to the reservoir system, which **stores the air until it is needed.**

The first tractor reservoir tank in a dual circuit air brake system is called **the main supply tank, or the wet tank. A second tank** called the primary holds compressed air for **the rear axle supply. A third tank** called the secondary holds compressed air for the **front axle supply. Both** these tanks are **also called dry tanks.** Wet tank and dry tank simply refers to how much condensed moisture and oil might still be found in these tanks.

You can see the tractor air reservoirs and the **front and rear axle trailer reservoirs** in Figure 4-2.

There are three types of valves in the air reservoir system: safety valves, check valves and air tank drain valves.

Safety valves protect the air tanks by **releasing excess pressure** if the air governor fails. Safety valves are usually set to open at 150 psi. If the safety valve releases air, that's a sign something is wrong.

Check valves allow air to flow in one direction only. All air tanks must have them. If there is a leak in a supply tank or in the air compressor discharge line, these valves prevent loss of pressure in the rest of the system. Check valves are placed in the lines going into the tanks.

An **air tank drain valve** is located at the bottom of each supply tank. The petcock, or draining mechanism, on these valves **must be opened manually so moisture can drain from the tanks.** Many new systems have spit valves or automatic moisture ejectors which can also be opened manually. From what you already know about the damage and problems condensed moisture and oil can cause in a brake system, you can see how important it is that the tanks be drained **daily.** There is, in fact, no more important maintenance you can do. If a tractor-trailer is equipped with automatic moisture ejectors, make sure you check them for proper operation whenever you service that vehicle.

Let's take a minute now and look at an explanation of how the service air brake system works. The spring brakes work differently. You'll learn how those work later in this section.

The compressor draws in surrounding air, compresses it and pumps it to the air dryer. The air dryer removes moisture from the compressed air, which then flows into the air reservoir system. When you operate one of the air control valves (the foot valve or the hand valve), the compressed air flows to the brake chambers. In the brake chambers, the compressed air moves the service brake linkages that press the brake shoes and linings against the brake drums. You'll get a more detailed look at how things work in the brake chamber later in this section.

THE SYSTEM PROTECTION VALVES

Four types of valves provide various kinds of protection in air brake systems.

- quick release valves
- relay valves
- tractor parking valve
- parking brake valve

Quick release valves are found near the brake chambers. When you apply the brakes, the air passes into the brake chambers. That compressed air applies the brakes and continues to apply them. Once you release the brakes, that air must be released very quickly so the brakes will release. The **quick release valve lets** this **air escape very quickly from the brake chamber.**

Air brake systems on tractors that have **dual air brake systems,** as in Figure 4-2, and on trailers, **use relay valves.** The relay valve functions somewhat like a quick release valve in that it causes the air to be delivered more quickly. With a relay valve, pressure is stored not only in the supply tanks but also in the lines that go up to the relay valve. When you apply the foot valve, a signal in the form of air pressure is sent to the relay valve. The relay valve opens and sends the air pressure to the brake chambers immediately. When you release the brakes, the relay works just like a quick release valve by immediately exhausting the air from the brake chamber. You can see why tractors and trailers with long service brake lines benefit from the use of relay valves. The length of time it takes for the relay valve to detect increased air pressure after you depress the foot valve is the brake lag time discussed on page 39.

Emergency or **spring brakes** are required on all heavy duty highway vehicles manufactured since 1975. You'll find spring brakes on all the trailer wheels and on at least one set of tractor drive wheels. They are **both parking and emergency brakes.** Figure 4-3 shows you how the spring brake rides on the back of the service brake air chamber.

The service brake part of the brake in Figure 4-3 works in the way we've already described. This is how the spring brake works. The **pressure that applies this brake** is **provided by a spring.** The spring is **held**

fig. 4-3
This is the type of brake you'll find on tractor drive wheels and trailer wheels. The front steering axles will have only the service brake chamber.

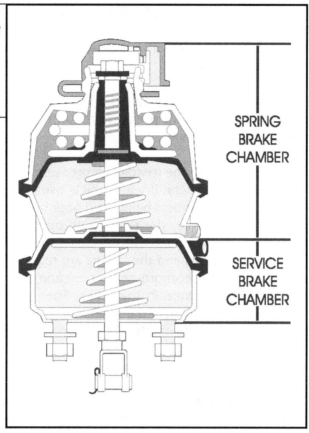

SPRING BRAKE CHAMBER

SERVICE BRAKE CHAMBER

back (the released position) by air pressure. When you apply the parking brakes, you **release that pressure and the spring presses forward** to apply the brakes.

The spring brakes are applied by pulling out the parking brake valve. All air brake systems have this valve. It's used to park the tractor and the trailer when they are coupled. It's a yellow push-pull diamond-shaped knob that you'll find on your dashboard. It's pictured in Chapter 2.

When you apply the parking brakes, you intentionally release air pressure from the spring brake chambers. However, in an emergency, **if the brake system air pressure drops to a range between 20 and 45 pounds per square inch (psi),** the spring brakes will automatically apply, bringing the truck to a stop. The parking brakes become emergency brakes. At the same time, the red trailer air supply control knob and the yellow parking knob on your dashboard will pop out automatically.

To release the parking brakes and recharge the system, you must push the parking brake and the trailer air supply knob back in. When the system recharges, the spring in the spring brake chamber is pushed back and held back by air pressure.

Never push the brake pedal down when the spring brakes are on. This is called "compounding." The combined force of the springs and the air pressure could damage the brakes. However some trucks are equipped with a compounding valve that would prevent the added pressure from damaging the chambers. The operator's manual can tell you if a vehicle you're servicing is equipped this way.

Rarely, you'll find a tractor with a **tractor parking only valve** for use when you're coupling and uncoupling. We pictured this control in Chapter 2, too. It's a push-pull blue round knob.

THE OPERATIONAL CONTROL VALVES

These controls are the brake pedal, the trailer hand valve control and the tractor protection valve that works with the trailer air supply control.

The **brake pedal** is also called a treadle or foot valve. It **operates a valve that supplies air pressure** to both the tractor's and the trailer's service braking system.

When you press on the treadle, air pressure is sent through the air lines to the brake chambers. If your vehicle uses relay valves, then the air is near the brake chambers being held back by the relay valves. When you press on the treadle, the relay valve opens and air speeds into the chambers. When you release the treadle, the air exhausts through the quick release valves and the brakes are released. This applying and releasing lets some compressed air escape out of the system and reduces the air pressure in the tanks. Then pressure must be built up again. This is why fanning the brakes leads to brake failure. You exhaust the compressed air faster than the compressor can replace it.

A tractor may have a **trailer hand valve.** It **operates the trailer brakes only,** letting you control the amount of air directed to the trailer brakes. This **must never be used as a parking brake.** The brakes will hold only if there is air pressure in the trailer air tank. When that leaks away, the brakes will release. You can use the trailer hand valve to lock the trailer brakes when coupling or uncoupling, or to test the trailer brakes.

The **tractor protection valve (TPV)** is controlled by the trailer air supply control. That's the push-pull, eight-sided red knob on your dashboard. You see one in Chapter 2. This TPV's job is to protect the tractor air supply in case of air pressure loss in the trailer's air lines. The TPV itself is located at the point under the tractor's frame where the flexible air lines that go to the trailer are connected by the glad hands. The valve **separates the tractor air supply from the trailer air supply.**

If anything goes wrong with the trailer system that causes it to lose air pressure below around 20 to 45 psi, a spring in the trailer air supply valve on the dashboard pops the valve out. This action sends a signal to the tractor protection valve between the tractor and trailer. It then closes off the air supply to the trailer. This has two effects. One, **it protects the tractor air supply from loss,** ensuring that the tractor's service brakes will work. Two, because the trailer is losing air pressure and no more is coming from the tractor, the **trailer emergency brakes activate.** So, the trailer spring brakes are on and you have control over the tractor service brakes. This lets you bring your rig to a controlled, safe stop.

All this happens automatically, but only after you have been warned by the low air pressure warning devices, which you'll learn about next.

The tractor protection valve can also be operated manually by pulling out the **trailer air supply control.** This shuts off the air supply to the trailer and puts on the trailer emergency brakes. To resupply the trailer brakes with air, simply push the red knob in.

THE WARNING DEVICES

Two devices warn you of **low air pressure: the warning light** and the **warning buzzer.** A truck will have at least one of them. They are located in the cab.

Some older vehicles have a low air pressure warning device called a **wig wag.** This is a signal flag that drops down from the top of the cab into the driver's view when the air pressure gets too low. It can't be reset it until the air pressure is restored to a safe level.

If the pressure in any one of the service air tanks drops below 60 psi while the ignition is on, these devices will go off. **If a low air pressure warning device goes off while you're driving, pull the vehicle off the road at the first safe place you find to stop.** Do not resume driving until you correct the problem.

THE GAUGES

All vehicles with air brakes have a **pressure gauge** connected to the air tank, so you can see how much pressure there is in the tank. A dual air brake system has a gauge for each tank, the primary (marked P) and the secondary (marked S), or one gauge with a separate needle for each tank.

The vehicle may be equipped with an **application pressure gauge.** This shows how much air pressure you are applying to the brakes when you depress the brake pedal. If you see you need increasingly more pressure to get the same braking effect, you should suspect brake fade.

THE BRAKE CHAMBERS

The brake chambers, or pods, hold some of the parts that make up the service brakes. They are listed below.

- an air inlet
- a push rod
- a clevis assembly
- a diaphragm
- a return spring

Pressurized air enters the brake chamber at the air inlet. The air then pushes against the **diaphragm.** The diaphragm **pushes** the **push rod** which is **connected to the slack adjuster** which is **connected to the braking mechanism.** You can see the push rod in both Part A and Part B of Figure 4-4. The **return spring returns the diaphragm to its proper position** once the quick release valve has released the pressurized air from the chamber. The **clevis assembly** provides a mechanism for **attaching the slack adjuster to the push rod.**

Besides the brake chamber, a slack adjuster, brake camshaft, S cam, brake shoes and linings and a brake drum make up a service brake. You know in general how service brakes work. As we cover each of these parts, you'll learn more specifically how they work. As you learn about each part, find it on Figure 4-4. Do this each time you read about a new part. Study the figure to see how the parts fit together and work.

THE SLACK ADJUSTERS

Slack adjusters **adjust the brakes** to **make up for brake lining wear.** A slack adjuster is a lever arm attached to the push rod of the brake chamber at the clevis assembly. You can see the clevis assembly on Part A of Figure 4-4. You can see the slack adjuster on Part B. Its job is to adjust the position of the S cam which then adjusts the distance of the brake shoe and lining from the brake drum.

Slack adjusters can be adjusted manually or automatically. Hand adjusted slack adjusters have an **adjusting nut.** To adjust this type, you must have special training and certification. Part 396.25 of the Federal Motor Carriers Safety Regulations (FMCSR) states the qualifications you need to inspect, maintain, service and repair brake systems of commercial motor vehicles. Part 396.25 is also specific about the push rod travel for the variety of makes and size of brake chambers used on tractors and trailers. Read and understand the sections that pertain to brakes in the FMCSR. When you pass the air brake knowledge and skills test for a CDL you are qualified to inspect the air brakes system.

Automatic slack adjusters make an adjustment automatically whenever the brakes are applied. They sense the distance the push rod travels each time and keep the brakes in constant adjustment. The FMCSR requires that commercial motor vehicles manufactured on or after October 20, 1994, be equipped with automatic slack adjusters. This is because of the difficulty of keeping manual slack adjusters in proper adjustment at all times. Often, only one or two brakes are in proper adjustment. Then they do all the work and the brakes that are out of adjustment fail to contribute to the braking effort. Repairs to automatic slack adjusters must be made by certified personnel according to FMCSR Part 396.25.

THE BRAKE DRUMS

Brake drums are made of iron or steel. They are bolted to the wheels, so the wheel and the drum rotate together. The **inside surface** of a brake drum should be smooth and uniform. If there are scores or ridges cut into the surface more than half the width of the friction area, the brake linings may not make complete contact with the drum. That could result in poor brake performance.

THE BRAKING MECHANISM

The braking mechanism, which consists of the brake shoes, the brake linings, the brake camshaft and the S cam, is found **inside the drum.**

You can see this in the cutaway view in Figure 4-4. It is the action of the brake shoes pushing the brake lining against the brake drum surface that produces friction and stops the vehicle.

The Brake Shoes and Linings
Each brake drum contains two brake shoes with attached linings that are made of metallic mineral fiber. Linings must be secure on the shoes and free of oil or grease. They should be no thinner than $\frac{1}{4}$ of an inch at the thinnest point.

The Brake Camshaft
The brake camshaft is attached to the slack adjuster. The **slack adjuster converts** the **pushing motion of the push rod into the twisting motion** of the brake camshaft. The brake camshaft **turns the S cam.**

The S Cam
The S cam is part of the brake camshaft. As the brake camshaft twists, it turns the S cam. This action **pushes the brake shoes and linings against the brake drum.**

Now you know enough to take a close look at how the service brakes work. You press on the treadle. This sends a signal to the relay valve. The relay valve opens and air enters the brake chamber through the air inlet. The pressurized air pushes the diaphragm. The diaphragm pushes the push rod. The push rod pushes the slack adjuster. The slack adjuster twists. This twisting action turns the brake camshaft, turning the S cam. The turning S cam pushes the brake shoes and linings against the brake drum. This creates friction which slows and stops the turning of the brake drum. Because the brake drum is attached to the wheel, the wheel also stops turning. When you release the treadle, the signal to the relay valve stops. The relay valve closes the air inlet and quickly exhausts the air from inside the brake chamber.

fig. 4-4
Part A shows the parts of a service brake chamber. Part B shows the parts of the braking mechanism (foundation brakes).

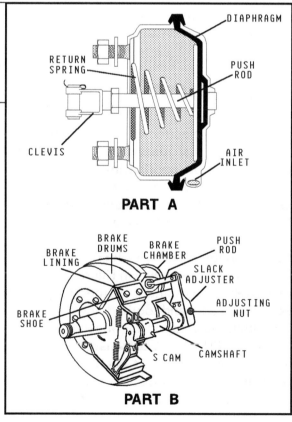

WEDGE BRAKES AND DISC BRAKES. Instead of S cam brakes, **a vehicle may have wedge or disc brakes.** In a wedge brake, the push rod pushes a wedge between the end of two brake shoes. The wedge pushes the shoes apart and against the inside of the brake drum. A disc brake has a power screw instead of an S cam. Air pressure acting on the diaphragm pushes the slack adjuster. The slack adjuster turns the power screw. The power screw clamps the disc between the brake lining pads of a caliper.

THE GLAD HANDS

Glad hands are the **coupling devices** on the ends of the air hoses on the back of the tractor and on the front of the trailer. These hoses **connect the service and emergency brakes of the trailer to the tractor air supply system.** They must be connected properly. Often they are color-coded. In that case, the service brake glad hands are colored blue and the emergency brake glad hands are colored red. The coupling device is a push, snap-lock type, similar to a radiator cap. When you're bobtailing, you can connect the hoses to the couplers on the back of the cab provided for that purpose. These couplers are often called dummy couplers. They protect the lines and keep water and dirt out. If the tractor doesn't have dummy couplers, just connect the lines together and secure them to the back of the tractor.

STOP LIGHTS

Although they don't help stop the vehicle, the stop lights are part of the brake system. Air pressure works a switch that turns on the brake lights when you step on the brake. This tells drivers behind the truck that the vehicle is stopping or slowing.

Anti-lock Braking System

Advancements in electronics have been put to use to improve the braking systems you just read about. **Before anti-lock braking systems (ABS), a hard brake application would often result in wheel lockup.** In Chapter 16 we touch on wheel lockup and skids. **Anti-lock braking systems do not shorten stopping distance** but they **do prevent wheel lockup** and reduce the chance of a skid or jackknife.

A microcomputer called **the electronic control unit (ECU)** is the brain of the ABS system as shown in Figure 4-5. The ECU constantly **receives signals from** sensors and a toothed ring located at the drum of **each wheel.** The sensors and toothed ring constantly measure wheel speed. During a brake application if a wheel tries to lock up, the sensor sends a signal to the ECU. The **ECU transmits electrical pulses to an ABS relay or modulating valve at each wheel which automatically apply, hold or release** brake chamber pressure up to as many as five times per second. This prevents wheel lockup. You'll find ABS on all tractors

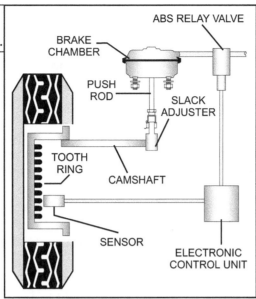

fig. 4-5
Basic parts of an anti-lock braking system.

ABS RELAY VALVE

BRAKE CHAMBER

PUSH ROD

SLACK ADJUSTER

TOOTH RING

CAMSHAFT

SENSOR

ELECTRONIC CONTROL UNIT

manufactured after March 1, 1997, and all new trailers manufactured after March 1, 1998.

Another feature that can be installed with the ABS system is **an automatic traction control system (ATC)**. The ATC system uses the sensors and toothed rings at the wheels, and a separate ECU for this system modulates the engine's throttle. This **helps keep wheels from slipping or spinning out during acceleration.**

Brake by Wire

Another improvement in the air brake system is **the electronic braking system (EBS)**, also known as brake by wire. The EBS system **uses a sensor at the brake pedal to measure braking demand.** The brake pedal signal is transmitted to yet another electronic control unit which calculates the air pressure needed to fill that demand. The ECU then electronically signals relay valves at each axle to provide the air pressure needed to meet the demand calculated by the ECU. The electronic signal sent by "wire" is much faster than the air signal you read about in the discussion of the basic air brake system earlier in this chapter. The brake by wire system greatly **reduces the time it takes for brakes at the wheel to respond** to the driver's pressing the brake pedal. In other words, it reduces brake lag. More than that, it ensures that braking force is evenly distributed among all the wheels by monitoring wheel sensors already installed in the system for the ABS.

If there is a failure in the EBS system, the brakes revert to normal dual air brake system operation.

Emergency Brake Situations

You know now what happens when the spring brakes are automatically activated because of an emergency situation. You also know what happens when the tractor protection valve activates. In this section, we're going to look at the emergency situations that call for the activation of these brakes.

If the trailer breaks away from the tractor, the tractor's air hoses for both the service and the emergency brakes will break away from the trailer. This will activate an immediate applications of the tractor protection valve to protect the air pressure in the tractor. That air pressure is needed to bring the tractor to safe stop. **A trailer breakaway** will activate the trailer emergency brakes and this will bring the trailer to a stop. Trailer breakaways are very, very rare. What is more likely is that one of the air lines will rupture.

If **a service brake air line ruptures,** nothing will happen until the brakes are applied. Then air will escape from the damaged service line instead of going to the trailer brakes. Should this happen only the tractor's brakes will work to slow the vehicle. You will notice the absence of the trailer's brakes. Repeated pumping or application of the service brake will reduce the air pressure. When the pressure falls below about 45 psi, the emergency brakes apply automatically and bring the vehicle to a stop.

If **an emergency brake air line ruptures,** there will be an immediate and rapid loss of pressure in the emergency brake lines. The tractor protection valve will activate, as will the trailer emergency brakes, just as if there had been a trailer breakaway.

If **the discharge line from the compressor to the main supply tank ruptures,** there will be a loss of air from this tank. The one-way check valve between the main tank and the dry tanks will prevent the loss of air from those tanks. When the main air tank air pressure drops below 60 psi, a low pressure switch will activate a warning device. There should be enough air pressure left in the tank to bring the vehicle to a stop. There will be enough for a limited number of brake applications.

Four Tests for Your Brake Systems

What **causes** emergency brake situations? **Rarely, a road hazard** will rupture an air line. For instance, a driver might run over a two-by-four that could then flip up and rupture a line. But the more likely and **most frequent** cause of emergency brake situations is **poor maintenance.**

What follows are four tests that will help you make sure the air brake systems are functioning properly.

Testing the Compressor
This procedure **tests pressure build-up time, the low pressure warning indicator and the air governor.**

- Open the petcocks and drain the wet air tank first. Then drain the dry air tanks until the gauges read zero and close the petcocks.
- Start the engine and run it at operating rpm. The compressor should start to fill the tanks.

- Watch the low air pressure warning device. If the warning stops before pressure reaches 60 psi, it needs to be adjusted.
- In a vehicle with a dual air system, pressure should build from 85 to 100 psi within 45 seconds. If the build-up takes longer, there's a problem somewhere. In older vehicles with single air systems, the pressure should go from 50 psi to 90 psi within three minutes with the engine at an idle speed of 600 to 900 rpm.
- Keep filling the tanks until the governor stops the compressor. If the governor continues filling the tanks above 120 to 130 psi, the governor needs to be adjusted.
- With the parking brake released (to avoid compounding), push and release the brake pedal until pressure in the system falls to just below 100 psi. If the governor is adjusted properly pressure should begin to rise again.

Drivers will report the results of failed tests to the Maintenance Shop. See that all indicated adjustments are made before they take the rig on the road.

Testing Air Loss Rate

With these simple steps, you can **test the brake system's ability to hold air pressure.**

- When the pressure is fully built up, typically 125 psi, turn off the engine, chock the wheels, release the brakes and let everything stand for one minute.
- Notice the reading on the pressure gauge and start timing.
- After one minute, note the pressure again.

The pressure should not have dropped more than two psi per minute for the tractor only. If the tractor is coupled to one or more trailers, the pressure should not have dropped more than three psi per minute. If the pressure drop is greater, something is wrong. Find out what is wrong and fix it before anyone drives rig.

- Next, press hard on the brake pedal and wait for one minute.
- Note the reading on the pressure gauge and keep pressing on the brake pedal. After one minute, note the pressure again.

If you're testing the tractor only, the pressure drop should not be more than three psi per minute. If you're testing a tractor-trailer combination, the drop should not be more than four psi per minute. For a double-trailer combination, it should not be more than six psi per minute.

Testing the Emergency System

These two steps **test your low air pressure warning device and your spring brake emergency application.**

- With air pressure at about 90 pounds and the engine off, push and release the foot brake until the low air pressure warning comes on.

If the warning device fails to come on below 60 psi, get it adjusted, repaired or replaced before you drive your rig. The warning should come on before the spring brakes are automatically applied.

- Continue pushing and releasing the foot brake until the spring brakes apply automatically.

Spring brakes should apply between 20 and 40 psi. If they apply above 45 psi, something is wrong.

Testing the Parking and Service Brakes
These tests will help determine if the parking and service brakes work properly.

- With the parking brake on, put the vehicle in a low gear and gently try to move the vehicle forward. If the parking brake works properly, the vehicle should not move.
- With normal air pressure in the system, release the parking brake and move the vehicle forward slowly. Check to see that the vehicle stops evenly when the brake pedal is firmly pushed and that nothing "feels" unusual.

Chapter 4 Quiz

1. Brake failures _____ .
   A. are the leading mechanical cause of accidents
   B. are most often caused by road hazards
   C. often lead to trailer breakaway
   D. are most often caused by brake fade

2. The purpose of the service brake system and the emergency brake system is to _____ .
   A. slow, stop and park the vehicle
   B. prevent breakaway trailers
   C. slow, stop and park the vehicle in a predictable, controlled way
   D. prevent the loss of air pressure from the tractor's braking system

3. The four factors of the basic theory of braking are heat, weight, speed and _____ .
   A. air pressure
   B. how many trailers are coupled to the tractor
   C. moisture content in the wet tank
   D. friction

For questions 4 through 8, please fill in the blanks in the illustration to the right with the correct labels.

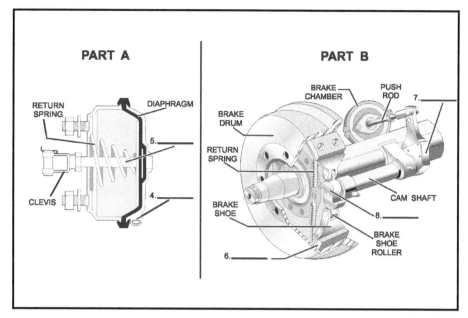

PART A

RETURN SPRING

DIAPHRAGM

5._____

4._____

CLEVIS

PART B

BRAKE CHAMBER

PUSH ROD

7._____

BRAKE DRUM

RETURN SPRING

CAM SHAFT

BRAKE SHOE

8._____

BRAKE SHOE ROLLER

6._____

9. "The slack adjuster twists. This twisting action turns the brake camshaft, turning the S cam." The quoted text is part of the explanation of how the brakes work.
    A. True
    B. False

10. If _____ , nothing will happen until you apply the brakes.
    A. the trailer breaks away
    B. a service brake air line ruptures
    C. the discharge line from the compressor to the main supply tank ruptures
    D. a spring brake air line ruptures

CHAPTER 5

ELECTRICAL

The Power Behind the Power

Of course, the power that runs a truck comes from the engine, but the fact is that the **power behind that engine power is electrical power.** You can't even start a truck without a starting circuit. You can't keep it going for long without a charging circuit. You can't run the lights without a lighting circuit and the dashboard instruments won't work without an instrument circuit.

As you can see, electrical systems in diesel trucks serve many necessary functions. They can also be quite complicated. Unless you understand the electrical system, it just looks like a maze of wires. But understand it you must, if only to keep some poor driver from having an electrical problem some dark night on a deserted highway.

The first step in understanding the system is to understand some of the basics of electricity.

The Basics of Electrical Current

An electron is a tiny particle of matter that carries a negative charge of electricity. **Electrical current is produced by electron flow.** All matter contains electrons, but some matter conducts electricity better than other matter.

To be a good conductor of electricity, the matter must have a large number of electrons that can be set in motion easily. Copper wire is a good conductor of electricity. Rubber is not a good conductor. That is why rubber is used as an insulator around copper wire.

Insulated **wires bring the current to the parts that need electricity** to operate. **Terminals are** the **connecting devices.** They are found on the ends of the wires and on the electrical components used to connect the wires to the parts. There is also a main terminal from which the wires originate and which contains all the system circuit breakers and fuses.

Pressure gets the electrons flowing. **Voltage is** another name for **electrical pressure.** Alternators or generators produce voltage. The term **amperage** or amps refers to the specified **amount of electric current** that is produced and carried by the wires.

The electrons flow through electrical circuits. A **circuit is a continuous path** basically made up of wire (the conductor), a source of power that drives the current around the circuit (the batteries and alternator or generator) and the devices that use the electricity (the radio and lights, for instance). This type of circuit is called a complete or closed circuit. **For current to flow, there must be a closed circuit.** For a circuit to be closed, all the components in that circuit must be grounded. That means there must be a wire or a conductor to bring the electrons back to where they started.

There are two other kinds of circuits: the open circuit and the short circuit. Electricity will not flow to its destination in either of these types of circuits and that usually means trouble.

An **open circuit** occurs when the normal **flow of electrical current is stopped.** A number of conditions can cause this. However, corroded connections and broken wires account for most open circuits. Open circuits account for most electrical problems.

A **short circuit** occurs when the electrical **current bypasses part of the normal circuit.** This means that instead of flowing to a light bulb, for instance, the current stops short of its destination and flows back to the battery. Shorts happen when the insulation has come off a section of a wire and it touches something outside the normal circuit, like another wire or part of the frame. Then the current takes the shortest route back to the source, using the other wire or frame to complete the circuit. It never does make it to the light bulb.

Any of these conditions can cause a short circuit.

- Two wires rub together until the insulation wears away and the bare wires touch each other.
- The wires in an electrical coil (like the starter winding) lose their insulation and touch each other.
- A wire rubs against the frame or other metal part of the truck until the bare wire touches another piece of metal.

Keep your eyes open for frayed or broken wires.

Circuit breakers and fuses protect the circuit from short circuits and from current overloads. A current overload happens when a circuit gets more current than it can handle. A short circuit is usually the cause of an overload. This is what happens. Turning on the lights, the starter motor or radio "uses" (actually, slows) the flow of the electricity. But if there is a short circuit, the bulb is not lit. The motor or the radio won't work. There is nothing to "use" the flow of current. This means there is more current in the wire than the wire can handle by itself and it will overheat and damage itself. Fuses or circuit breakers are placed in each circuit to prevent this.

fig. 5-1
A short circuit will keep current from getting to the device it's meant to operate.

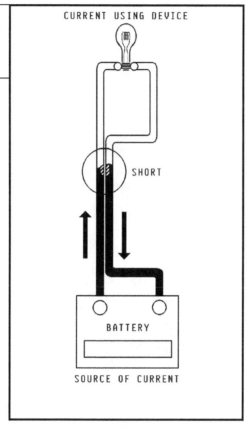

Here's how they work. Fuses are rated by their amperage carrying capacity. In other words, they can handle only so much current. By design, this is even less than the wire can handle. If there is an overload, the **fuse will blow and open or break the circuit before the wire can be damaged.** When the circuit is open, current can no longer flow. Once a **fuse** is blown, it **must be replaced.**

Circuit breakers are also rated by their amperage carrying capacity. A circuit breaker used on a circuit will have the same amperage carrying capacity as the circuit. If there is more current load than the circuit breaker can carry, the circuit breaker opens and breaks the circuit. Once a **circuit breaker** has opened, it usually **resets automatically.** This is an advantage circuit breakers have over fuses.

A Truck's Basic Electrical System

Wires, circuit breakers, fuses, components and terminals make up the circuits in a truck. There is one main terminal block that contains all the circuit breakers and fuses. From this terminal block, wires run out in bunches to connectors. At the connectors the wires split and go to other connectors or to parts that need electricity to operate.

All the wires in a truck's electrical system are color-coded. Color coding makes it easier to trace a wire from one connector to another and to components. You'll learn more about color coding and tracing wires later in this chapter. Right now, we're going to look at the basic component of the truck's electrical system: the battery system.

THE BATTERIES

Most trucks have a basic 12-volt electrical system. Many of the system's parts are the same as the ones in the humble family car. One of the major components is the battery system. **Batteries convert stored chemical energy into electrical energy** and then supply power to the rest of the electrical system.

Major battery parts are a case, a number of individual cells, cell connectors and two terminal posts. See Figure 5-2.

fig. 5-2
The components of a typical battery.

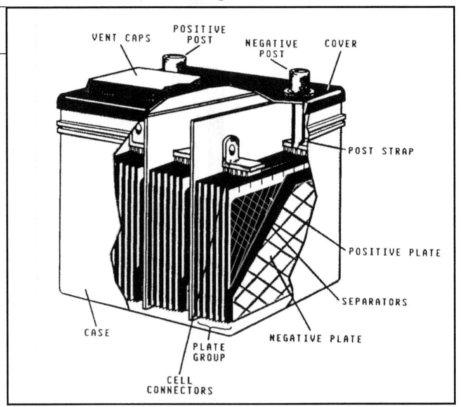

The **two posts on the top part of the battery** are called main battery terminals or battery posts. The **positive (+)** post **is** the **larger** one. The other is the negative (-) post. The battery **cables** are **connected to** these **posts.**

The vent caps are also on the top part of the battery. Gases build up when the battery charges. The **vent caps let** these **gases escape.** You will remove the vent caps to check the battery liquid level.

Batteries are dry-charged, wet-charged and maintenance free. The dry-charged battery has no electrolyte solution in it when it leaves the factory. The dealer adds the electrolyte solution to the battery upon selling it. The wet-charged battery has the electrolyte solution already in it when it leaves the factory. With these types of batteries, you must check the level of the solution whenever you service the truck. The maintenance free battery does not usually require this periodic maintenance.

Good maintenance practices will extend a battery's life. Make sure the cable connectors are not corroded. If they are, clean them or replace them. **To prevent corrosion, keep the exterior of the battery clean. Coat the battery terminals with** a high temperature **grease,** petroleum jelly or a terminal protector.

Check and **replace any cables that are frayed, worn or cracked.** Check to **make sure the battery connections are tight.** Unless the battery is maintenance-free, **check the electrolyte level regularly.** Check the hold-down bars to make **sure the battery is snug.** This keeps it from being damaged by vibration.

The electrolyte solution is acid and very dangerous. Electricity is always dangerous. So here are some important safety practices you should use around batteries to avoid serious injury.

- Never put your face directly over the battery when you are working on or around it.
- Disconnect the battery ground strap before you begin any electrical or engine work.
- Connect the ground strap last when you install a new battery.
- Disconnect the battery cable before fast charging the battery.
- Never use a fast charger as a booster to start the truck.
- Never hook up the battery backwards.
- Do not lay metal tools or other objects on the battery.
- Keep sparks and fires away from batteries. Gas from the electrolyte can catch fire.
- Use only distilled water to refill the battery.
- Avoid spilling the acid electrolyte solution. It will burn your skin.

The battery is the power source for a truck's electrical system. It supplies power to start the engine. Then the alternator or generator supplies power to charge the battery and to run the truck's systems. Older trucks may have generators. Newer trucks have alternators.

We'll talk about these two components later. Right now, let's take a look at the starter. The battery's main job is to supply power to the starting circuit.

The Starting Circuit

The starting circuit supplies electrical power to the starter motor, or starter. The **starter's job is to crank the engine.** That's why the starting circuit is also called the cranking circuit.

fig. 5-3
A 12-volt starting system includes the batteries, the ignition switch, the starter solenoid, the starter motor and the engine flywheel.

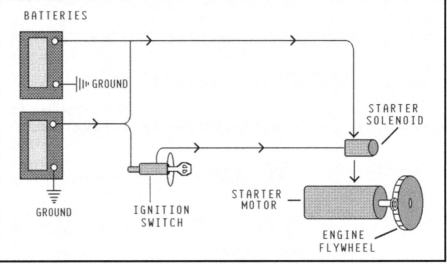

The parts of the starting circuit are listed below.

- the ignition switch
- the starting solenoid
- the starting circuit wiring
- the battery
- the starter motor

The **ignition switch opens and closes the circuit between the battery and starting solenoid,** which lets electrical current flow to the starter motor (the starter). When you turn the key all the way to the right, the ignition switch is in its "start" position. That action completes a circuit between the battery and the starter. After the truck's engine has started, the ignition switch goes back to the "run" position. This breaks the circuit between the battery and the starter.

The **starting solenoid opens and closes the starter circuit.** It's installed between the battery and the starter. The solenoid starting switch is the one used in most starting circuits. The purpose of the **solenoid switch** is to **control the starting motor.**

It takes only a small amount of current to close the solenoid switch. That means light, low amperage wires can be used to lead to this switch. The batteries are usually mounted close to the solenoid. That way the heavy, high amperage cables to the solenoid can be very short. The shorter heavy duty wires are better, especially on cold days when the starter needs to draw a lot of current to get the engine started. With shorter wire, there is less resistance and more current flow. That means short, heavy duty wires from the batteries to the solenoid will result in faster, more reliable starts.

There are two commonly used types of starting circuits: the 12-volt and the 24-volt. The 12-volt circuit connects all the batteries in parallel. The batteries are connected positive to positive and negative to negative. Figure 5-3 hows the components of a 12-volt starting circuit. In this circuit, the **voltage is kept at a constant 12 volts.**

fig. 5-4
(A) Batteries connected in series for starting and (B) batteries connected in parallel for normal use.

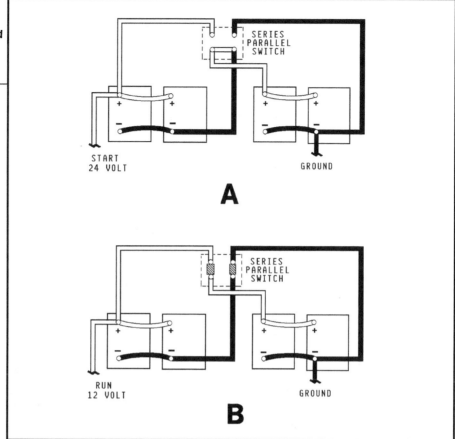

The 12-volt starter circuit works like this. You turn the key to the start position on the ignition switch. Current flows directly from the battery to the starter. The starter then engages and cranks the engine flywheel.

Some heavy duty diesel engines need more starting power. So they use a 24-volt starting circuit **with a 24-volt starter.** These starters supply faster engine cranking speeds. The **normal voltage is 12,** but the voltage does not stay at a constant 12 volts. It's **increased to 24 volts for the purpose of cranking the engine.**

You may wonder how a 24-volt starter could be used with a truck's basic 12-volt electrical system. The series-parallel switch makes this possible. Figure 5-4 on the next page shows a typical 24-volt starting circuit. In View A, the batteries are connected in series for starting. They are hooked up positive to negative. In this way, the starter motor is supplied with 24 volts. In View B, the engine has started and the series-parallel switch has changed the circuit to a 12-volt parallel system.

The Charging Circuit

Once the engine has started, an **alternator supplies the power that keeps the battery charged and runs the truck's systems.** The charging circuit is very important. It replaces the current that starting the engine uses up. Older trucks had generators while newer trucks have alternators. Whichever the truck uses, the circuit it's in is called the charging circuit (which makes sense since it charges the batteries).

THE ALTERNATOR
The components of the alternator charging circuit are listed below.

- the battery
- the regulator
- the alternator
- the ammeter or voltmeter
- the ignition switch

The alternator can produce almost maximum current even at very slow engine speeds. This is important to drivers who work in heavy city traffic. Figure 5-5 shows an alternator charging circuit.

The major disadvantage of the **alternator** is that it **produces alternating current.** "Alternating" means the voltage is continually changing back and forth from positive to negative Direct current is the only type that can charge the battery.

This problem is overcome by using **silicon diodes** to **change the alternating current into direct current.** These diodes act as one-way valves for electricity. They permit electricity to flow in only one direction and will stop it if it tries to go the other direction. So when the electricity comes to the diode, it is going back and forth. When it leaves the diode, it's going in only one direction.

fig. 5-5
Alternator charging circuit.

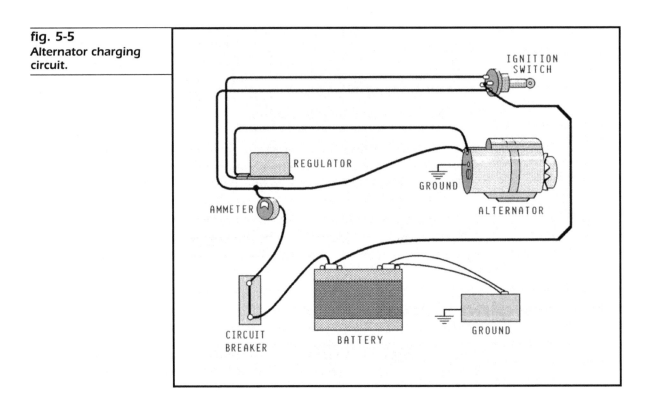

The alternator has a voltage regulator that controls the amount of current it puts out. However, the alternator regulator only has two electro-magnets. One stops excessive voltage output. The other stops excessive current output.

The Lighting and Instrument Circuits

Another circuit in the electrical system is the lighting circuit. The **lighting circuit is composed of circuit breakers, fuses and the wiring that connects to the various lights** on the truck. These lights include:

- the headlights
- the backing lights
- the turn signals
- the interior lights

- the parking lights
- the brake lights
- the emergency flashing lights
- the auxiliary lights

The **instrument circuit consists of the battery, the alternator (or generator), gauges and switches** on the dashboard **and the connecting wiring.** The gauges and switches vary from truck to truck.

Tracing the Wires

First of all remember never to work with an electrical circuit unless you know what you're doing. You can make things worse. Having said that, we can assure you there are some things you can do and should do. You should be able to troubleshoot electrical problems in a truck. To do this, you need to know about wiring and wiring diagrams.

fig. 5-6
So you can understand the symbols used, the wiring diagram will include a symbol chart similar to this one.

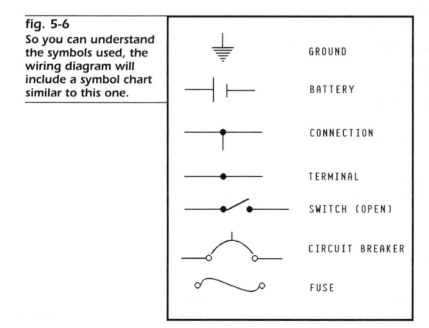

GROUND

BATTERY

CONNECTION

TERMINAL

SWITCH (OPEN)

CIRCUIT BREAKER

FUSE

Electrical systems use various sizes of wire. Wire is sized according to its diameter, or thickness, not including the insulation. Wire size is shown in terms of gauge, which is a series of numbers ranging from 0000 to 36. The larger the gauge number, the smaller the wire. For example, a No. 1 gauge wire is larger than a No. 36 gauge wire.

Larger wire has more current carrying capacity than smaller wire. Take the wire that goes from the battery to the starter. It is a heavy cable. Because of its size, we determine that it carries a heavy load.

Each **wire is color-coded.** This makes it easier to identify wires when you troubleshoot an electrical system. The **wiring diagram** for each truck and trailer **shows the color code** and the sizes of the wires. Although each manufacturer uses its own color coding system, most use red for power wires and white for ground wires.

Wiring diagrams **trace the flow of electrical current.** All wiring diagrams have the same basic information. They all use the same symbols to designate electrical parts. See Figure 5-6. When an electrical device fails, you can use the wiring diagram to figure out which wires might be involved.

You will use a wiring diagram to do troubleshooting. You might have to service a truck, for instance, whose clearance lights suddenly stopped working. If that happens, here's what you should do in the order in which you should do it.

- Most circuit breakers reset automatically, and you can hear them click on and off. Check the circuit breakers and fuses. If the breaker is off, reset it. If the fuse has blown, the glass window will be darkened, or you'll be able to see the broken metal ribbon inside. Replace broken fuses.
- Check the bulbs. If the bulbs are bad, they will have darkened. Or you'll be able to see the broken filament or hear it rattling around inside. Replace bad bulbs.
- If the breaker trips again or the fuse blows again, check for loose connections or broken wires.
- Using the truck's wiring diagram, follow the clearance light wires from the main terminal toward the lights.
- If you find a loose connection, tighten it.
- If you find broken wires, use wire connectors to reattach properly. Turn off the switch controlling that series of wires before you reattach the wires.

You can use the same basic procedures to solve many other simple electrical problems.

When a driver fixes a broken wire on the road, it is only a temporary fix. You will need to correct the problem fully upon the driver's return.

The Current Path

Taking what you've learned about the electrical system, let's trace the path of current through a truck's electrical system. The path begins at the battery. When the ignition switch is turned to the start position, the current flows from the battery to the starter. The starter cranks the engine. After the engine has started running, current flows from the alternator back to the battery to replace the current used to start the engine and to the other parts that need electrical power.

Chapter 5 Quiz

1. _____ refers to the specified amount of electric current that is produced and carried by the wires.
    A. Voltage
    B. Electronics
    C. Amperage
    D. Resistance

2. _____ circuits account for most electrical problems.
    A. Open
    B. Closed
    C. Complete
    D. Short

3. Circuit breakers and fuses protect the circuit from _____ .
    A. overloaded circuits
    B. closed circuits
    C. open circuits
    D. complete circuits

4. Most trucks have a basic 24-volt system.
    A. True
    B. False

5. The starter's job is to _____ .
    A. supply electrical power to the ignition switch
    B. crank the engine
    C. operate the starter switch
    D. operate the alternator

6. The 12-volt circuit connects all the batteries in parallel.
    A. True
    B. False

7. Once the engine has started, the _____ supplies the power that keeps the battery charged and runs the truck's systems.
    A. series-parallel switch
    B. engine
    C. 24-volt system
    D. alternator or generator

8. The _____ uses a voltage regulator that has three separate electromagnets.
   A. alternator
   B. 12-volt battery system
   C. generator
   D. starter

9. Wire is sized according to its length.
   A. True
   B. False

10. The bulb in the picture to the right is not lit up. Why?
    A. The current (wire) is not connected to the source (battery).
    B. The switch has not been turned on.
    C. The fuse has blown.
    D. The current is overloaded.

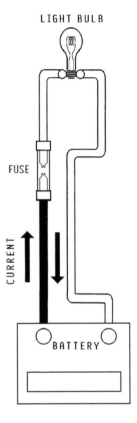

CHAPTER 6

ENGINES

The Heart of the Truck

In this chapter, you'll learn about the heart of the truck—the engine. You'll learn about the parts, the principles of operation and the auxiliary systems.

In terms of operation and parts, the **diesel engine** in a truck is **in some ways like the gasoline engine** in a family car. Both are internal combustion engines. Both use air and fuel in the combustion process. How the air and fuel mixture is ignited is one of the main differences between diesel and gas engines. Diesel engines depend on heat created by air compression for ignition. You'll see how later in this chapter.

Diesel and gasoline engines have many similar parts. They both have pistons and valves, for instance. However, **there are differences.** Diesel engine parts are placed under greater stresses than the ones in gasoline engines. These stresses are higher temperatures and compression pressures. To withstand these stresses, diesel engine parts must be stronger.

Diesel engines also usually have higher maximum torque and higher compression ratios than gasoline engines. They **are more efficient.** They turn slower and last longer. They need servicing less often. That is why the diesel engine is relied on to provide economical power whenever a job calls for an engine high in horsepower and reliability.

The Engine Parts

Before you learn about the principles of engine operation, you need to know more about its parts. Then we can talk about how these parts work together to produce power.

The main parts of the diesel engine are :

- the cylinder block
- the connecting rods
- the valve train
- the pistons
- the crankshaft

and all the smaller components that comprise these parts. We're going to look closely at each of these parts.

THE CYLINDER BLOCK

As you can see in Figure 6-1, the **cylinder block** consists of many smaller components. It **contains the cylinder bores** (or piston holes), the **water jackets,** the **oil passages** and the top half of the **crankcase.** The lower half of the crankcase is an oil pan that is bolted to the bottom of the block. One feature of engine design is the number of cylinder bores used. Diesel engines may have four, six or eight cylinders.

fig. 6-1
The cylinder block is a single casting that includes the crankcase and is the main part of the engine.

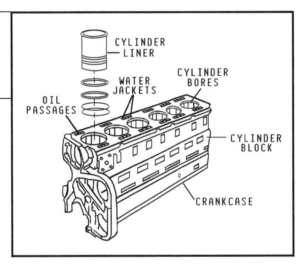

Notice the cylinder bores in Figure 6-1. These bores go down into the engine block. The pistons, which you'll learn about next, fit into these bores. In some types of blocks, the pistons run directly in the bores. In other types, **liners** are used. Then the liner can be replaced if the cylinder bore should become scored or worn. Scoring occurs when the piston scrapes the cylinder during movement. Replacing a liner is much less costly than repairing the bores or replacing the block.

Dry liners can be used with this type of engine design just described. The cylinder bores are made larger and then the liners are press-fitted into the bores and held there by friction. However, diesel engines are usually designed to use wet liners, and wet liners are preferred because they are easier to replace and cool faster.

To understand the difference between the wet liner and the dry liner, you first need to know about the **water jackets.** The water jackets are the spaces in the block that surround the cylinder bores with coolant to carry away some of the engine heat. Dry liners are very thin and simply fit inside enlarged cylinder bores. Wet liners are much thicker and actually form the outer parts of the water jackets.

Cylinder blocks that use wet liners are basically hollow inside. The block has a shoulder at the top of each cylinder bore. The edges of the liners slip down over these shoulders, hold the liners in place and form a seal at the top of the liner. The bottom of the liner has an O-ring that makes a seal between the liner and the block. The coolant then flows between and around the liners.

THE PISTONS

The arrangement of the pistons is a major factor in engine design. There are two types of engines based on piston arrangement: the V-type engine and the in-line engine. With the **V-type, half the cylinders and pistons are on one side** and the **other half are on the other side.** The engine we use in our illustrations in this chapter is an **in-line** engine. In this engine, the **cylinders** are **all in a straight line.**

Diesel engine pistons are designed to be very **durable.** They **must withstand high compression pressures** of up to 900 psi **and temperatures** that can exceed 1,000 degrees Fahrenheit. Depending on the weather, pistons can be exposed to very cold temperatures, too.

Pistons are usually made of malleable iron or aluminum. Aluminum pistons are lighter than iron ones, which reduces the load on the engine bearings and crankshaft. Aluminum pistons conduct heat better than iron ones; in fact, they cool off two times faster. Vibration has less of an effect on aluminum pistons.

Aluminum pistons do wear out faster than iron ones, and they cannot withstand heat as well as iron pistons. However, their ability to resist scoring and the other advantages we've listed far outweigh these disadvantages. Aluminum pistons and piston parts are built heavier to compensate for faster wear, and special rings are used to reduce the negative effects of heat. A nickel iron alloy is used for piston ring inserts because it expands at the same rate as aluminum, but is stronger and wears better under heat. Also, heat treated steel bands are used in the crown of the piston. These bands add strength and increase piston life.

Let's take a close look at the two major parts of the piston: the crown (top) and the rings.

Pistons have formed crowns or flat crowns. **Diesel engines** most often **use formed crown pistons** because they create better air turbulence for combustion. Air turbulence is the swirling of the air in the combustion chamber. This helps mix the fuel sprayed into the cylinder with the air. Good air turbulence means **more complete combustion.** It also makes for more even cylinder pressure and cleaner emissions.

The two types of piston rings are compression rings and oil rings. **Compression rings** are usually made of cast iron and are often chrome plated to cut down on scoring and decrease wear. Installed near the top of the piston, they **make the piston fit the cylinder wall** so that compression is created and maintained. In other words, they keep the compressed air in the cylinder from escaping and thus **maintain compression pressure in the combustion chamber.** Many pistons only use one or two compression rings; however, some designs have several rings.

Oil rings are usually very thin, made of cast iron and can come in one or two pieces. Most use an expander which forces the oil ring against the cylinder wall. **Oil rings spread oil along the sides of the cylinder** so there is always a film of oil between the piston and the cylinder as the piston moves up and down. This serves both **to cool the engine** and to **prevent scoring** of the cylinder walls. On some piston designs, these rings are installed right below the compression rings. On other designs, more oil rings are installed below the piston pin. You'll learn about the piston pin when we talk about connecting rods. Figure 6-2 shows you both the piston and the connecting rod in relation to the cylinder block.

As we said, oil is used to **keep pistons cool.** Engines use one of three methods to do this: circulation, splash or spray. Most diesel engines use the spray method. Oil is sprayed through a jet in the block. This **oil is sprayed on the underside of the piston head.** To provide better cooling, the bottom of the piston heads are finned, which also adds strength to the piston.

Because the piston slides up and down the cylinder 2,000 times or more a minute at full speed, all pistons and cylinders will eventually wear out, even with good lubrication. However, there are ways to prolong the life of the pistons and cylinders or cylinder liners. Here's how.

- The oil should be changed frequently. This removes impurities that could build up in the oil, score the cylinder walls or cause the oil to lose some of its lubrication ability.
- Having a clean air filter helps. If dirt from the air gets into the cylinder, it may score the cylinder walls.
- Avoiding engine overheating will also preserve the pistons and cylinders. When metal heats up, it expands. That means the cylinder bore size will decrease while the piston size increases, decreasing the clearance between the piston and the cylinder. The piston may scrape hard against the cylinder, damaging both parts.

THE CONNECTING RODS

The piston is connected to the crankshaft by the connecting rod and the connecting rod is connected to the piston by the piston pin. You can see this in Figure 6-2 on the next page.

Connecting rods are made of forged steel. They **transfer the piston's up and down motion to the crankshaft's rotary, or turning, motion.** The two types of connecting rods are the I-beam and the tubular. The type used depends on engine design. The main parts of the connecting rod are the piston pin and the bearings.

The **piston pin connects** the top end of the **connecting rod with the piston.** Piston pins are made of chromium steel and come in various diameters (sizes). The size of the pin used depends on the load it has to carry.

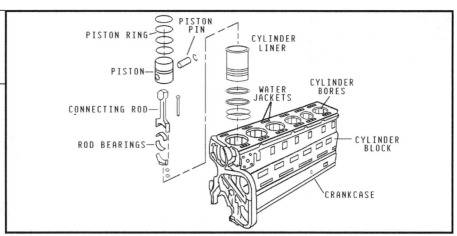

fig. 6-2
The piston and connecting rod parts fit together and then go inside the cylinder liner.

Wherever you have moving parts in an engine, you'll find bearings. The **connecting rod bearings** are the thin wall type. They reduce friction, **protect the crankshaft and the connecting rod from excessive wear** and ensure that the crankshaft and connecting rod turn freely. These bearings have holes in the center through which oil flows to lubricate and keep parts cool.

THE CRANKSHAFT

The crankshaft is forged or cast heat-treated steel. The crankshaft is the **main shaft** of the diesel engine. Its **rotating motion is used to drive the truck's wheels.**

Crankshafts have drilled **oil passages** and so does the cylinder block. The crankshaft passages line up with holes in the connecting rods and main bearings. Crankshaft holes are used to **supply lubrication** to the crankshaft bearings and the pistons. The **crankshaft bearings** are the main bearings of the engine. They **reduce friction** and ensure that the crankshaft turns freely.

The **flywheel** is connected to one end of the crankshaft. It does three jobs. When you start the engine, **the starter engages it** to start the crankshaft turning. It **forms one face of the clutch.** As the engine runs, it **dampens** the **vibration** of combustion.

THE VALVE TRAIN

The **valve train** is that series of parts which **operates the intake and exhaust valves.** First let's look at the parts; then we'll describe how they work.

Each cylinder has at least one intake and one exhaust valve. **Intake valves let air into the cylinders.** The **exhaust valves let burned gases out** of the cylinders after combustion. Two-stroke cycle engines have no intake valves. They use intake ports instead.

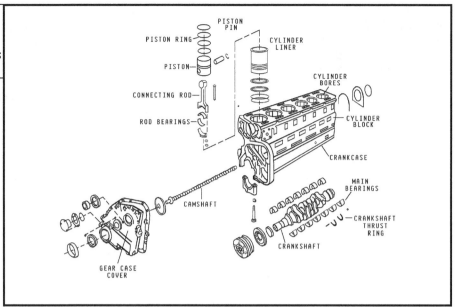

fig. 6-3
Now we've added the crankshaft and its parts and the camshaft and its parts.

Because valves are exposed to high temperatures and pressures, they are made of special alloys, usually in two pieces. The valve head and face make up one piece; the fillet and stem make up the other piece.

The valve head rests on the valve seat. Many engines use replaceable valve seat inserts. These inserts are used so seat life can be lengthened. It is important that you install valve seats properly. If you don't, a valve leak could occur.

The valve guide keeps the valve in alignment with the valve seat. Valve springs pull the valves closed.

The **camshaft** is a straight steel shaft on which there are a number of bearings and cams. Each cam has a **cam lobe,** or bump, on it. Each cam rotates as the camshaft turns.

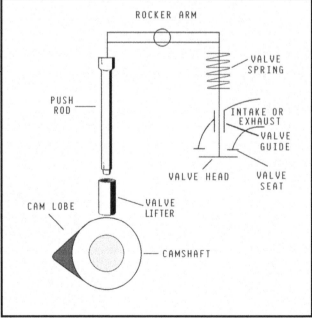

fig. 6-4
The purpose of the valve train is to open and close intake and exhaust valves.

The push rod is just that — a straight rod. One end sits on top of the valve lifter or cam follower which sits on top of the camshaft. The other is connected to a **rocker arm.** The rocker arm acts like a teeter-totter to **open and close valves.** It works like this. The camshaft turns and the cam lobe contacts the push rod, pushing it up. The push rod pushes one end of the rocker arm. The other end pushes the valve down, opening it. As the camshaft continues to turn, the lobe moves on and the push rod returns to its normal position. The rocker arm rocks back and the spring under the valve pulls it back into place.

Principles of Operation

As we discussed in Chapter 5, the starter cranks the engine and gets the crankshaft turning. The turning crankshaft pushes the pistons down in the cylinders. While the pistons are moving down, air is pulled into the cylinders. Then, as the pistons start to move up again, the air intake stops. The moving pistons squeeze the air in the cylinders into a smaller and smaller space. As the air is being compressed, it also begins to heat up. By the time the pistons reach the top of the cylinders, the air will be very hot.

When the pistons get near the Top Dead Center (TDC) of the cylinders, the fuel is injected into the cylinders. The hot compressed air ignites the fuel. This is called combustion. The temperature and pressure increases as the fuel burns. The pressure forces the piston down and the connecting rod transfers this downward thrust to the crankshaft. The turning force is transferred to the engine flywheel. In Chapter 3 we show how this force then goes through the clutch and the transmission where it's turned into torque that is transmitted to the wheels through the drive train.

THE TWO-CYCLE AND FOUR-CYCLE ENGINES

The method used to obtain power is a feature of diesel engine design. Some engines use the two-stroke cycle for power. Other engines use the four-stroke cycle. However, both use the compression/combustion method just described to make power. The term stroke refers to the up and down movement of the piston.

In a **two-stroke cycle engine** the piston makes two strokes in its combustion process: the **compression stroke** and the **power stroke.** With the power stroke, the piston moves down the cylinder. Combustion has already taken place. As it gets close to the bottom, the exhaust valves open and the intake ports are uncovered. Two-stroke cycle engines use intake ports instead of intake valves. After the ports are uncovered, air is forced into the cylinder by the supercharger. The exhaust gases are pushed out by the forced air. While this is going on, the piston is still moving down the cylinder.

When the piston gets to the Bottom Dead Center (BDC) of the cylinder, it begins its upward, or compression stroke. While the piston continues upward, the exhaust valve closes. Forced air continues to enter the cylinder until the piston's upward movement covers the intake ports. The remaining air is compressed. Just before the piston reaches Top Dead Center (TDC), the fuel is injected and combustion occurs, starting the process over again.

As the name implies, the **four-stroke cycle engine** uses four piston strokes: **intake, compression, power and exhaust.** On the intake stroke, air enters the cylinder as the piston moves down. As the compression stroke starts, the intake valve closes and then the piston moves up the cylinder, compressing the air. The piston continues up until just before it reaches TDC. Fuel is then injected into the cylinder, and combustion takes place. The high pressure caused by combustion forces the piston down the cylinder for the power stroke. As the piston reaches BDC, the exhaust valve opens. The piston moves up the cylinder again, pushing out the burned gases through the exhaust valve for the exhaust stroke.

Each of these engines has advantages and disadvantages. The **two-stroke engine is able to produce more power from a smaller engine.** This is because it requires only two strokes to get one power stroke. The four-stroke engine needs four strokes for each power stroke. So in effect each piston provides twice as much power in a two-stroke engine. This means the engine can be built smaller and still provide the same power output as a larger four-stroke engine. The disadvantage of a two-stroke is that it **is less efficient** than the four-stroke engine. This is mainly because the two-stroke **requires a supercharger that** is driven by the engine. This **uses some power that could go to the wheels. Four-stroke engines usually use a turbocharger that** is driven by the exhaust gases and so **does not rob any power from the engine.**

Auxiliary Systems

Just learning about the engine is not enough. You must know about the other vehicle systems that work with the engine. These are referred to as auxiliary systems. The electrical system covered in Chapter 5 is one of the auxiliary systems. The rest of this chapter will discuss the other auxiliary systems.

COOLING
All engines have some type of **cooling system** that **controls the engine's temperature and prevents overheating.** Two types of cooling systems are the air cooling system and the liquid cooling system. The **liquid cooling system is** the one **most often used.**

The parts that make up the liquid cooling system are listed below:

- the radiator
- the radiator cap
- the fan and fan belt
- the water pump

- the thermostat
- the engine water jacket
- the water hoses
- the coolant

The radiator, the largest component in the cooling system, consists of an upper and lower tank, a core, a filler cap, an overflow tube and connections for water hoses. The coolant absorbs heat as it travels through the cylinder block. **In the radiator,** the **coolant releases heat** into the surrounding air.

To fill the radiator, you pour coolant into the filler neck of the upper tank. An overflow tube on one side of the filler neck lets excess coolant or pressure escape. The radiator cap fits on the filler neck. The radiator cap seals the radiator and provides a way to release excess pressure. Inside the cap is a spring-loaded seal. If the pressure gets too high the pressure overcomes the spring and raises the seal. This allows coolant and pressure to flow out. When the pressure drops, the spring pushes the seal back in place and stops the flow. The pressure cap allows the coolant to reach a higher boiling point.

You'll find the fan and fan belt behind the radiator. The fan belt drives the fan.

There are two types of fans. One type starts turning as soon as the engine is turned on and continues to turn until the engine stops. The second type is the **clutch fan.** It's thermostatically operated. This means the fan **doesn't begin turning until the engine temperature reaches the clutch fan's preset temperature.**

The first type of fan uses the most power from the engine because it is always turning whether the engine requires cooling or not. This is why the other type is used. It saves power and increases fuel economy. The savings can be great because the engine fan on a big truck can use up to 25 horsepower.

The **water pump moves the coolant through the cooling system.** The thermostat controls engine temperature. The thermostat fits into a housing in the water jacket.

The water jacket is found in the engine head and cylinder block and consists of passages around cylinders and valves through which the coolant flows.

The **water hoses connect the cooling system components.** They are also called radiator hoses.

Most of the **coolant is 50% water and 50% antifreeze** plus chemical additives. Most manufacturers recommend distilled water and low silicate ethylene glycol or propylene glycol antifreeze.

Now let's look at how all these parts work together to cool the engine. Look at Figure 6-5 as we discuss this process.

fig. 6-5
The radiator and its parts work together to control engine temperature and prevent overheating.

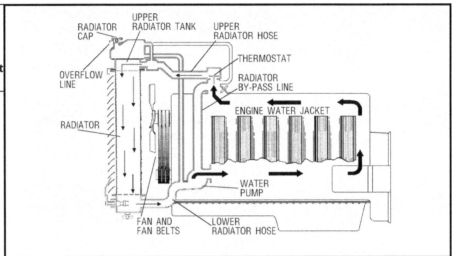

When you start a cold engine, the thermostat is closed. The coolant in the water jacket begins to circulate around the cylinders and valves. As it circulates it flows past the thermostat. **When the coolant reaches the thermostat's preset temperature,** around 180 degrees Fahrenheit, the **thermostat opens the passage to the radiator** and **directs** some of the **coolant to** flow through the **radiator to cool off the coolant.**

The hot coolant leaves the engine through the upper water hose. It goes through the hose into the top tank of the radiator and down through the radiator's core. The forward motion of the truck and the **fan pull air in through the radiator and cool the coolant.**

When the coolant reaches the bottom tank, the water pump draws the coolant through the lower water hose. The coolant passes through the water pump and is forced through the water jacket. Then the process begins again.

The whole idea of the thermostat is to direct the flow of the water. When the water is below about 180 degrees Fahrenheit, the thermostat directs the water to flow only through the block and pump, without going through the radiator. Then as the water temperature increases to about 180 degrees Fahrenheit, the thermostat opens and permits some water to flow into the radiator. The thermostat continually opens and closes slightly to direct the flow of the coolant and thereby control engine temperature.

THE FUEL SYSTEM

The **fuel system delivers the fuel to the engine.** The parts of the fuel system are as follows:

- the fuel tank
- the fuel filter or filters
- the fuel pump
- the fuel lines
- the fuel injectors
- the fuel

The **fuel tank holds the fuel** and the **filter cleans it** before it reaches the fuel pump. The fuel system on a diesel engine is a precision piece of equipment with very close tolerances and small holes. If dirt, gum or water gets into the system, damage or at least poor performance will result. Fuel with this kind of sludge in it will plug up the system. You can see why there are sometimes two filters.

The **fuel pump delivers the fuel to the engine.** The two types of fuel pumps are the constant volume type and the metering type. **Fuel lines carry the fuel from the pump to the cylinders.** The fuel **injectors spray the fuel into the combustion chambers.**

Let's examine two grades of diesel fuel. **Grade 2 diesel fuel** is the **most widely used.** It's a little less costly and thicker than Grade 1. The only advantage to Grade 1 is that the temperature has to drop much lower for #1 fuel to thicken or jell than it would for #2. But this does not make up for the risk of using such a thin fuel. Its thinness means it doesn't do as good a job of lubricating as #2. That means more wear. Grade #1 also does not produce as much power. Performance suffers.

During the winter, refineries change the mix of #2 diesel so it will stay fluid at colder temperatures. Also, the fuel stations will mix Grade 1 and 2 to achieve the same end. Grade 1 fuel should be used only in below zero degree temperatures. Trucks designed to run in such cold weather will use fuel heaters and additives to keep #2 diesel from jelling.

Ultra-low sulfur diesel (USLD) made its appearance in 2006 in a move to lower emissions. The Environmental Protection Agency mandated USLD to be used in model year 2007 and newer engines. You'll read more about USLD in Chapter 18.

Let's trace the flow of the fuel through the fuel system. The fuel leaves the fuel tank and runs through the fuel lines to the check valve. From there, it flows through the filter and into the fuel pump. The pump forces it through the fuel lines and into the fuel injectors. The injectors spray a measured amount of fuel into the cylinders.

THE LUBRICATING SYSTEM

The **lubricating system cleans, cools and oils the engine's moving parts.** It helps the piston rings seal the combustion chamber and **reduces wear on metal parts** by keeping a thin film of oil between them.

Lubricating systems differ depending on the make and model of truck, but they all consist of the components listed below.

- the oil pan
- the oil filters
- the oil

- the oil pump
- the oil cooler

You'll use the type of oil recommended by the manufacturer of your engine. Diesel engine oils are readily available. The oil must be changed according to the manufacturer's directions, or more often.

fig. 6-6
A typical lubrication system for a heavy duty truck.

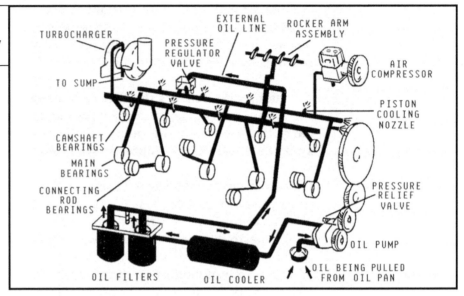

Changing the oil is one of the **most important** things you can do **to improve the performance and lengthen the service of your engine.** The oil gets dirty largely because of the by-products of combustion. But the residue of unburned fuel on the cylinder walls also mixes with the oil. This tends to dilute the oil so it doesn't lubricate as well. Coolant can ruin oil very quickly. If you notice a light foam in the oil or an increased amount of oil on the dipstick, change it immediately and check the cooling system. It could be a sign of a slight internal leak.

The oil pan holds the oil. The **oil pump,** under pressure, **pumps the oil from the oil pan through the oil cooler.** After leaving the cooler, the oil moves **through the filters.** Oil filters strain out metallic particles and dirt from the oil. The filtered oil then goes **through the lubricating lines into the engine.**

Some parts, like crankshaft bearings and camshaft bearings, get oil under direct pressure from the oil pump. Others, like the cylinder walls and pistons, have oil sprayed or splashed over them. Most engines use both direct pressure and splashing in their lubricating system.

THE EXHAUST SYSTEM
The **exhaust system provides an outlet for engine heat, burned gases and other waste products.**

The parts of a typical exhaust system are the exhaust manifold, the exhaust pipe and the muffler. **The exhaust manifold receives the exhaust gases from the cylinders.** From the exhaust manifold, these **gases pass through the turbocharger, the exhaust pipe and into the muffler.** The muffler's job is to reduce exhaust noise.

SUPERCHARGERS, TURBOCHARGERS AND AFTERCOOLERS
Both **superchargers and turbochargers** are blowers used by both two-stroke and four-stroke cycle engines to **increase engine power by packing more air into the cylinder.** Both help to make an engine burn cleaner and cooler.

Let's look at superchargers first. A **supercharger is a mechanically driven** blower. An accessory shaft from the engine drives the supercharger. The supercharger both **provides pressurized air to the cylinder and forces exhaust gases out** of the cylinder. This is used primarily on two stroke engines.

The **turbocharger is** a supercharger that is **driven by the exhaust gases.** A turbocharger is more efficient because no power is drawn off the engine to run it.

Many diesel truck engines have an aftercooler located between the turbocharger and the intake manifold. An aftercooler is a heat exchanger. **It takes the hot air leaving the turbocharger and cools it before it goes to the engine.** This **increases power** because cooler air is denser and more oxygen can be packed into the cylinder. That means more fuel can be burned and that means more power from the engine.

Chapter 6 Quiz

1. The main part of the engine is the _____ .
   A. rocker arm
   B. valve
   C. cylinder
   D. cylinder block

2. Installed near the top of the piston, the oil rings make the piston fit the cylinder wall so that compression is created and maintained.
   A. True
   B. False

3. The _____ dampens the vibration of combustion and is engaged by the starter when you start the engine.
   A. crankshaft
   B. flywheel
   C. camshaft
   D. connecting rod

For Questions 4, 5, 6 and 7, fill in the blanks in the figure below to identify the components.

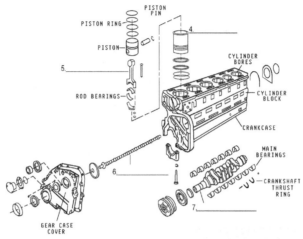

For Question 8, fill in the blank in the figure to the right.

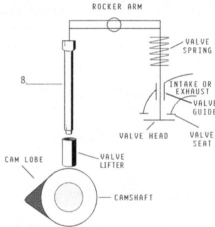

9. The job of the _____ system is to control the engine's temperature and prevent overheating.
   A. lubricating
   B. turbocharging
   C. fuel
   D. cooling

10. The oil gets dirty largely because of _____ .
    A. the by-products of combustion
    B. dirt left in the engine from the manufacturing process
    C. coolant leaks
    D. the practice of mixing Grade 1 and Grade 2 fuels

CHAPTER 7

DRIVE TRAIN

From the Engine to the Wheels

That's what the drive train is, everything from the engine to the wheels that actually makes the truck move. So, the drive train is made up of the engine,

- the clutch
- the transmission
- the drive shaft

- the differential
- the inter-axle differential
- the axles

and the wheels. The engine was covered in the last chapter and the transmission in Chapter 3. In this chapter, you'll learn about the rest of the drive train up to the wheels. You'll learn about the wheels in Chapter 9. We'll also cover the axles, the frame and suspension systems.

The Clutch

The clutch is the component that **connects or disconnects the engine from the transmission and the driveline.** When the clutch is engaged, the power produced by the engine is transmitted through the clutch to the transmission. When the clutch is disengaged, the power flow stops at the flywheel. The clutch provides the driver with an easy way to shift gears.

The clutch is made up of the clutch housing, the flywheel, the clutch disc (or discs), the pressure plate, the release assembly and the controls. The clutch forces plate surfaces together under pressure.

The **pressure plate** assembly is bolted to the flywheel. It provides the necessary force to **keep the clutch plate in constant contact with the flywheel** while the clutch is engaged.

The clutch disc or discs consists of a smooth disc or discs, or plate, a facing material attached to the disc surface and a splined hub. The clutch disc is also called the driven plate assembly, the clutch plate and the driven disc or discs. It's attached to the transmission input shaft with the splined, or grooved, shaft.

A single-plate clutch is one that has only one driven disc activated by the cover assembly. A **dual-plate clutch** has two driven discs separated by a smooth surfaced center plate. The dual-plate clutch greatly **increases the amount of engine torque the clutch is able to absorb and transfer to the transmission.** Dual-plate clutches are used with heavy duty truck engines.

fig. 7-1
The friction disc type clutch is the type most commonly used with manual transmissions.

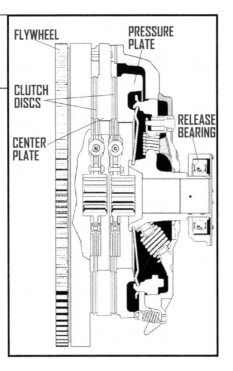

We will discuss the **friction disc clutch,** the type most commonly used **in trucks with manual transmissions.** It is shown in Figure 7-1. The major components of this clutch are the flywheel, the clutch disc or discs, the pressure plate assembly and the clutch release bearing. The flywheel is attached to the engine's crankshaft. It is the driving member of the clutch.

The **clutch release assembly** includes the release bearing assembly and the clutch release mechanism. When the clutch pedal is pressed, the release fingers rotate and pull on the release bearing. This forces the release bearing against the clutch release levers. The release members move the pressure plate to the rear of the clutch assembly, **disengaging the clutch.** See Figure 7-2.

fig. 7-2
A clutch release mechanism. Depressing the clutch pedal moves the pressure plate to the rear of the clutch assembly.

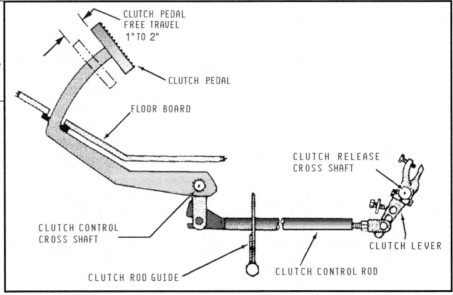

Let's look at the clutch controls. The clutch control you'll use most often is the **clutch pedal** in the cab. This **activates the clutch linkage** between the pedal **and the release mechanism** on the clutch.

There are two types of mechanical clutches: the direct and the cable operated. **Direct clutch controls** are made up of a manually operated assembly of levers, rods and springs that connect the pedal to the clutch release mechanism. The arrangement of the **mechanical linkage** components varies. **Conventional tractors use the direct control** because the pedal is physically close to the clutch.

Cable operated clutch controls use a cable to **replace part of the linkage. Cabovers sometimes use a cable** because it's several feet from the clutch to the pedal. Also, the cable provides a way for the linkage to flex when the pedal tilts up with the cab.

HOW THE CLUTCH WORKS

Now that we know the basic components of a clutch, let's see one in action. First of all, the driver **pushes down on the clutch pedal** to **disengage the clutch** so the gears can be shifted. This **activates the clutch release assembly** which **separates the pressure plate from the clutch plate.** This means that the **power from the engine is also separated from the transmission.** After the driver has made the shift, the **clutch pedal is released.** The **pressure plate** is now forced against the **clutch plate,** which is forced against the **flywheel.** That means that all three parts will **rotate as a unit.** The engine's **power is now being transmitted by the clutch to the transmission** gears. The gears cannot be shifted when there is power on the gears.

The Driveline

The driveline consists of all **the components that connect the transmission to the differential.** The driveline **transmits the engine's torque from the transmission to the differential.** You'll learn about the differential next. Right now, look at Figure 7-3. You can see that the main components of the driveline are the drive shaft, the universal joints and the flanges or yokes. How many drive shafts and universal joints are used on a truck depends on the wheelbase length, the types of transmission and rear axle combination, and what auxiliary equipment is used. Now let's look at each component individually.

DRIVE SHAFT

Most drive shafts are made of hollow steel tubing because such tubing provides maximum torque-carrying capacity at minimum weight. The hollow shaft is the strongest and it has a great resistance to twist.

The drive shaft spins three to four times faster than the wheels or tires, which means the drive shaft must be exactly balanced. At the factory, drive shafts are dynamically balanced and permanent weights are attached to prevent vibration.

The **basic drive shaft** assembly is a **two U-joint and shaft assembly,** which is a drive shaft with a universal joint at each end. The principal parts of this two U-joint and shaft assembly are the slip joint, the tubular shaft and the permanent joint, as you can see in Figure 7-3.

fig. 7-3
The driveline consists of the drive shaft, universal joints and yokes or flanges.

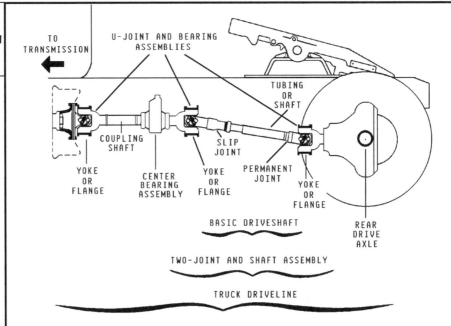

The U-joint is a flexible coupling used to transfer the rotary motion between one rotating shaft and another while allowing for changes in the driveline operating angle. This is necessary because the differential moves up and down when the truck goes over bumps causing the angle between the transmission and the differential to change. U-joint is short for universal joint. These connectors are also referred to as "Cordon Joints."

The slip joint provides a way for the drive shaft to change its length slightly while operating, thus making up for the movement of the rear axle and the suspension.

In other words, the **U-joint allows a change in the angle between the transmission and the rear end. The slip joint permits a change in length.** Both these actions are needed because the rear end moves up and down in relation to the transmission.

The **center bearing assembly supports the driveline** when two or more drive shafts are used. The **coupling shaft** is an extension shaft used to **connect the transmission output shaft to the differential on**

long wheelbase tractors, because the distance is too great for a single shaft. A center bearing assembly connected to the truck's frame is usually used to support the coupling shaft.

The Differential

There are two types of differentials. One is called simply the differential. It divides the drive axle in half and allows each half to spin independently. The other is the inter-axle differential. It divides the two axles and lets each turn independently of the other.

THE DIFFERENTIAL

The axle differential is a gear mechanism that does two main jobs. It **transmits power** from the drive shaft to the axles. It splits the drive axle in half and then **lets each axle half turn at a different speed than the other.** This means that each wheel can rotate independently of the other under certain conditions. Take cornering, for example. When a truck takes a corner, the outside wheel must rotate faster than the inside wheel. Figure 7-4 shows you how the differential operates when cornering. Without the differential, you'll drag at least one set of tires around the corner. That will mean the tires will wear out very quickly.

Before we explain the differential and how it works, let's take a minute to clear up a couple of common misunderstandings. First, a differential does not divide the drive power equally between the wheels. Second, it does not send all the power to the wheels that have the most traction.

What a differential does do is send **all the power to the wheels with the least traction.** That means if you jack up one side of the drive axle, start up the tractor and engage the clutch, the tractor will just sit and spin. The same thing can happen if just one set of wheels is on a patch of ice and you try to start the truck moving.

There are several types of differentials, but the major components of a typical differential are the drive pinion, the ring gear and four spider gears. These parts are enclosed in a differential case that is mounted at the center of the drive axle housing.

fig. 7-4
When you turn a corner, the differential will let the outer drive wheels turn faster than the inner drive wheels.

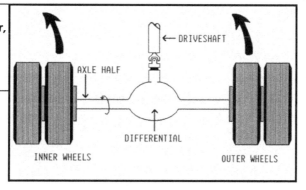

INNER WHEELS   OUTER WHEELS

DRIVESHAFT

AXLE HALF

DIFFERENTIAL

The drive pinion is connected to the drive shaft and it drives the ring gear. The four spider gears are attached to the ring gear and mesh with gears on the ends of the drive axle halves. Each spider gear is free to rotate. Each axle gear meshes with all four spider gears. So the **power is transferred from the ring gear through the spider gears and into the axles halves.**

When wheels turn at the same speed (traveling in a straight line), drive pinions rotate with the spider gears. However, the spider gears do not revolve because both wheels are turning at the same rpm. In other words, **both axles halves revolve at the same speed.**

When the **truck makes a turn,** the **inner wheels** begin to **slow.** As one axle half begins to spin at a slower speed than the other, the **spider gears** begin to **rotate, allowing** the **axle halves to spin at different speeds** and allow a truck to turn without scrubbing the tires. In other words, the spider's gears that are attached to the axle shaft of the inner wheel slow, too, and begin to rotate in a direction that adds speed to the opposite spider gears and the other wheel.

Another way to look at this is to say that the spider gears have acted as balancing levers. To illustrate this, let's say that the vehicle is traveling at a constant speed going into a curve. The inner wheels slow to only half of the vehicle speed. The differential increases the speed of the outer wheels to twice the vehicle speed. The differential has transmitted the decrease in speed of the inner wheels as a proportionate increase in speed.

The types of gears and gear teeth used in differentials are the hypoid, amboid and spiral beveled. The most common type of ring-and-drive pinion gearing used in differentials are the hypoid and amboid. See Figure 7-5. The hypoid is used mainly on the forward axle of the tandem drive. The amboid is often used on the rear axles of a tandem drive assembly.

fig. 7-5
Most trucks use hypoid gearing because it provides quieter operation and more torque-carrying capacity.

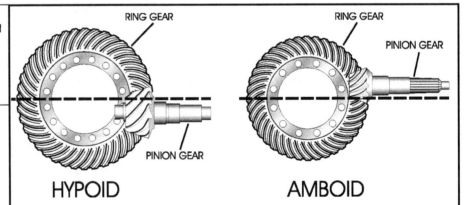

THE INTER-AXLE DIFFERENTIAL
The inter-axle differential is **used on tandem rear-drive axle trucks.** It's also called a power divider.

The **tandem assembly** on trucks with tandem rear-drive axles has two parts: the front rear axle and the rear rear axle. Both of the axles are called drivers.

When a tractor has two drive axles, a differential and the inter-axle differential are housed together in the differential case assembly on the front rear axle. Another differential is mounted on the rear rear axle. A short drive shaft connects the drive unit of the front rear axle to the drive unit of the rear rear axle.

In terms of function, the inter-axle differential is really just another differential. It does the same thing the axle differential does, but between two axles rather than between two axle halves. It is needed because just as the inside and outside tires rotate at different speeds sometimes, so do the front and rear axles. The inter-axle differential **compensates for slippage, mismatched tires between axles and cornering.** It can also be used to improve traction when trying to couple to a loaded trailer and when adjusting sliders.

The main difference between the differential and the inter-axle differential is that the inter-axle differential can and should be used **to manage slippery road conditions.** Chapter 2 shows that there is a control in the cab that lets you **lock the inter-axle differential** and there is a warning light that reminds you when it is locked.

With normal road conditions, the inter-axle differential should remain unlocked. Along with the front rear differential and the rear rear differential, the inter-axle differential provides the capability for each set of wheels to spin independently of the others. This eliminates tire scrubbing when taking a curve or making a turn.

However, with slippery road conditions, the inter-axle differential should be locked. This forces the front rear differential and the rear rear differential to turn together. This doubles the traction on a slippery road surface because it ensures that power will go to each axle. Now for the tractor to spin out, two wheels (one on each axle) will have to spin. If the inter-axle was not locked, one wheel could spin and that would mean a loss of traction. Figure 7-6 shows you what we mean.

The Axles

Truck axles can be divided into two categories: drive axles (also called live or power axles) and non-drive axles (also called dead or non-power axles). The three main parts of a drive axle are the axle halves, the axle housing and the differential. One job of the differential is to transmit the torque from the drive shaft to the drive axles.

fig. 7-6
The large black arrows show you where the power goes on a slippery road surface when the inter-axle control is locked.

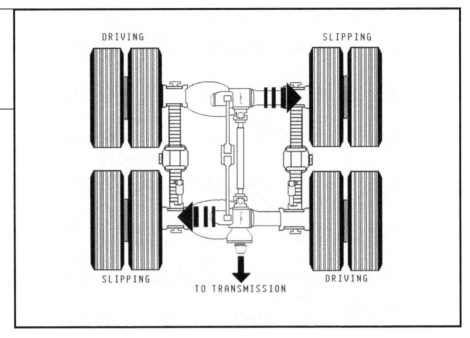

Axles are also labeled by their position on the truck: front or rear. Front axles are either drive or non-drive steering axles. The most common is the non-drive front axle. Its construction is an I-beam crossmember mounted between pivot centers. Front axles are rated by their weight carrying capacity, normally 12,000 pounds.

Many trucks have one drive axle. Many are equipped with two rear drive axles, one behind the other. This is the tandem arrangement we discussed when you learned about inter-axle differentials.

The Frame

The frame is **the foundation of the truck.** The truck body, engine, drive train, steering system axle, wheels and tires, brake assemblies, suspension system and other components or assemblies are all directly or indirectly mounted on the frame or suspended from it.

The major parts of the frame are the side rails and crossmembers. The **side rails carry the load.** A number of crossmembers are bolted or riveted to the side rails. These **crossmembers stabilize the frame.** They also support the engine, transmission, cab and other heavy components. **For added strength, gusset plates** are welded or riveted at the points **where the crossmembers are joined to the side rails.** The gusset plates are actually angular pieces of metal.

Frames are made of steel or aluminum. Brackets and hangers are bolted or riveted to the frame to support shock absorbers, springs, fenders and running boards.

The Suspension System

The suspension system serves many purposes. It **supports the weight of the vehicle,** keeping the frame from resting directly on the axles. The suspension also **provides a smoother ride** for the driver and the cargo. **It absorbs the shocks** and jolts of traveling over the road's surface and **keeps the wheels and tires from bouncing on rough terrain.** It also helps maintain proper frame alignment. Thus, the suspension system protects the wheels and tires from undue wear.

Two common suspension systems are the leaf spring and air ride. There are a variety of leaf spring and air ride suspensions for the different positions of the axles on tractors and trailers. Each suspension, spring or air, has a load rating based upon the number of pounds it can safely support. A single axle suspension will generally be designed to support less weight than that of a tandem axle. Heavy-duty suspensions are designed to handle much more weight for off-road trucks, tractors and trailers involved in heavy-duty applications such as construction, mining and forestry.

THE LEAF SPRING SUSPENSION
The leaf spring suspension is made up of two or more long **metal strips,** or leaves, that are **shackled together with clamps.** Typically the leaf springs are bowed with the outer ends of the spring curved upward connecting to shackles or hangers on the frame of the vehicle. The middle of the leaf spring connects to the axle or a center beam between two axles. **As weight from the vehicle pushes downward on the hangers, the springs' outer ends are forced downward.**

The number of leaves on each assembly will vary depending upon the type of metal they are made of and the amount of weight they must bear. **The weight that the springs must bear depends on the axle position on the vehicle and the type of hauling the tractor or trailer will be doing.** The fewer the leaves and the more flexible they are, the more road shocks and bumps can be absorbed. This contributes to a smooth ride for the driver and the cargo.

Taper Leaf Suspensions
Taper leaf springs are used on single and tandem axles of tractors. They **are the most often used suspension on the steering axle** of on-road tractors because they are light, inexpensive and provide for a smooth ride. They have metal strips of equal length that are thinner at their ends than at their center. A typical steering axle taper leaf spring suspension might use two or three long, flexible leaves.

Multi-leaf Suspensions
Multi-leaf springs use many leaves and are common on drive and tandem axles of tractors and trailers. They are bigger and heavier

than taper leaf springs and **are often used for heavier loads.** Because of their many leaves, multi-leaf suspensions are also much stiffer than taper-leaf suspensions which makes for a rough ride, particularly when there is an empty load.

fig. 7-7
A typical taper-leaf and multi-leaf suspension.

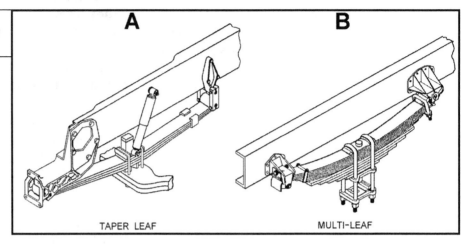

TAPER LEAF   MULTI-LEAF

THE AIR RIDE SUSPENSION

Air ride suspensions are designed for all types of axles and are common on tractors and trailers. The air ride suspension system uses air springs that consist of a rubber-fabric bag that holds air. The top of the bag is attached to a metal plate that is connected to the vehicle frame. The bottom of the bag rests on the suspension assembly (see Figure 7-8). **A height control valve adjusts the amount of air in the bag.) When weight is put on a tractor or trailer axle, the height valve automatically opens and compressed air flows into the air bag supporting the weight of that axle, raising the tractor-trailer to its unloaded height. When weight is removed or the cargo is unloaded, the valve exhausts air from the bag, keeping the tractor and trailer balanced and level at all times.**

fig. 7-8
Air suspensions give a smoother ride and provide better balance to the vehicle than spring suspensions.

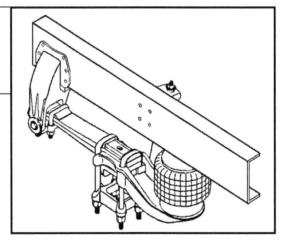

Electronic vans (trailers), used to haul very sensitive electronic equipment, were some of the first trailers equipped with air ride suspensions. Over the years other types of trailers have been equipped with air suspension.

Spring Suspension with Torque Rods

Figure 7-9 shows a typical tandem axle spring suspension using torque rods. Torque rods transmit torque and braking effort to the truck's

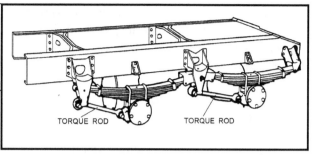

fig. 7-9
Torque rods absorb and transmit the effect of axle wind up to the frame and help maintain correct alignment.

TORQUE ROD   TORQUE ROD

frame. When a heavily-loaded truck is put in motion, as well as during braking, the axles tend to turn forward or backward. This is called "Axle wind up." **Torque rods absorb and transmit the effect of axle wind up to the frame and correct alignment is maintained.** Putting the truck into motion and stopping the vehicle gently instead of abruptly also helps reduce the stress on the suspension system.

Chapter 7 Quiz

1. The _____ is the mechanical component that allows the engine to be connected to, or disconnected from, the transmission.
    A. inter-axle differential
    B. differential
    C. clutch
    D. driveline

2. When you press down the clutch pedal, you _____ .
    A. engage the clutch, which allows power to flow from the transmission to the differential
    B. disengage the clutch, thereby stopping power flow at the flywheel
    C. engage the clutch, thereby stopping power flow at the flywheel
    D. disengage the clutch, which allows power to flow from the transmission to the differential

3. _____ refers to all the individual components that connect the transmission to the differential.
    A. Driveline
    B. Power train
    C. Drive shaft
    D. Drive train

4. The air ride suspension system constantly adjusts itself as the vehicle is loaded and unloaded, to maintain correct vehicle height.
    A. True
    B. False

5. The _____ is a flexible coupling used to transfer the rotary motion between one rotating shaft and another while allowing for changes in the driveline operating angle.
   A. flange
   B. yoke
   C. short coupled joint
   D. U-joint

6. The _____ is a gear mechanism that transmits power from the drive shaft to the axles. It splits the drive axle in half and then lets each axle half turn at a different speed than the other.
   A. driveline
   B. differential
   C. drive train
   D. inter-axle differential

7. The _____ does the same thing the axle differential does, but between two axles rather than between two axle halves.
   A. U-joint
   B. transmission
   C. inter-axle differential
   D. clutch

8. The three main parts of the _____ axle are the axle-halves, the axle housing and the differential.
   A. drive
   B. front
   C. non-drive
   D. driveline

9. The _____ is the foundation of the truck.
   A. driveline
   B. frame
   C. inter-axle differential
   D. pinion shaft gear

10. The weight of the vehicle is supported by the _____ .
    A. frame
    B. wheels
    C. drive shaft
    D. suspension system

CHAPTER 8

STEERING

How the Wheel in Your Hands Controls the Wheels on the Road

The early chapters in this book describe how the truck goes and how it stops. They show how the engine's power moves through the transmission and the drive train to the truck's wheels and tires. What controls that power are the steering components. In this chapter, you'll learn about the types of steering and the steering components. You'll also learn about alignment, or what keeps the steering components working properly.

The **steering system enables the tractor to change direction and get around corners.** A good steering system **provides precise rolling, without slipping,** when turning a corner or negotiating a curve. We're not going to talk about how to turn corners. Instead you'll learn about what happens when you turn the steering wheel. In other words, you'll learn how the wheel in your hands controls the wheels on the road.

Steering Components

The wheel in your hands is the steering wheel. It controls the steering wheels on the road that are connected to the steering axle. Between the steering wheel and the steering axle are the components that make steering possible. Figure 8-1 on the next page shows the basic steering components and how the steering action flows through the system. Refer to it as you proceed through the following discussion.

The steering system starts with the **steering wheel,** which is **connected to** the **steering column** by a spline or shaft and held by a nut. The steering wheel transfers the driver's instructions to the steering system, allowing you to control the tractor's direction.

As you turn the steering wheel, the column turns in the same direction. This **turning motion** continues **through the U-joint to** the **steering gear shaft.** From there the motion continues **through another U-joint to the steering gear box. The steering gear box,** also called the steering sector, **changes the rotating motion** of the steering column **to the**

fig. 8-1
These components make up all types of steering systems, whether manual or power.

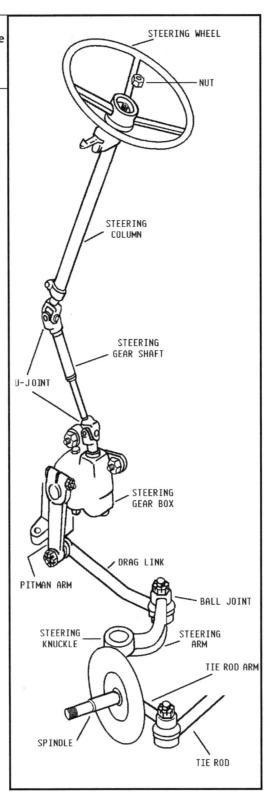

STEERING WHEEL

NUT

STEERING COLUMN

STEERING GEAR SHAFT

U-JOINT

STEERING GEAR BOX

DRAG LINK

PITMAN ARM

BALL JOINT

STEERING KNUCKLE

STEERING ARM

TIE ROD ARM

SPINDLE

TIE ROD

back and forth, or reciprocating motion, of the Pitman arm. The **Pitman arm** is a lever attached to the steering gear box. The **drag link** joins the Pitman arm and the steering arm.

The steering arm is the first steering component that is part of the **steering axle.** The steering, or front axle, does two jobs. It **carries a load** just like other axles. In addition, however, it **steers the truck** and so it has different components and looks different. Steering axles use an I-beam construction. The components of the steering axle are listed below.

- the steering arm
- the steering knuckles
- the spindles
- the tie rod arm
- the tie rod

The **steering arm turns the front wheels left and right** when the Pitman arm pulls it back and forth. The steering arm is connected to the **steering knuckle,** which is a moveable connection between the axle and the wheels that **lets the wheels turn left or right.**

There is a steering knuckle at the end of each axle. The steering knuckles are very important because they contain the seals, bushings and bearings that support the weight of the tractor. The steering knuckles transfer motion to the tie rod arm and the tie rod.

The spindles are the parts of the steering axle knuckles that are inserted through the wheels.

A **tie rod holds both wheels in the same position.** As the left wheel turns, the right wheel moves in the same direction. In addition, the **kingpin,** which is contained in the steering knuckle, **allows each wheel to have its own pivot point.** As you can see in Figure 8-2, the spindle, or stub axle, on which the wheel rotates is attached to the kingpin.

fig. 8-2
The steering knuckle includes the kingpin (A), the bushings (B) and the tapered roller bearings (C). The steering knuckle is attached to the spindle (D) and to the cross steering lever (E). A ball joint (F) connects the cross steering lever to the tie rod (G).

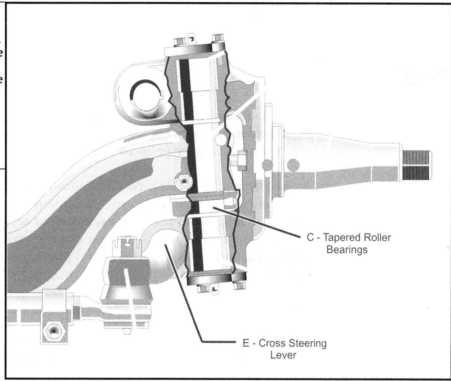

C - Tapered Roller Bearings

E - Cross Steering Lever

Types of Steering

The two types of steering are manual and power. In this chapter, we'll focus on manual steering because the manual system is the basis for the power system. So, if you know the manual system there are just a few things you need to know about power systems.

As you've just learned, the **manual steering system multiplies steering wheel effort** through gears and mechanical linkage. Just imagine the strength you would need if you got down on the ground, grabbed the wheels and tried to move them with 12,000 pounds of load resting on them. The steering system "multiplies" the fairly small effort you exert at the steering wheel into this greater force needed to move the front wheels. At the same time, the **motion** at the steering wheel **is reduced** at the front wheel. In other words, you may turn the wheel completely around two or three times to make your front wheels move through only a few degrees of a circle.

Power steering systems go this one better. **Power steering systems use hydraulic pressure to assist** the mechanical linkage in making the turn. This way even less effort comes from your arms.

When hydraulic pressure is used to assist steering, the steering gear box is replaced with a hydraulic unit. A hydraulic pump is added to the engine to supply the pressure used to help turn the wheels. So, when you turn the steering wheel to the right, the hydraulic valve senses this. A valve opens and the pressure of the oil is used to help turn the wheels to the right.

Alignment

When you **align** the steering system, you **put** the **components at the right angles to maintain** assembly **balance.** Keeping the steering system in alignment is essential to safe and proper operation of the truck.

As a mechanic, you will probably perform steering system repairs and alignments. You must know when a system needs repair or alignment. **Improper alignment leads to excess wear** on both the steering components and on the tires. The next chapter covers tires and wheels in detail. What you need to know now is that improper alignment can very quickly ruin a tire that may cost as much or more than $350.

Four angles that affect alignment are listed below.

- toe in
- toe out
- caster
- camber

If any of these angles is out of alignment, problems will result. Another angle that affects steering is the turning angle. We'll cover that angle in this chapter, too.

TOE IN AND TOE OUT
Picture a steering axle with wheels and tires mounted. To understand toe in and toe out, think of the fronts of the tires as the toes and the backs of the tires as the heels. **Toe in** means **the distance between the toes of the tires is less than the distance between the heels** of those tires. **Toe out** means the **distance between the toes of the tires is greater than the distance between the heels** of those tires.

Too Much Toe In or Toe Out
Not only does too much toe in or toe out make the truck **hard to steer,** it also **causes the tires to wear** rapidly and unevenly. If you notice that the edges of the tires look like feather edges or like the teeth of a saw, the alignment needs adjusting. **Feathered or saw-toothed tire edges** that point inward often indicate too much toe in. Feathered or saw-toothed edges that point outward often mean too much toe out.

Excessive toe out can be caused by a bent tie rod. If it is bent, it may need to be replaced. Usually the toe in can be adjusted. To do this, you will usually adjust the threads on the tie rod end of the steering linkage.

Proper Toe In
You do, however, want a little toe in. It will balance the camber. What's camber? We'll talk about that next.

CAMBER
Camber is the position of the top of the tire. When there is **zero camber,** the top of the tire sits directly over the bottom of the tire. If you were to draw a dotted line from the top of the tire to the bottom, it would be a vertical line. When there is **positive camber,** the tire leans slightly away from the body of the truck. So would your imaginary line. When there is **negative camber** the tire leans toward the body of the truck. Negative camber is also called reverse camber.

If you draw a line from the top to the bottom of a tire that has positive or negative camber, it will create an angle when compared to the straight line of zero camber. This angle is called the positive or the negative **degree of camber.** Figure 8-4 shows you what we mean.

Improper Camber
Improper camber causes road shocks, uneven tire wear and steering wander. A driver who reports feeling an impact in the steering wheel every time the front tire hits a bump is experiencing road shock. Under these circumstances, there's probably a problem with the degree of camber.

fig. 8-3
Too much toe in or too much toe out makes the truck hard to steer.

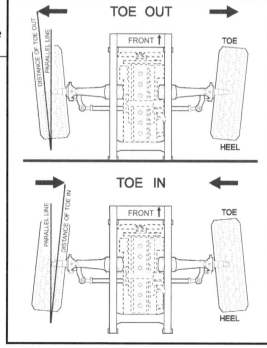

Too much or too little camber causes uneven tire wear. **Too much camber wears away tread on the outside edge** of the tire. If there is **too little camber,** the **inside edge will be smooth.**

Steering wander occurs when a tractor pulls to one side on a flat road. It's most often caused by uneven camber. That is, **one tire has more or less camber than the other.** The truck usually pulls to the side with the highest positive camber.

97

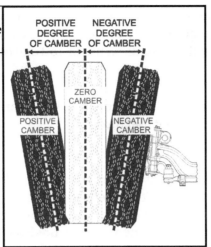

fig. 8-4
Degree of camber can be positive or negative.

Uneven camber is caused by using:

- different sized tires
- improperly inflated tires
- unevenly worn tires

Improper cambering can also be caused by:

- worn steering knuckles
- knuckle pins that are not in correct position
- worn kingpin bushings
- bent axles

Camber cannot be adjusted like toe in. To correct an improper camber, you must find the cause and repair or replace the part or parts.

Proper Camber

Remember that **all the alignment angles work as a unit.** When the steering components are properly aligned, the tractor maneuvers easily. Just as proper alignment calls for a little toe in, it also calls for a little positive camber. Positive camber causes the wheels to pull away from the tractor, and a little toe in will balance that.

CASTER

Caster is the position of the tire in relation to the steering knuckle kingpin. Look at Figure 8-5. When there is **zero caster,** you can draw a line through the center of the steering knuckle kingpin and that line will hit the ground at the center bottom of the tire. When there is **positive caster,** a line through the center of the kingpin hits the ground in front of the center bottom of the tire. When there is **negative caster,** a line drawn through the center of the kingpin will hit the ground in back of the center bottom of the tire.

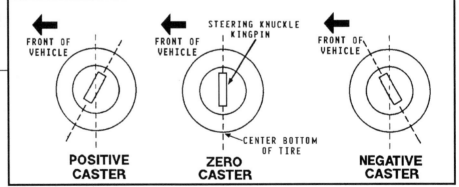

fig. 8-5
Caster is the position of the tire as it relates to the steering knuckle kingpin.

Positive Caster

You have probably noticed in your car that the steering wheel will try to come back to a straight ahead position after you turn a corner. This is caused by **positive caster.** Caster makes the front wheels more stable, especially as the **wheel returns to a straight ahead position after turning a corner.** It also curbs the wheel's natural tendency to move from side to side at the back as the vehicle moves.

Too much positive caster:

- makes steering hard
- increases road shock
- can cause wandering at high speed
- can cause a chattering sound in the power steering.

Improper Caster
Zero or too much negative caster causes the **front** to **shimmy** and wander at low speeds. At high speeds, it causes front end instability. With zero or negative caster, the wheels will be slow to straighten after negotiating a turn or curve.

Proper Caster
Just as **both wheels should have** equal, or even, camber, both should have **equal caster.** If the **positive caster** is **uneven,** the **vehicle will pull toward the side** that has the least caster.

Incorrect caster will not affect tire wear, so you can't rely on looking at the tires to tell you about caster. Caster is usually made with a tapered caster plate placed between the suspension springs and the axle. The caster angle is corrected by replacing the caster plate with a plate that will provide the proper caster. For proper alignment, caster should be slightly positive.

THE TURNING RADIUS
Toe in, toe out, camber and caster affect how easily the vehicle can make turns and curves. They affect the handling of the truck on straightaways too. Toe in, toe out and camber affect tire wear. **Turning radius** is the **size of the circle the tractor makes while turning around.** It is determined by the length of the tractor and the maximum angle the wheels can be turned. The turning radius is the distance from the center to the outside tire marks of a circle made by a turning tractor.

The turning radius **determines** the **maneuverability** of the tractor. The turning radius is determined by the turning angle. The **turning angle** is the **number of degrees to the right or left that the front wheels can be turned from a straight ahead position.**

Correct setting of the turning angle is important. **Too small an angle** makes the tractor **hard to steer. Too large an angle** will **allow the tire to turn too far** and hit the chassis or steering linkage. In addition, the angle must be adjusted for both right and left turns.

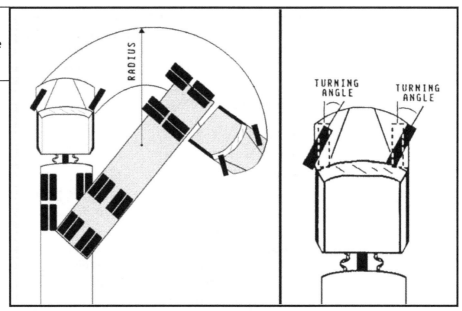

fig. 8-6
Turning radius and turning angle affect the maneuverability of the vehicle.

THE SET-BACK FRONT AXLE

A cabover tractor tends to have a tighter turning radius than a conventional model mainly because the tractor design calls for a shorter wheelbase. A recent development in tractor design allows for a set-back front axle on conventional tractor models. Figure 8-7 shows you a comparison of a conventional tractor with a regular front axle and one with a set-back front axle. These may be offered as an option or as an entirely different model.

To allow for this set-back axle on conventional tractors, design changes were made to the hood, the steering linkage, the front suspension mounts and the front bumper.

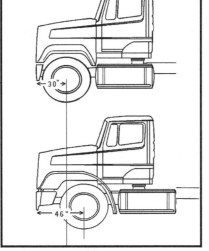

fig. 8-7
A regular front axle is set back about 30 inches from the front of the tractor while a set-back axle is set back about 46 inches.

The set-back front axle results in several advantages. The front axles can carry a heavier load, increasing the payload. The ride is more comfortable because the set-back axle lets the suspension system work better. Maintenance is easier because the engine compartment is more open and easier to get to.

But the advantage to notice here is that the set-back axle narrows the turning radius by as much as 26 percent. This is because the set-back axle tightens the steering angle and shortens the wheelbase. Because of improved clearances between the steering components and the tires, set-back wheels can make a turn that is up to $7\frac{1}{2}$ degrees tighter than conventional wheels.

Add that to the 16 inch shorter wheelbase and the result is a greatly improved turning radius.

This greatly improved turning radius means **maneuverability is greatly improved.** This is a real boon in any tight driving situation like city loading docks and heavy in-town traffic.

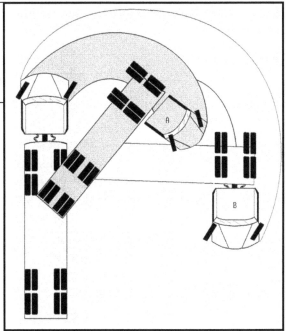

fig. 8-8
The set-back front axle of Tractor A leads to a much tighter turning radius than the conventional front axle of Tractor B.

STEERING GEOMETRY

Steering geometry refers to how the truck responds to its steering system. It refers to all the angles of alignment you've just learned about and how they work together to improve the maneuverability of the truck and to protect the tires from undue wear. It includes how the movement of the steering wheel is changed to the left or right movement of the wheels of the tractor.

Keeping the steering system in good mechanical condition is very important to safe, efficient tractor operation. The signs of improper alignment you've learned about in this chapter will warn you of problems in the steering geometry. Those signs are:

- difficulty steering
- front end instability
- feathered edge tire wear
- chattering in the power steering
- increased road shock
- saw-tooth tire wear
- steering wander
- shimmy

Difficulty straightening out after negotiating a turn or curve, tread worn away on the inside or outside edges of the tires and an improper turning angle are also signs of steering problems. These signs tell you that repairs or adjustments are needed.

Chapter 8 Quiz

1. The power steering system uses oil pressure to assist steering.
   A. True
   B. False

2. _____ describes a steering axle assembly wherein the distance between the toes of the tires is less than the distance between the heels of those tires.
   A. Caster
   B. Toe in
   C. Toe out
   D. Camber

For questions 3 through 6, please label the unlabeled steering components in the figure at the left.

3. _____
4. _____
5. _____
6. _____

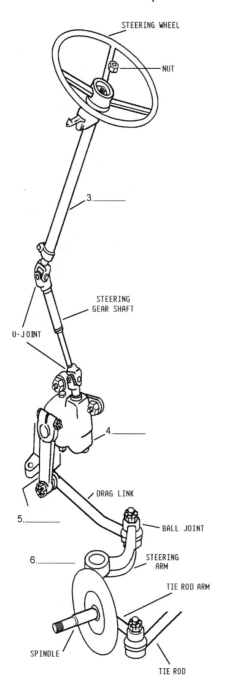

STEERING WHEEL

NUT

3. _____

STEERING GEAR SHAFT

U-JOINT

4. _____

DRAG LINK

5. _____

BALL JOINT

6. _____

STEERING ARM

TIE ROD ARM

SPINDLE

TIE ROD

7. _____ describes a steering axle assembly wherein the distance between the toes of the tires is greater than the distance between the heels of those tires.
   A. Caster
   B. Toe in
   C. Toe out
   D. Camber

8. _____ describes how the tire leans in relation to the truck.
   A. Caster
   B. Toe in
   C. Toe out
   D. Camber

9. _____ is the position of the tire in relation to the steering knuckle kingpin.
   A. Caster
   B. Toe in
   C. Toe out
   D. Camber

10. A tractor with a set-back axle _____ .
   A. has a faulty alignment
   B. has a tighter turning radius
   C. requires power steering
   D. uses a steering sector instead of a steering gear box

CHAPTER 9

TIRES AND WHEELS

If It Goes, It Probably Has Tires and Wheels

The engine's power goes through the drive train to the wheels and finally to the very surface of the tires. Not only does the engine's power end up there, but so does the weight of your rig and the cargo. You can see the importance of the 18 tires on the typical rig. They

- provide proper traction
- dampen vibration
- absorb road shock
- transfer braking force to the road surface

as well as transfer driving force to the road surface.

BASIC CONSTRUCTION

Now that you know what tires do, let's look at how they are built. There are many different tire designs, but the basic principle of tire construction is the same.

Tires are made up of plies, bead coils, beads, sidewalls, tread and the inner liner. Plies consist of **separate layers of rubber cushioned cord** and make up **the body of the tire.** All of the **plies** are **tied into bundles of wire called the bead coils.**

Bead coils form the **bead,** which is **the part of the tire that fits into the rim** and **secures the tire to the rim.** Bead coils provide the hoop strength for the bead sections so that the tire will hold its shape when it's being mounted on a wheel.

The **sidewalls** are **layers of rubber covering** which **connect the bead to the tread.** Sidewalls protect the plies in the sidewall area. The **tread** is the part of the tire that **contacts the road.** Treads are designed for specific applications. Some applications require that the tread provide extra traction. Others call for a tread designed for high-speed use. The **inner liner** is the sealing material that **keeps the air in the tire.**

TUBE OR TUBELESS

Tires can either be tube type or tubeless. **Tubeless tires weigh less,** have fewer components and have a slower rate of pressure loss from punctures. Tires constantly flex when they are in use and this flexing creates heat, which leads to breakdown. With fewer parts to flex and create heat, tubeless tires **last longer.** Tubeless tires are less dangerous to repair because they have a single rim instead of a split rim.

Now that you have learned the basics of tire construction, let's move on and discuss the different types of tires. The three basic types are the bias ply, the belted bias ply and the radial. Each type is available with tube or tubeless construction, although radials are usually tubeless.

fig. 9-1
The components of the tubeless and tube-type tires.

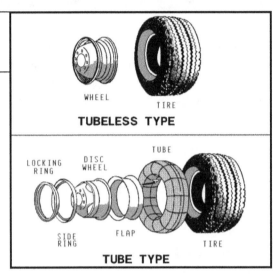

BIAS PLY TIRES
Let's look at the bias ply first. In Figure 9-2(A), you can see the bias **plies** running at a **crisscross** or bias **angle.** This **makes the sidewall and tread rigid.**

Figure 9-2(C) is the **belted bias** ply tire. Like the bias ply tire, its **plies cross at an angle.** However, an **extra layered belt of fabric or steel** is **placed between the plies and the tread.** The belts **make** the **tread** of this tire **more rigid** than the bias ply tire. The tread will last longer because the belts reduce tread motion when the tire is running.

THE RADIAL TIRE
The radial tire is shown in Figure 9-2(B). The **plies** on this tire **do not cross at an angle.** The ply is laid from bead to bead, across the tire. Like the belted bias ply tire, the radial also has a number of belts. The construction of the radial tire **supports the tread better** than that of either the bias ply or the belted bias ply. The radial design means the sidewalls flex with less friction. That requires less horsepower and **provides greater fuel economy.** Radial tires also:

- hold the road better
- resist skidding better
- give a smoother ride

than the bias types.

Low Profile Radial Tires
Radials are available in two standing heights: standard profile and low profile. Low profile radials lower the center of gravity which improves handling and directional stability and makes the ride more comfortable. Low profile radials also reduce the vehicle's overall height, which allows

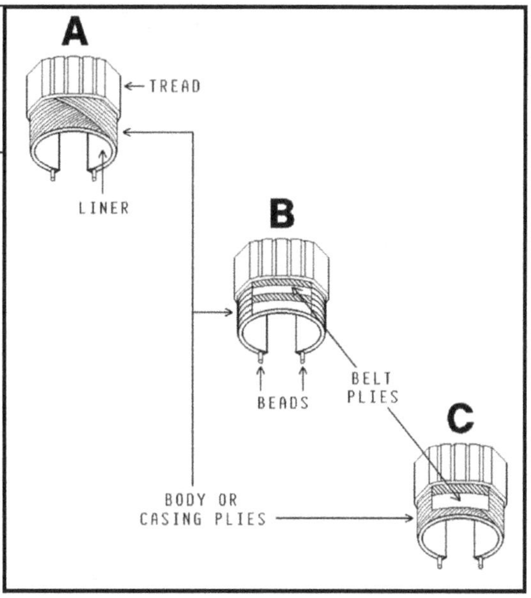

fig. 9-2
The types of tires are
(A) the bias ply,
(B) the radial, and
(C) the belted bias ply.

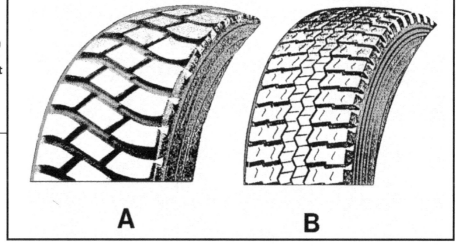

for more clearance room under bridges. They **weigh less** and offer a lower rolling resistance (the friction between the tire and road), which makes for **still greater fuel savings.**

TREAD DESIGN

Tire tread design takes two main factors into account: the job the tire must do and the conditions the tire will normally face. Tire **treads are designed to do specific jobs.** Steering tires need to roll well and provide good traction for cornering. Drive tires need to provide good traction for both braking and acceleration. Trailer tires primarily need to roll well. Tire treads are also designed **to face specific road conditions.** For example, drive wheel position tires need maximum traction in rain, snow, sleet and ice.

TIRE SIZE AND LABELING

Tire Size

Tire size is shown by either a numerical designation or a series design designation. You find this information on the sidewall of the tires.

fig. 9-3
Two driving tire tread designs. "A" is designed for maximum traction in adverse road conditions such as rain, snow, sleet or ice while "B" is designed for general road and weather conditions.

An example of the **numerical designation** is a 10.00 x 22 tire. The first number is the **tire's width.** This means the inflated tire measured 10 inches from the farthest outside point on one sidewall to the farthest outside point on the other sidewall. The second number in the numerical designation is the **rim size.** Our example tire will fit a 22-inch diameter rim.

The **series designation** system was developed because of the **low profile tire,** which is wide in relation to its height. Once again, let's take an example to look at this. The sidewall of our example tire reads 295/75 R 22.5. This means the section width is 295 millimeters (low profile tires are measured in millimeters rather than inches). The aspect ratio is 75, the construction type is radial and the rim is 22.5 inches in diameter. Figure 9-4 should clear up any confusion you may have about what the series designation system tells you about the tire.

Tire Labeling

The **government requires tire manufacturers to label all tires** with the information listed below:

- the brand and manufacturer
- the maximum load
- the wheel position
- whether the tire is tube or tubeless
- the material used in the ply construction
- the load range
- the maximum pressure
- the size
- the DOT's code

Load range refers to tire strength, which is rated from A to Z, Z being the strongest. The maximum load the tire can carry in terms of weight is shown in pounds. The maximum pressure is shown in psi and is given for cold tires that have been driven for less than one mile. That should clue you in as to why tire pressure should be checked before the tire is ridden on. Wheel positions are listed as S for steering tire, D for driving tire, A for an all-wheel tire and T for trailer tire. The DOT code is a series of numbers and letters that stand for most of this information. It's useful mainly in tire sales.

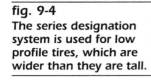
fig. 9-4
The series designation system is used for low profile tires, which are wider than they are tall.

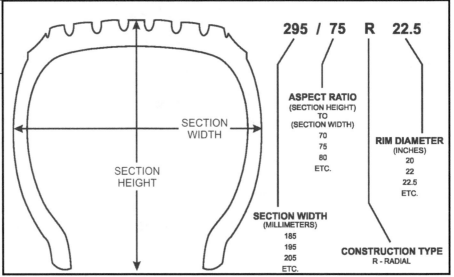

As you can see, the sidewall of the tire will tell you everything you need to know about that tire.

USED TIRES

Basically our discussion of tires has focused on new tires. Used tires can sometimes be restored to like-new condition. These are recaps or retreads.

A retreaded, or recapped, tire has had the old tread surface removed. Then new tread is bonded to the outside layers of the belts or body plies.

Tire Wear

No tire, no matter how expensive or well-maintained, will last forever. **In normal service, some tires simply wear faster than others.** For instance, studies of radial tires show that the tires on the steering axles of tandem axle trucks wear twice as fast as those on single-axle vehicles. This is a result of the tandems pushing straight ahead and scuffing as the front wheels are turned. On tandem axles, rear axle tires wear faster than those on the forward axle. This is because when it turns, the vehicle pivots on the forward axle.

Excessive wear, on the other hand, can result from poor driving or maintenance practices. Let's look at that next.

Tire Damage

As a mechanic, you must know how to **diagnose tire damage.** Tires are very costly so their proper maintenance is important **for economic reasons.** However, tires are even more vital **for safety reasons,** so you must be able to spot damage on tires. Chapter 8 covers some of the causes of tire damage, such as improper alignment, balance, toe-in and toe-out, and camber and caster. In this chapter, we'll take a close look at another major cause of tire damage: improper tire inflation. Then we'll give you a chart that will help you locate tire damage, its possible causes and possible remedies.

IMPROPER TIRE INFLATION

Improper inflation is a leading cause of tire damage. **Under-inflated tires,** or tires with too little air in them, **wear rapidly at the sides of the tread.** An under-inflated tire will sag under heavy load conditions. If it's part of a dual wheel set-up, the under-inflated tire may contact the tire next to it. This will cause heat to build from the friction of the two tires. In this situation, a driver may be heading for a blowout. At the very least, more precious **fuel will be burned** than would with properly inflated tires.

Even if it's not part of a dual wheel set-up, the heat build-up of running an under-inflated tire can be tremendous. This is because the sidewalls flex up and down as the tire rolls.

Overheating leads to the problems listed below:

- faster wear
- tire fires
- tread separation
- blowouts
- cord separation

Overinflated tires, or tires with too much air in them, **wear rapidly at the center of the tread** because the center of the tire is forced to carry more than its share of the load. This clearly also shortens the life of the tire. Over-inflation causes extreme strain on the body plies. The extra pressure **increases the chances a blowout** will occur and that the tire will be damaged by road hazards, such as stones or potholes. An over-inflated tire simply cannot withstand the normal shocks of driving. Fabric separation or tread separation or both can occur.

Many companies will have instructions regarding inflation of tires on company equipment.

How To Check Tire Pressure

You already know you should always **check the tire pressure when the tires are cold.** When a tire is rolling, it heats up and the air inside expands, increasing the air pressure. Do not hit the tires with a stick or a billy or kick them to check for proper pressure. Using a billy is a good way to quickly determine a tire is not completely flat. But it is not an accurate way to check the tire pressure. **Use a calibrated tire gauge.**

Figure 9-5 on the next page is a tire problem chart. It lists the symptoms of some tire problems and possible causes and remedies. Most are problems a driver can correct or avoid. Others require your attention. If you see any of these symptoms while doing your routine inspections, it is up to you to check them out.

With tube tires, poor mounting can result in a torn or leaking tube. If the tube tire is very low or flat, it could be for any of these reasons:

- rubbed, pinched or creased tubes
- fold at edge of tube flap
- tube is sized larger than tire
- screw or nail in tire
- foreign matter caught between tube and the tire casing
- a stretched, used tube installed in new tire

fig. 9-5
Use this chart to identify common tire problems, their possible causes and remedies.

COMMON TIRE PROBLEMS

POSSIBLE CAUSE	POSSIBLE REMEDY
SYMPTOM: RAPID TIRE WEAR	
A. High-speed driving	A. Reduce speed
B. Improperly inflated tires	B. Inflate properly
C. Rapid starts and stops	C. Correct poor driving habit
D. Front end misaligned	D. Repair and realign
E. Wheels out of balance	E. Balance wheels
F. Excessive load	F. Reduce load or replace tire
SYMPTOM: UNEVEN OR SPOTTY TIRE WEAR	
A. Incorrect caster or camber	A. Adjust
B. Damaged front suspension	B. Repair and align
C. Wheels out of balance	C. Balance wheels
D. Tires under-inflated	D. Inflate properly
SYMPTOM: SAW-TOOTH TREAD WEAR	
A. High-speed driving	A. Reduce speed, rotate wheels
B. Excessive braking	B. Correct poor driving habit
SYMPTOM: SIDE WEAR	
A. Incorrect camber	A. Adjust camber
B. Under-inflated tire	B. Inflate properly
C. Cornering too fast	C. Correct poor driving habit, rotate wheels
SYMPTOM: FEATHERED TREAD EDGES	
A. Excessive toe-in, toe-out	A. Check alignment, repair/adjust as needed
SYMPTOM: ROUNDING/ROUGHING OF TIRE EDGES	
A. Cornering too fast	A. Correct poor driving habit, rotate tires
B. Incorrect camber	B. Adjust camber

DOT Tire Regulations

The Department of Transportation has established some very specific regulations regarding the tires to be used on a rig (stated in Subpart G, Miscellaneous Part and Accessories, Sec. 393.75). No vehicle that operates under DOT regulations may use tires that

- have any fabric exposed through the tread or sidewalls.
- have less than $\frac{4}{32}$ of an inch of tread measured at any point in a major tread groove on the steering axle.
- have less than $\frac{2}{32}$ of an inch of tread measured at any point in a major tread groove on all other axles.

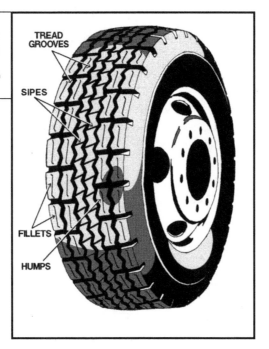

fig. 9-6
A "legal" measurement of tread depth must be taken in a major tread groove, not on a hump or in a fillet or sipe.

When measuring grooves, you must not measure where tie bars, humps or fillets are located. A hump is a pattern of tire wear that looks a little like a cupped hand. The hump is the edge or higher part of the cupping. Tie bars and fillets are not patterns of tire wear but design factors. A sipe is yet another design factor. Sipes are cut across the tread to improve traction on wet roads.

You must **take the tread depth measurement on a major tread groove** where the way is clear to the body of the tire. See Figure 9-6.

Types of Wheels

The two types of wheels used on medium and heavy duty trucks are the cast spoke wheel and the disc wheel. As you can see in Figure 9-7, not only do the wheels differ, but so do the wheel assemblies. The purpose of the wheel is to **provide a mounting device for the tire.** The purpose of the wheel assembly is to **support and connect the tire to the truck axle.**

THE SPOKE WHEEL
Although many companies now manufacture the spoke wheel, some people refer to any cast spoke wheel as a **Dayton** because the Dayton Co. originated it. Spoke wheels are also called "spokes." Most people agree that **spoke wheels have more strength** than disc wheels. That's why they're used for heavy duty applications.

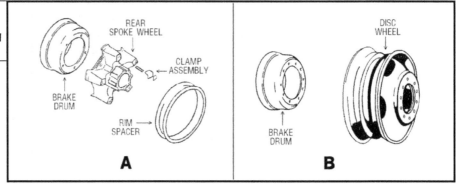

fig. 9-7
(A) Cast spoke wheel assembly; (B) disc wheel assembly.

On a spoke wheel, the wheel consists of a **one-piece casting** which **includes the hub and spokes.** Spoke wheels are made of ductile iron, cast steel or aluminum. A **separate rim** supports the tire. It has no center disc and is clamped onto the cast spoke wheel.

Cast spoke wheels can have five or six spokes. The **five-spoke** wheel is standard **for the steering axle** and the **six-spoke** is used **for driving wheels.** The additional spoke provides greater rim clamping.

Compared to disc wheels, spoke wheels are:

- less costly
- easier to service
- stronger

A cast spoke wheel assembly consists of the wheel, a separate rim and a clamp assembly. When cast spoke wheels are **dual mounted,** the **rims are kept apart by a rim spacer band.** Whether the cast spoke wheel is bolted to the brake drum or the axle depends on the wheel design. As the brake drum turns, so does the wheel.

THE DISC WHEEL

The Budd Company originated the disc wheel, although many other companies now manufacture it. So, many people refer to the disc wheel as a **Budd.**

Disc wheels are made of steel or aluminum. Aluminum wheels are forged. Aluminum discs have increased in popularity because they weigh less than steel discs. The idea here is that anything done to lighten the weight of the equipment means the truck can carry more cargo weight. **Aluminum wheels** are a common way to **reduce weight** and dress up the truck (make it look pretty). Like other lightweight options, aluminum wheels cost more than the standard steel wheels. So the buyer must decide if investing in aluminum wheels will pay off in the long run.

As the last section explained, spoke wheels use separate rims. They are clamped onto the wheels with wheel clamps. If you don't install the clamps just right, the wheel may be out of round and wobble. Because the rim and center portion of the disc wheel are one piece, no clamp is used and so there is less chance of the wheel being out of round. When a wheel is out of round or wobbling, we say it is not true running. The main advantage of the disc wheel over the spoke wheel is that the **disc wheel is true running.** That means the **tire will wear more evenly and last longer** and the **ride will be smoother.**

So, on a disc wheel, the **rim is part of the wheel** and the wheel is bolted to the hub and brake drum assembly. You can see this in Figure

9-7(B). A Budd-type disc wheel assembly consists of the wheel and a stud bolt and nut assembly.

Disc wheels are **mainly used with drop center rims and tubeless tires,** although they can be used with multi-piece rims and tube-type tires.

Types of Rims

The rim's job is to **support the tire bead and the lower sidewall.** The two types of rims used on heavy trucks are the drop center rim and the multi-piece rim.

The **drop center rim** is a single piece rim and the one **most often used** on heavy trucks. It is part of the wheel. This type of rim can be used with either type tire. But it is most often used **with tubeless tires** because the center has a smaller diameter to provide room to remove the tire. These wheels are built the same as most car wheels, only larger.

There are two types of multi-piece rims: the two piece rim and the three piece rim. The **two piece rim** consists of the rim and a split side ring. Two piece rims cannot be made airtight so they're **used with tube tires only.**

The **three piece rim** consists of the rim, a continuous side ring and a split lock ring. Three piece rims cannot be made airtight either, so they, too, **take a tube tire.** Figure 9-8 shows you what these three types of rims look like.

fig. 9-8
(A) Drop center rim;
(B) two piece rim;
(C) three piece rim.

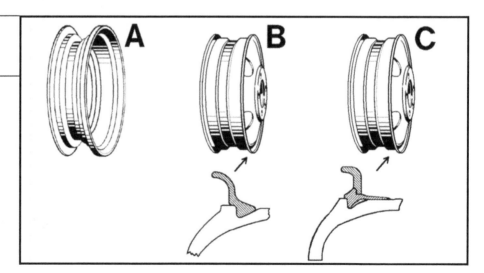

As with tires, wheels and rims share some common problems. Figure 9-9 on the next page lists the symptoms of some of these problems, along with possible causes and remedies. As with the tires, some of the problems are within the driver's power to control or correct. The others need your attention to ensure the continued safe operation of the truck.

fig. 9-9
Use this chart to identify common wheel problems, their possible causes and remedies.

COMMON WHEEL PROBLEMS

POSSIBLE CAUSES	POSSIBLE REMEDIES
SYMPTOMS: CRACKED OR CORRODED RIMS	
A. Overloading	A. Reduce load, replace wheel
B. Pitting by water or chemicals	B. Clean rim or replace wheel
SYMPTOMS: DAMAGED OR SPRUNG RINGS	
A. Rings mounted improperly	A. Replace rings, remount properly
B. Rings dismounted improperly	B. Replace rings, remount properly
SYMPTOMS: CRACKED OR ERODED SIDE RINGS	
A. Mounted improperly	A. Replace side rings, remount properly
B. Collision with road hazards	B. Replace wheel
C. Excessive clamping	C. Replace side rings, remount properly
D. Overloading	D. Reduce load, replace side rings
SYMPTOMS: CRACKED, RUSTED OR WORN STUD HOLES	
A. Loose running wheel	A. Replace wheel, tighten properly
B. Overloading	B. Reduce load, repair or replace wheel
C. Worn ball seats	C. Repair or replace
SYMPTOMS: DAMAGED WHEEL STUDS (OR BOLTS) AND NUTS	
A. Excessive tightening of studs	A. Replace studs if threads are stripped and tighten to proper specification
B. Loose or excessively tightened nuts	B. Replace all studs if one or more are broken, tighten to proper specification
C. Improperly seated wheel	C. Replace wheel, tighten to proper specification
D. Loose mounting	D. Replace damaged nuts and studs, check wheel ball seat, replace wheel if necessary

Mounting and Dismounting

For the most part, when tires need service, the driver will note it on the inspection report and you or someone else from the company shop or service garage will take care of it. The Office of Safety and Health Administration (OSHA) requires that mounting and dismounting of tires be done only by someone who has been trained for the task. So it is against the law for drivers to perform these procedures themselves unless they receive special training.

However, many drivers will want to stay around whenever their tires are mounted or dismounted. They'll want to **make sure this is done properly** because they are the ones who'll be riding on those tires and wheels and they are ultimately responsible for their rig. Following are some things you should look out for when mounting or dismounting tires.

MATCH TYPES OF TIRES
If a dual is replaced on the road, make sure that the replacement tire is the same type as the one already in place. In other words, the **duals should match according to ply type.** Put radials with radials, bias ply with bias ply and so forth. The same concern holds true for the steering axle—don't put a radial on one side if you have a bias on the other. On the other hand, it's acceptable to have different types of tires on the tractor than you have on the trailer.

Follow any specific rules your company may have when replacing tires.

MATCH DIAMETERS OF DUAL TIRES
What will happen if you put tires with different diameters on the same side of an axle? Both tires will wear faster than they should. The larger tire will carry most of the weight, causing it to wear out very quickly. **Make sure both tires on a dual set-up are the same diameter.** "Eyeball" the newly inflated tire to compare it with the one that's in place. If the diameters don't match, you need a different tire.

SAFETY FIRST AND ALWAYS
You should always use a safety cage when a tire is being inflated. Never stand in front of a rim and tire assembly while you're inflating or deflating it. The pressure on the wheel parts is tremendous. If a ring should come loose, it can do so with enough force to go through the wall or the roof.

PRE-INFLATING THE TUBE
If the tires are tube tires, make sure to pre-inflate them. You should insert the tube and inflate it just enough to make it round before proceeding with the mounting process. This **helps to prevent folds and creases** in the tube. As you learned, folds and creases in a tube can tear the tube, causing it to leak.

THE PROPER BOLT TIGHTENING SEQUENCE
Figure 9-10 shows you the proper bolt tightening sequence for the three types of wheels you may see on a tractor-trailer. Using the proper sequence for tightening wheel bolts **helps to ensure that the wheel is**

square on the hub and that each bolt is taking its share of the load. When the tire is square on the hub, it runs true. If the wheel is not square on the hub, the tire will wobble. If the tire wobbles, it will wear rapidly and unevenly.

fig. 9-10
Make sure you use the proper bolt tightening sequence when mounting wheels.

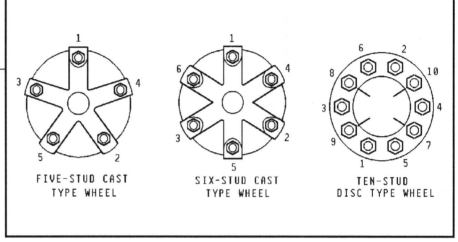

FIVE-STUD CAST
TYPE WHEEL

SIX-STUD CAST
TYPE WHEEL

TEN-STUD
DISC TYPE WHEEL

If you mount **spoke wheels** make sure you do a **lateral run-out check.** This is easy to do. Just place a hammer close to the tire, spin the tire and watch the space between the tire and the hammer. If the tire is not running true, you will see it wobble in that space.

Check all the bolts and tighten any that are loose as part of your normal maintenance routine. Do not use an air-impact wrench for the final torquing.

CLEANING THE RIM

Make sure you check and, if necessary, clean the rim before mounting a tire on it. This is important with both types of tires, but especially with tubeless tires. If there is corrosion and dirt on the rim, the rubber edge of the tire will not be able to seal properly against the rim. Cleaning the rim **ensures a good seal,** which **protects against leaks.**

RUNNING A LOADED TRUCK UP ON BLOCKS

Eventually, you will change a flat on an outside tire of a loaded rig. When this happens, you may wish to run the truck up on blocks. It's easier for you and it's probably okay as long as the rig is empty.

However, if the truck is loaded, tire manufacturers recommend that it be jacked up to change that flat. Why? When you run the inside dual up on blocks to get the outside dual off the ground so you can change it, you put all the weight of that axle on one tire. Asking one tire to hold an amount of weight intended for two tires can result in serious damage to the tire plies. Your best bet in this situation is to be guided by your company policy.

Chapter 9 Quiz

1. _____ consist of separate layers of rubber cushioned nylon cord and make up the body of the tire.
   A. Beads
   B. Plies
   C. Treads
   D. Bead coils

2. Match the types of tires in the illustration to the right with the correct labels.
   A. _____
   B. _____
   C. _____

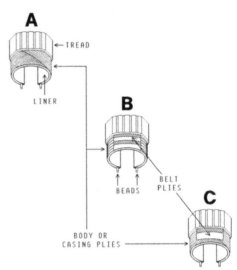

3. Radial tire construction provides less support for the tread than does bias ply type construction.
   A. True
   B. False

4. The number and letter combination 295/75 R 22.5 is an example of _____ designation labeling.
   A. series
   B. numerical

5. _____ refers to tire strength, which is rated from A to Z, Z being the strongest.
   A. Load range
   B. Maximum load
   C. Maximum pressure
   D. Series designation

6. Improper inflation is a leading cause of tire damage.
   A. True
   B. False

7. _____ tires wear rapidly at the center of the tread.
   A. Under-inflated
   B. Overinflated

8. Tread measurements must be taken in a _____ .
   A. major tire groove
   B. tire hump
   C. fillet sipe
   D. tread tie bar

9. Label the types of wheels in the following illustration with the correct name.
   A. _____
   B. _____

A   **B**

10. To prevent folds and creases in a tire tube, which cause it to leak, make sure you _____ when mounting a tube tire.
    A. grease the rim
    B. use the proper bolt tightening sequence
    C. pre-inflate the tube
    D. match the diameters of the dual tires

CHAPTER 10

TRACTORS

The Power Unit

Every truck tractor has an engine, a frame, axles, a suspension, a transmission and a cab. Beyond that, the tractor is assembled from what you could almost call a tractor kit. In fact, most truck tractors have been put together with a particular job in mind. Unlike a car, which you pretty much get as a complete piece of equipment, a truck is put together component by component to meet the challenges it will face on the job.

The average Class 8 tractor, the heavy duty type we most often think of when we think "truck," weighs upwards of 13,000 to 20,000 pounds and costs about $80,000. It's a lot to handle. A truck must be inspected and registered, which involves some pretty hefty fees. It will get about 6 miles to the gallon, a lot less than your little subcompact, and diesel fuel doesn't cost much less than gasoline. Most trucks will probably have two fuel tanks. Since each holds between 50 and 150 gallons, a fill up can run up quite a bill. Buying and operating a tractor-trailer takes no small amount of money. Keeping the tractor and trailer in prime condition will be your primary concern.

Above all, you will observe the special care and handling of a tractor. Treat every tractor as if you owned it. So, on the theory that to know a tractor is to love it, let's investigate some of its many designs and specifications.

What Is a Tractor?

First, however, let's get specific about the difference between a "truck tractor" and a plain old "truck." According to the DOT, a **truck tractor is a motor vehicle used to draw or pull other vehicles.** Except for the part of the weight it is drawing (the part resting on the fifth wheel), the truck tractor is not used for carrying a load. By itself, the tractor has no real commercial use. In other words, it **doesn't carry cargo.** The tractor is the power unit of a full rig. Its calling in life is to pull a trailer, and the trailer is what carries the cargo. For the sake of simplicity, the term "truck tractor" is usually shortened to "tractor."

To drive a commercial tractor of 26,001 pounds or more gross vehicle weight rating (GVWR) and pull a trailer of over 10,000 pounds GVWR, you must get a Class A CDL. A Class B CDL will license you to drive an equally heavy tractor pulling a trailer weighing 10,000 pounds or less. You may have to take a special knowledge and skills test on combination vehicles.

A plain truck is a simple, self-contained piece of equipment that consists of the power unit as well as the truck body or bed. These are sometimes called "straight trucks." Although straight trucks may often be quite large and powerful, they do not articulate and there is no fifth wheel. Trailers can be towed by straight trucks by means of a tow bar, partial hitch or ball.

Different sizes of **trucks are grouped into classes, based on weight.** We've already mentioned Class 8. These are the extra heavyweights, the over-the-road sleepers, dump trucks, cement trucks and the like. The eight classes of vehicles are described in the chart below. These classes are different from the vehicle groups used in CDL licensing.

In addition to size, trucks can be grouped into on-road and off-road types. We'll look at that next.

The On-road and the Off-road Tractor

Tractors are built to go either on the road or off the road. You see on-road tractors pulling their trailers full of cargo over the highways.

VEHICLE CLASSIFICATION

CLASS	GROSS VEHICLE WEIGHT RATING (IN POUNDS)	EXAMPLES
CLASS 8	over 33,000	Heavy duty over-the-road tractors, construction vehicles
CLASS 7	26,001-33,000	Medium-size conventional tractors, residential fuel service vehicles, trash removal trucks
CLASS 6	19,501-26,000	Small-size cab-over-engine vans, single axle vans, furniture vans
CLASS 5	16,001-19,500	Landscaping service vehicles, beverage rack vans
CLASS 4	14,001-16,000	Large-size walk-in vans
CLASS 3	10,001-14,000	Medium-size walk-in vans, milk trucks, bakery trucks, compact vans
CLASS 2	6,001-10,000	Small walk-in vans
CLASS 1	under 6,000	Compact vans, pickup trucks, utility vans

But of course tractors are also used in the logging, mining and construction industries. The load could be logs, coal, equipment or rocks. The trailers pulled may be end dumps, bottom dumps, flatbeds, lowboys or pole trailers.

Basically, **off-road tractors** are built to **withstand more abuse** than the on-road tractor. They have a heavy duty construction to hold their own against the inevitable rough terrain and hard work. Of course, tires, axles, suspensions, transmissions, drive shafts and engines are all heavy-duty. Power is a main consideration.

While off-road tractors spend most of their working lives on rough terrain, most of them use public roads to get to and from the job site. They therefore **must still be "street legal."** This means they have to have the safety equipment, components and construction specified by DOT regulations.

The on-road tractor is built to **perform well on the road.** Some of its equipment **does not have to stand as much abuse as the off-road tractor.** This means that some parts can be built lighter so the tractor will weigh less. The reduced weight can mean better fuel economy, which for the on-road vehicle may be more important than power.

Because it is often used for long hauls, the cab of the on-road tractor is designed for driver comfort. There are adjustable cushioned seats and a roomy sleeping berth. Many on-road tractors have air ride suspension which makes for a smoother ride. The wheels and tires are also made for highway use.

Part for part, let's compare features of both types of tractors.

THE ENGINE
With its larger horsepower requirements, the **off-road tractor** has a **larger engine,** radiator and air cleaner than does the on-road tractor.

TRANSMISSION
The transmission of an **off-road tractor** is built to deliver more power in the low gear ratios since it does most of its work in that range. Often there will be **more low speed gears.** They are therefore able to pull a very heavy load up a steep, rough grade. In an **on-road vehicle,** the emphasis is on efficient operation at **highway speeds.**

SUSPENSION
The **suspension of** the **off-road tractor** must also be **heavy duty** to absorb the shock of unpaved roads. Rugged steel springs help the driver maintain control. Suspensions are rated by the amount of weight they can safely haul. Off-road tandem axles are usually rated at 44,000 pounds. An **on-road vehicle's suspension** would more likely be required to **deliver a smooth ride.** That way, the driver doesn't tire over the long haul.

TIRES AND WHEELS

Because of the tremendous loads and rough terrain the **off-road** trac-tor must handle, **tires and wheels** are always **heavy-duty** and designed for traction in dirt. **Tires** are generally **wider** than the on-road tire to avoid sinking in loose dirt. Most off-road **wheels** are **made of steel.** Aluminum would be no match for the rocks and uneven terrain. These tires must be strong enough to support heavy loads. On the other hand, **on-road** trucks use **tires** built to **stand up to the heat generated by rolling at higher speeds.** They have more grooves in the tread for better traction on pavement.

THE HYDRAULIC SYSTEM

Hydraulic systems are found **more often in off-road** than on-road trac-tors. The hydraulic system includes a tank, lines from the tractor to the trailer, and a pump. This is called a wet kit.

FUEL TANKS

An **on-road tractor** will have at least one and most probably **two fuel tanks.** These are located under the cab or the sleeper on each side of the truck. Each tank will hold at least 50 gallons and the large ones can hold 150 gallons. When fueling you have to fill each one separately. The fuel lines from the engine usually go to the tank on the driver's side of the truck. If there are two or more tanks they will be **interconnected. This way the fuel level is pretty much the same in all the tanks even though the engine is taking fuel from only one tank.**

Axles

Tractors are not only classified by their uses (on-road or off-road), but also by the number of drive axles. Tractors that you will be working with can be classified as single axle tractors or tandem axle tractors.

SINGLE AXLE TRACTORS

The **single axle tractor has one drive axle and one steering axle.** Be-ing **smaller** and **easier to handle** than the tandem, it is used for pulling two or more trailers, or for short distances and light loads. It has a **smaller turning radius.** Turning radius depends on wheelbase. For a single axle tractor, wheelbase is the distance between the center of the steering axle to the center of the rear drive axle. (For a tandem, wheel-base is from the center of the front axle to the center of the tandem.)

A single axle tractor is **cheaper to buy and operate.** Repair costs are lower since there are fewer parts on the single axle to repair.

fig. 10-1
The wheelbase of a
single axle tractor.

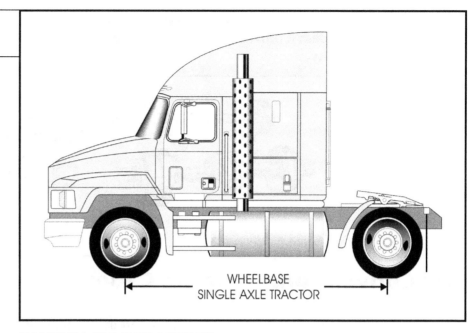

WHEELBASE
SINGLE AXLE TRACTOR

TANDEM AXLE TRACTORS

For heavy loads and long distances the tandem axle tractor is generally used. The **tandem axle provides four more drive tires.** That gives not only **more strength** but **more traction.**

The average wheelbase of a tandem axle tractor is 196" to 220" for a cabover and 220" to 260" for a conventional tractor. The **wide turning radius** of the long wheelbase tandem axle can make it a little **harder to maneuver** a truck within a limited space.

fig. 10-2
The wheelbase of a
tandem axle tractor.

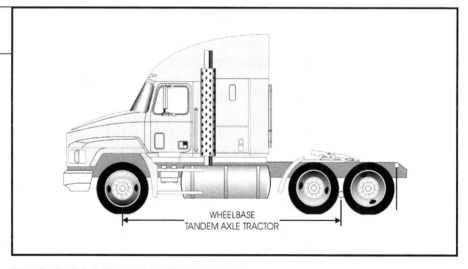

WHEELBASE
TANDEM AXLE TRACTOR

SINGLE DRIVE AXLE TRACTORS

One other configuration is a single drive axle with an tag axle. A tag axle is a dead axle. It isn't powered by the engine, but rather freewheels. The **tag axle** has certain advantages of both the single and the tandem drive axles. Like the single, it is **not as heavy** and requires **less maintenance** than the tandem. Since it doesn't require any engine power, it

doesn't increase fuel use the way the tandem axle does. Like the tandem it provides four more wheels and a **greater load-carrying capacity.**

fig. 10-3
Tandem axles. (A) Single drive with tag axle and (B) two drive axles.

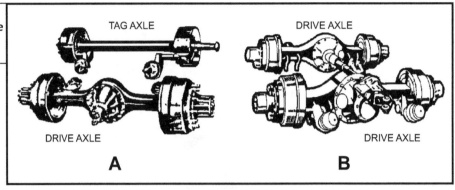

The Conventional and the Cabover

There is yet one more important system of classification. That is whether a tractor is a conventional or a cabover.

THE CONVENTIONAL
In the conventional tractor, the **cab sits behind the engine. Sleepers** are easier to get into and out of and are sometimes **larger.** The length of the hood can be classed as long, medium or short.

Road **visibility** is **not as good** as in the cabovers, but having the engine in front can be safer if a collision occurs.

THE CAB-OVER-ENGINE
Although it was called the cab-over-engine when it was introduced just before World War II, people eventually shortened that to the "cabover," or COE. The cabover has a **shorter wheelbase** and **greater visibility** for the driver.

Cabovers are used for all types of hauling. With their shorter wheelbase and **turning ease,** they are often preferred for in-city deliveries and for pulling long trailers. Plastic, fiber glass and aluminum are often used to reduce the weight of the cabover. That **lighter weight** means more of the allowable weight can be payload.

Its one-time advantage was that since the cabover tractor itself was shorter in length than the conventional, it could pull a longer trailer without the length of the entire rig exceeding limits set in certain states. That was a real plus for a while. Then came standardization. In 1982 the Surface Transportation Assistance Act meant states had to allow semi-trailers up to 48 feet in length on all interstate and U.S. highways, including all roads within access of the pickup or delivery point. (States can set length limits beyond the 48-foot limit, however.) Having a shorter tractor was no longer of any particular advantage.

The Heavy Straight Truck

The **straight truck** is an "all-in-one" vehicle with **no articulation** (coupling device). It can be quite heavy and powerful. For example, the straight truck is paired with front end loaders in garbage collection and in construction to haul dirt and gravel. It is also used for hauling specialized items such as cranes, sheet rock, dressed stone, cinder block and petroleum products.

Driver comforts are important in the straight truck. The truck is generally smaller in size and therefore less intimidating to the new driver. In fact, straight trucks may have fully synchronized transmission gears which might seem "too easy" for the professional driver.

Specifications

Every item on the tractor has a distinct purpose. The **tractor** has been **"spec'ed out" for the job** it will be doing. A tractor that travels up, down and across the Rocky Mountains will have different specifications than a truck that travels the flatland. Specification of the frame, axles and springs is based on the weight of the load, type of cargo and the sort of terrain over which the tractor will run.

Climate also plays an important role. If the tractor will be running in very cold weather, it is likely to have such add-on features as an engine block heater, fuel line heater, brake system air dryer and battery warmer. For fragile cargo such as electronics equipment or medical supplies, air ride suspension is a must. Tractors that haul extremely heavy cargo are fitted with thicker frames and stronger rear end differentials.

AERODYNAMICS AND FUEL ECONOMY
The word **"aerodynamics"** refers to the **moving** of objects **through the air** (aero = air, dynamics = movement). When a tractor pushes against the wind it **burns up a lot of fuel.** If the tractor can be made "slicker" to glide more easily through the air, significant **fuel savings** can be realized. This **can be achieved with a few changes in the truck design.** Wherever possible, the cab will have rounded edges instead of flat surfaces. An aerodynamic design tucks in the fuel tank, exhaust stack and all protruding parts to keep them from catching the wind and holding back the tractor. The truck on the cover of this book exhibits many aerodynamic features.

Add-on accessories include wind deflectors, automatic engine fan shut-off, formula diesel engines and even lighter-weight cabs, frames, wheels and components. Because of the importance of fuel savings, research in the field of aerodynamics is fierce and ongoing.

ACCESSORIES

Tractor accessories serve many purposes. They can **make the vehicle safer,** as well as **easier to operate and maintain.** Some accessories are strictly for driver comfort, while others just make the tractor nicer looking.

Gauges, radios, cab styling, auxiliary brakes, fuel tank heaters and power take-offs are some of the tractor accessories available. With some tractors, cab size will limit the accessories to be added.

COLD AND HOT WEATHER ACCESSORIES

In cold or hot weather, it's tempting to keep the engine running so the engine or cab will stay warm or cool while the truck is parked. But all that idling wastes a lot of precious fuel, and can cut a year off the truck's life. An **auxiliary power unit** can be added to **keep the engine or cab warm or cool** while the truck is parked for extended periods **with the engine turned off.** Not having to idle the engine for those long periods will save fuel. A fuel heater can be added to keep the fuel from thickening up in sub-zero weather.

THE DRIVER'S SEAT

Tractor **seats** are scientifically engineered and adjustable to **provide** the best possible **support** for long hours of driving. Some of these have high backs and arms that fold up or down.

Nearly every truck you see will have an air ride seat on the driver's side. This works just like the air ride suspension and the purpose is the same, to provide a better ride. Under the seat you will see a small air bag. Air pressure from the air supply system inflates the bag.

There are several different designs. There will be a knob or lever that can be moved one way to add air to the bag and the other way to re-lease air. On some seats this knob is used to adjust the seat to suit the driver's weight. These seats have a separate lever adjusting the height. Other seats will use the air supply knob to adjust for weight and height. All seats will have a separate lever to move the seat forward and back.

Drivers will be spending a lot of time in that seat, so make sure all of its controls are working. Be able to adjust it so it is comfortable to you when you must drive.

GAUGES AND CONTROLS

The switches and gauges are usually located on the dash of the truck. One manufacturer's main gauges are in front of the driver with the aux-iliary gauges to the driver's right. Other makers curve the dash to the right so that all gauges and switches are within easy reach.

The basic gauges are air pressure, speedometer, tachometer, oil pressure, fuel level and water temperature. Then there are gauges to measure transmission fluid temperature, rear axle fluid temperature, manifold pressure and temperatures of various mechanical parts. **Gauges indicate how the tractor is running.** They make it possible for drivers to take better care of their equipment. **Switches are used to control or operate the truck.** Among these are switches for lights, high beam indicators, engine stop control, auxiliary brakes and the power take-off switch (PTO).

Chapter 2 covers gauges and controls in greater detail.

THE HEADACHE RACK

A headache rack is the **cab guard** that **protects the back of the cab** if the load shifts forward during a sudden stop. Obviously, this accessory could save someone from getting a very bad headache! It provides not only a safer truck but it also serves as a safe handy place to hang chains and binders. Safety regulations require that a tractor have a headache rack when pulling a flatbed trailer that does not have a front bulkhead.

fig. 10-4
A cab guard will stop the forward motion of cargo that's not securely loaded on the trailer.

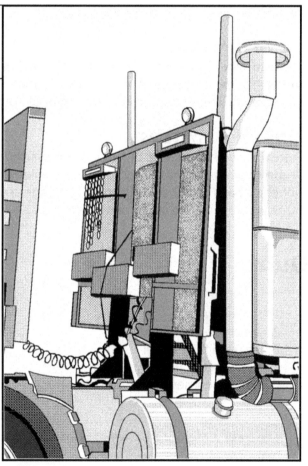

THE JAKE BRAKE

"Jake brake" is a term you'll hear used for engine retarders or engine brakes in general. It really refers to one particular manufacturer's product, and there are several different types of engine retarders. This accessory is almost a necessity for tractors that travel up and down mountains and steep grades. Using the engine's own compression to slow the vehicle, the **engine brake controls speed on a downgrade** and can **save wear on the brakes.** A switch inside the cab will turn it on or off.

Several chapters in this book contain more information about this important accessory, such as Chapter 16.

THE POWER TAKE-OFF (PTO)

Another option is the **power take-off** for hydraulic powered equipment. The PTO **activates a hydraulic pump** that pumps fluid from the tractor to hydraulic equipment such as a dump trailer.

THE SLEEPING BERTH

The sleeping berth ("**sleeper**") **for rest periods out on the road** has gotten pretty fancy over the years. There was a time when it was little more than a stuffy little compartment with a lumpy cot. These days, a sleeper can be plain enough for a missionary or designed to warm a lonely driver's heart. There is heat and air conditioning, often TV and stereo. Some even feature sinks, running water, microwave ovens and queen-sized beds. Extra insulation shields against outside noise and temperature extremes.

As you will see, a lot of money can be spent on the sleeper. Larger sleepers have stand-up space, closets and drawers, writing table, carpeting. One thing a sleeper normally doesn't have is a shower (but showers are available at most truck stops).

THE FIFTH WHEEL

The **fifth wheel provides the point of rotation where the trailer fits on the tractor** and is used for load distribution. It's a very basic accessory and you'll learn much more about it in Chapters 13 and 15.

SUSPENSION SYSTEMS

There are two basic types of suspension systems: air ride or leaf spring. Of the two, air ride is the most comfortable. The air ride system uses rubber air bags rather than springs. The bags are located just inside the frame where the drive axles meet the frame.

Chapter 10 Quiz

1. The truck tractor _____ .
    - A. is a self-contained unit
    - B. has no fifth wheel
    - C. consists of the power unit
    - D. is sometimes called a straight truck

2. The basic difference between on-road and off-road tractors is that _____ .
    - A. one type must be "street legal" and the other never is
    - B. off-road tractors are built to withstand more abuse
    - C. off-road tractors are built for speed
    - D. off-road tractors have no passenger seat

3. The single-axle tractor is ideal for _____ .
   A. lightweight cargo
   B. mountain driving
   C. safety during winter storms
   D. cross-country driving

4. For hauling extremely heavy equipment, a tractor must have _____ .
   A. a brake system air dryer
   B. a heavy-duty differential
   C. an automatic engine fan shut-off
   D. a mechanical suspension system

5. The device that helps slow the truck is the _____ .
   A. engine retarder
   B. coupling device
   C. tag axle
   D. power take-off

6. A typical fuel-saving add-on device is _____ .
   A. a shorter wheelbase
   B. an air ride suspension
   C. an air ride seat
   D. a wind deflector

7. The cab guard is required by law when the _____ .
   A. road involves steep grades
   B. trailer being pulled has no auxiliary brakes
   C. flatbed being pulled has no bulkhead
   D. tractor has no power take-off

8. The distance between the rear drive axle and the center of the steering axle is the _____ .
   A. first gear ratio
   B. load-carrying capacity
   C. GVWR
   D. wheelbase

9. The COE enjoyed greater popularity _____ .
   A. during World War I
   B. before conventionals were introduced
   C. before 1982
   D. with those who preferred not to stand while driving

10. In a tractor, aluminum, fiber glass and plastic are used to _____ .
    A. create a stylish interior
    B. reduce the tractor's weight
    C. strengthen the rear end differential
    D. provide off-road durability

VEHICLE MANAGEMENT SYSTEMS

Computers and Change in Trucking

Computers — they're everywhere! They're in your car, of course, and your VCR. They're in many household appliances, in the supermarket, in vending machines...As the Y2K hysteria showed at the turn of the millennium, there are few things that don't have microprocessors in them. You aren't likely surprised to learn that there are computing devices in trucks.

As computer systems have changed almost every aspect of our lives, so have they changed the trucking industry. The computer has changed the business management department of the carrier company. It has changed the way drivers work. Onboard computers, or **vehicle management systems,** are one way carriers **monitor and determine profits.** Every day, the industry learns something new about the positive effects of technology. Computers prove to be a good investment in terms of money management for the carrier. They relieve the driver of a lot of paperwork. They **help improve driving habits** and thus **save fuel and promote safety**. They help the carrier and the driver **provide better customer service**. They assist mechanics in their work. And, it appears they will be able to do much more in the future.

Computers in the Trucking Industry

Running a trucking business involves a lot of work. The company manager takes charge of the business. This person makes the decisions that affect company profits. But the manager needs lots of help to run the company well. The manager needs other people to carry out the decisions and to handle the different areas of the business. This list of workers includes not only the drivers but also salespeople, dispatchers, billing clerks and of course, mechanics.

With this many areas of work at one company, the paperwork can be both time consuming and expensive. This is especially true for dispatch and billing. **Computers** offer managers a much **more efficient and prompt** way to take care of business **than paper.** As it turns out, it's also a less costly way.

So, at modern trucking companies, computers are everywhere. **In the maintenance department,** the computer generates inspection and other needed forms. It keeps an accurate record of inspections and maintenance performed on each piece of equipment. Computers keep track of parts and accessories. And, they do that without reams of paper and walls of file cabinets. Plus, as you'll see, a computer can help determine what needs to be maintained.

In the sales department, the computer is used for word processing to write letters and generate promotional materials and proposals. **In dispatch** it's used to keep track of where the drivers, the equipment and the freight are at all times. **In billing** the computer generates bills and keeps track of accounts receivable.

Computers are used in all these parts of the terminal, but they're also mounted inside the cabs of the trucks. The **onboard computers gather information that you and your employer can use to do a better job. This information enables drivers to operate more efficiently and safely**. You and the carrier will use the data collected to file required reports and keep the equipment in good condition.

Computers even help those in the industry to comply with federal regulations. Electronic onboard recorders called EOBRs help automate the process of keeping drivers' hours-of-service logs.

When computers are mounted in trucks, they are called onboard computers.

Functions of the Onboard Computer

The two main purposes of the onboard computer are to **monitor vehicle performance** and to **monitor driver performance**. They do this by reading, recording and storing information from special sensors that are located so that they monitor most of the truck's systems. For instance, these sensor and probes can monitor all the performance factors listed below:

- fuel consumption
- periods of stop-and-go driving
- departure and arrival times
- vehicle stop time
- road miles
- cruise control time
- idling time
- speed
- rpm
- driving time
- brake use
- fan clutch use
- number of stops that are longer than a set time
- number of times the exhaust goes above a certain temperature
- engine warm-up and engine cool-down times

The onboard computer is the modern, electronic answer to the older tachograph, which monitors many of the same factors.

Often the information gathered by the onboard computer can warn you that a system is close to failure. It's almost always less costly to prevent a breakdown than to repair one. If the data shows that a truck system is not performing up to par, you can look into it and make adjustments. You can see how such a system would improve vehicle performance.

The same system improves driver performance because it **lets a driver see where habits might be changed or improved**. While drivers almost always know when they are speeding, they don't always realize how much of the time they may drive just a little too fast. Lowering speed improves fuel consumption, of course, but even more important, it promotes safety.

Types of Onboard Computers

Most onboard computers consist of two major components: the sensors and the recorder. The sensors monitor vehicle and driver performance and send the data to the recroder. The recorder stores the information. Some computers only accept information from the sensors. Others are designed to let the driver enter information too. Drivers make preprogrammed entries by pressing different keys on a panel. For example, on crossing a state line, a driver would enter a code for the state mileage report and then the code for the state. **Time and date clocks** stamp the entries with the precise time and date. The odometer keeps track of the miles. Data is transmitted to a recording medium or storage device such as a removable module or cartridge. That device can then be inserted into a main computer and report can be generated from the data. Figure 11-1 pictures one of these early onboard computers. Wireless technology now allows data to be transmitted directly from the vehicle to the main computer.

fig. 11-1
An early onboard computer lets the driver input information by pushing button.s Data was stored on removable cartridges.

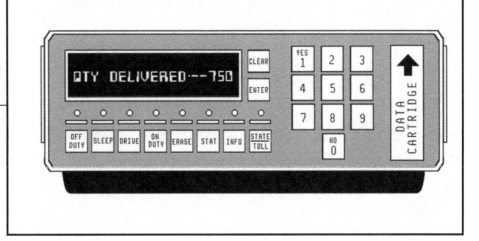

Reports Generated by Onboard Computers

Many helpful reports can be generated from the data gathered by the onboard computer. Types of reports this information leads to include:

- driver's trip reports
- trip over/short/damage reports
- driver's expense reports
- driving performance reports
- state mileage reports

Drivers who work for a carrier will not see all these reports. Some are useful mainly to management or to an owner/operator. Drivers will see driving performance reports, especially when the carrier wants to congratulate them for a good job. Or, this report can pinpoint problem areas where the driver may be falling behind in driving performance.

During your career as a mechanic, you may not see all of these reports either. Still, it's always a good idea to have a basic understanding of all aspects of your chosen profession. So we'll take a quick look at each of these reports so you can get a clear idea of just how they fit in and how helpful onboard computers can be.

The data for driver's trip reports and driving performance reports is gathered by sensors. The driver does not input any data for these reports. However, for the trip over/short/damage reports, the state mileage reports and the driver's expense reports, the driver may need to give the computer some information. These last three reports all save paperwork for the driver. The driver's trip report shows the total miles driven, the average speed, driving time and the stopping time.

The **driving performance report** is very detailed. It includes the information listed below.

- total miles driven for this report
- total hours driven for this report
- engine idling time
- how long the engine ran and its rpm in each speed category
- how often and for how long the driver exceeded the speed limit

You can see how this report **would help** the carrier, mechanics and drivers **pinpoint performance problems** that could lead to equipment damage, loss of profits and safety hazards.

How the Onboard Computer Helped One Company

A few years ago, a trucking company in Oregon decided to look for new ways **to reduce costs and increase profits**. To achieve their goal, they knew that they had to make a change in the driving habits of their drivers. They installed a Vehicle Management System into each of the trucks in their fleet.

The mechanics met the challenge of interpreting and working with the information that these onboard computer provided. Because of this information, they were able to catch potential problems on the truck early. They were able to make adjustments and repairs in the shop, saving costly over-the-road repairs and delays in shipping.

The reports also shows quite a bit or money being wasted by speeding and excessive idling time. The company developed speed limit policies. Although this addressed the problem of excessive speeding, the problem of excessive idling had to be corrected too.

Comfort means a lot to a person whose "home" is the cab of a truck. Weather conditions can range from sizzling hot to freezing cold. Idling the engine can provide the driver with the comforts of heat or air conditioning. However, idling burns expensive fuel and it shortens engine life.

The company made changes on the fleet trucks that improved driver comfort. The company installed auxiliary power units on the tractors to run the air conditioning and heating systems while each tractor was parked with its engine turned off. You'll read more about these systems in the chapter on air conditioning.

Drivers no longer needed to idle their engines to keep the cab comfortable. That saved the company money. The company introduced an **incentive plan that rewarded drivers who save the company money with extra pay each month** Driver performance greatly improved. The company looks back with satisfaction at the success that began with computer reports.

Computers in Trucking

Today, critical information is collected and made available for use using any or all of these devices:

- onboard computers
- portable computers
- handheld devices

ONBOARD COMPUTERS

The technology used in heavy equipment is becoming more sophisticated with the increased use of electronic components to control a growing variety of functions. Increasingly, you'll need training in electronics in order to make engine adjustments and to diagnose problems.

The **latest onboard computers** record much the same data as before, only with more accuracy, more detail and often less input from the driver. Some systems **use satellites and global positioning technology** (GPS) to pinpoint the vehicle's precise location. To generate a state mileage report, for example, a driver used to have to enter a code at each state line crossing. With GPS, this information is entered automatically. All the driver has to do is to confirm the information later.

The systems can store much larger amounts of information internally. As you read earlier, some systems don't use data storage cartridges. Instead, data is transmitted by

- wireless communication
- direct cable connection
- handheld devices
- removable memory cards

Communication between the company and the truck **can be two-way, and almost instantaneous.** The in-truck system can advise the dispatcher if drivers are on schedule. Route and cargo information can be sent to the drivers to keep them on track or reroute them around unforeseen obstacles.

The onboard computer pictured in Figure 11-2 shows a system with an alphanumeric (letters and numbers) keyboard that the driver can use to communicate with the dispatcher. This system also has a display that transmits alerts from the dispatcher back to the driver. The onboard computer shown in Figure 11-3 on the next page pictures a touch screen which lets the driver input data. The system will prompt the driver through the process of entering information.

fig. 11-2
This onboard computer offers the driver an alphanumeric keypad for making detailed entries. The display advises the driver about messages that have been sent to or received by the dispatcher.

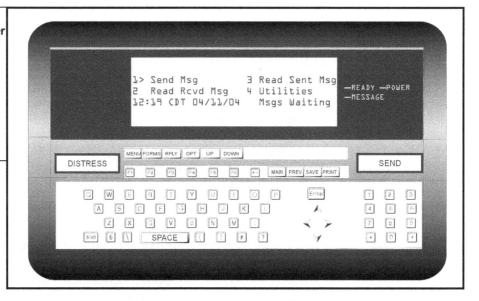

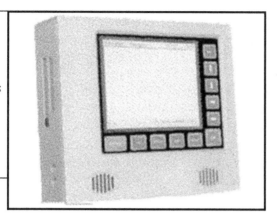

fig. 11-3
With this onboard computer, part of the Cadec Mobius TTS system, the driver makes entries using a touch screen. Messages displayed on the screen prompt the driver through the data-entry process.

Onboard **computers** can do more than simply record information from the vehicle's systems. They can **relay instructions back to the vehicle.** For example, managers may study driver performance reports only to find that some drivers have a habit of speeding, or idling too long. Both practices are fuel-wasters, and speeding is unsafe. The computer can be used to program the vehicle not to exceed a preset speed as long as the truck is in gear, or to shut off the engine after a certain period of idling. (That the drivers have undesirable habits is not likely to be forgotten by the managers who read the reports!)

PORTABLE COMPUTERS

Today's truck drivers tote around the same laptop computers that desk jockeys and college students use. Well, they're not exactly the same. Trucker's **laptops** are "hardened" — able to take the bounces and jolts that come with riding in a cab. They can handle being exposed to harsh chemicals, extremes in temperature, moisture, greases and vapors. They're also outfitted with displays that work well in less-than-optimal lighting conditions. Their operating systems are specially designed to work with the type of software that the industry uses. However, like consumer laptops, they can give access to the Internet.

You'll see laptop computers in the yard, too. Some systems will use wireless connections to transmit data from the onboard computer while the vehicle is still on the road. However, many will wait for the truck to reach a terminal. The laptop is connected to the onboard computer by a cable. Data can be downloaded — collected — that way.

HANDHELD DEVICES

You may find yourself using handheld devices in your work. These small computers serve as the link from technician to vehicle. They can be plugged into an onboard computer to diagnose any component that needs adjustment or repair. You may also find yourself using a tablet computer. Instead of jotting notes on a small notepad, you'll write them on the tablet with a stylus — a special electronic pen — and the computer will store the information for later retrieval.

Personal data assistants (PDAs) are small computers that fit in the hand. Smaller than even laptops, they can still hold huge amounts of information like entire manuals, with room to spare.

The functions of all three items — the scanner-equipped handheld, the tablet computer and the PDA — are sometimes combined into one powerful and convenient piece of equipment.

Another common handheld device is the cellular phone. The cellular phone hasn't put the CB radio completely out of business for drivers. However, for making long distance calls, a cell phone is often more convenient and less expensive than a landline connection. **Cell phones equipped with cameras and able to respond to voice commands are even more useful.**

Onboard Computers and the Future

As you've seen, simple onboard computer systems were designed to read and record data from the three gauges listed below:

- tachometer
- odometer
- speedometer

More complex systems monitor these three gauges and can gather a variety of other information. To the many examples we have already listed, you can add engine water temperature and oil pressure. Going even further, sophisticated systems can control the starter, door locks, lights — even the wipers and the horn. Using GPS, it's possible to program trailer doors to open only when the cargo has reached its destination.

More and more, devices are being equipped with GPS, wireless technology, voice recognition and video capabilities. Instead of making an entry into an electronic log by pushing a button or hitting a key, drivers may simply speak the words, "On Duty." A truck-mounted video camera could let them see into blind spots or keep them centered in a lane. A truck may be equipped to exchange data wirelessly every time it passes a "hot spot" that can receive and transmit. Using such a system, mechanics could diagnose a problem with a truck while it's still on the road. Wireless and GPS **technology can** keep the driver in constant contact with the home terminal, **offer**ing **greater comfort, safety and security** while out on the highway.

Chapter 11 Quiz

1. The computer is a more efficient way to take care of paperwork, but it's also more costly.
   A. True
   B. False

2. In _____, computers are used to write letters and generate promotional materials.
   A. Sales
   B. Maintenance
   C. Dispatch
   D. Billing

3. Two main purposes of the onboard computer are to monitor vehicle performance and _____.
   A. idling time
   B. fuel temperature
   C. driver performance
   D. engine water temperature

4. The parts of the onboard computer that monitor vehicle and driver performance are called the _____.
   A. gauges
   B. sensors
   C. cartridges
   D. trackers

5. The part of the onboard computer that stores the data is called the _____.
   A. input device
   B. download cable
   C. recorder
   D. sensor

6. Even the simplest onboard computer can read and record data from all the truck's systems.
   A. True
   B. False

7. The _____ report shows engine idling time.
   A. trip over/short/damage
   B. state mileage
   C. driver's expense
   D. driving performance

8. Onboard computers improve driving habits, save fuel and promote safety.
   A. True
   B. False

9. Drivers often let their trucks idel so they can leave their heating or air conditioning on, making the cab more comfortable.
   A. True
   B. False

10. An onboard computer that monitors idling time can help a
   _____ .
   A. motor carrier increase sales
   B. motor carrier control expenses
   C. driver get more rest
   D. driver with log books

TYPES OF TRAILERS

The Towed Unit

The first chapters in this book explored the power unit, the tractor. In this chapter we will turn our attention to the towed unit, the trailer.

As you must have noticed even before deciding to become part of the trucking industry, **there are many different types of trailers** on the road today. The simplest of these trailers is basically just a box container on wheels. You've seen these rolling boxes heading for the warehouse full of anything from shoes to television sets.

No doubt you've also noticed the refrigerated trailers that actually look like big freezers on wheels. Their job is to make sure fresh and frozen food stays that way during the trip. Another recognizable trailer type is the big tank. The tanks are filled with liquids and pressurized gases. Milk is carried in tanks, and so are flammable materials such as gasoline and other petroleum products.

Construction and Components

Transporting goods on the road **calls for** a **light, strong, flexible and spacious** container. The **materials** used to build a trailer make a very big difference. They dictate how the equipment will operate and how long it will last. They also determine its weight, strength and method of upkeep.

Steel, aluminum, wood, plastic, fiber glass, polyester and stainless steel are the basic materials used in the construction of a trailer. **Aluminum** has just lately replaced steel as **the most common metal** found in the van. A very notable savings in weight can be achieved by using aluminum for skin sheets, roof sheets and frame rails.

Many unseen parts may also be of aluminum — or even composite materials — including side posts, crossmembers and roof bows. In some trailers, even the main frame rails are aluminum. However, aluminum is not the most practical metal for certain components. These parts must be as strong as possible.

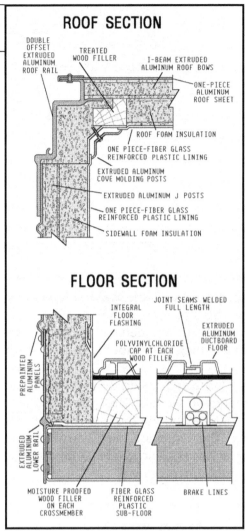

fig. 12-1
Van trailers are made of a variety of materials.

ROOF SECTION

DOUBLE OFFSET EXTRUDED ALUMINUM ROOF RAIL

TREATED WOOD FILLER

I-BEAM EXTRUDED ALUMINUM ROOF BOWS

ONE-PIECE ALUMINUM ROOF SHEET

ROOF FOAM INSULATION

ONE PIECE-FIBER GLASS REINFORCED PLASTIC LINING

EXTRUDED ALUMINUM COVE MOLDING POSTS

EXTRUDED ALUMINUM J POSTS

ONE PIECE-FIBER GLASS REINFORCED PLASTIC LINING

SIDEWALL FOAM INSULATION

FLOOR SECTION

JOINT SEAMS WELDED FULL LENGTH

INTEGRAL FLOOR FLASHING

EXTRUDED ALUMINUM DUCTBOARD FLOOR

POLYVINYLCHLORIDE CAP AT EACH WOOD FILLER

PREPAINTED ALUMINUM PANELS

EXTRUDED ALUMINUM LOWER RAIL

MOISTURE PROOFED WOOD FILLER ON EACH CROSSMEMBER

FIBER GLASS REINFORCED PLASTIC SUB-FLOOR

BRAKE LINES

Keep in mind that even though **trailers** come in many different shapes and sizes, they are **made up of the same basic parts. They all have running gear, a frame and similar body construction.**

RUNNING GEAR

The running gear includes **those parts that** actually **allow the trailer to be pulled down the road.** To run, a trailer must have **tires, wheels, axles, brakes and springs.** Most trailers have **landing gear.** Some also have an optional assembly, the sliding tandem, which helps distribute weight.

Tires

Most commonly, **trailers have dual tires on each axle end.** Two tires are often required to support the weight of the cargo. Also available are extra wide tires. One wide tire is made to carry the same load as duals. These wide tires are called super singles. Super singles faded out for a while but they're coming back into popularity these days with weight savings more important than ever.

Wheels

As a general rule, **trailers use the same Daytons and Budds — spoke and disc wheels — as tractors.**

Axles

Most trailers have two axles. These axles are made very much like tractor axles. The big difference is that **trailer wheels are free-rolling** rather than driven by the engine.

Axles help support the **weight** of the trailer and the load. **Most axles** are built to **carry the legal limit of 20,000 pounds each.** Trailers that will be hauling very heavy loads will have two or more axles. Trailers that haul very light loads may need only one.

Brakes

Mechanically, the **trailer's brakes work the same way the tractor brakes do.** There are service brakes (air brakes) and emergency brakes (spring brakes). The **trailer brakes have their own air tanks** which are charged in response to a control in the tractor. The tractor protection valve separates the tractor air supply from the trailer air supply. Should there be a break in the trailer air lines, this valve would "protect" the tractor's air supply so at least the tractor would still have braking power.

Suspension Systems

Suspension systems provide a smooth ride for driver and cargo by **absorbing bumps from the road.** These systems must be strong enough to **carry the weight of the cargo and to flex under the cargo's weight.**

A suspension system is **used to attach the axles to the trailer.** A trailer may be equipped with **either a leaf spring or air ride suspension.**

Sliding Tandems

The **slider assembly** allows the driver to slide the tandems back and forth to adjust the wheelbase of the trailer. This **helps distribute** the **trailer weight correctly.** (You'll learn more about sliding tandems in Chapter 15.)

Landing Gear

Landing gear is sometimes called trailer supports or even dolly legs. The **landing gear holds up the front of the trailer when the trailer isn't hooked to the tractor.** It is usually cranked into place with a crank found on the side of the trailer. The crank has a low gear and a high gear. Use the high gear when no trailer weight rests on the landing jacks.

Aerodynamic Options

Since the early 1970s when the price of fuel flew skyward and kept going, trucking companies have been **making** their **trailers,** as well as their tractors, **more fuel efficient.** Sometimes a wind foil device is added to the top front wall of the trailer. This directs the flow of air over the top and around the sides of the trailer. That way the trailer "slides" through the air with less resistance.

Front corners of vans are often rounded or tapered to cut down on wind drag. A smooth exterior skin is another important design factor. The search for more fuel-efficient trailer design continues. During your career with the trucking industry, you are bound to see more interesting discoveries in the area of aerodynamics.

FRAME

The main beams and stringers of a trailer are made of steel or aluminum. It is the job of the **beams and stringers** to **support the load.**

Inside or Outside Rails

Inside rail trailers have supporting beams near the middle of the trailer. Most vans and reefers and some platform trailers have an inside rail. Other platform trailers have outside **rails.** They both **provide** about the same level of **support.** Outside rails provide perhaps a somewhat stiffer trailer. The choice often comes down to a matter of personal preference, much like the choice between cabover and conventional tractors.

fig. 12-2
Inside rails (A) and outside rails (B) provide about an equal amount of support.

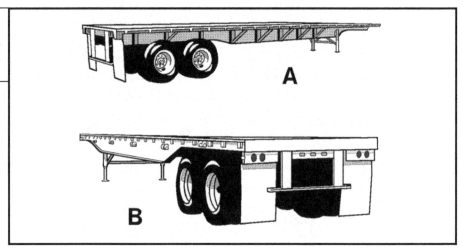

Kingpin

The kingpin is located underneath the front of the trailer in the middle of the bed plate, which is a metal plate attached to the frame. It will always be made of high strength carbon steel. Aluminum is too light and flexible.

When a tractor is backed underneath the trailer, the **kingpin slides through the slot up to the center of the fifth wheel.** At that point, locking jaws lock into place and hold the kingpin into position so that it cannot slide forward or backward but is able to turn freely.

BULKHEAD, FLOOR, WALL AND DOOR CONSTRUCTION

Bulkhead

The bulkhead is the short wall **on** the front edge of a **platform trailer.** It keeps whatever the trailer is hauling from sliding too far forward. In an emergency stop, the **bulkhead must hold the cargo back** so that it won't slam into the tractor and possibly injure the driver.

Flooring

Depending on what the trailer is used for, the trailer **floor** can be **made of various materials.** A popular choice is hardwood flooring made of narrow strips of wood. Another common flooring is a ribbed aluminum, found in refrigerated trailers. Besides giving strength to the metal, the ribbing allows air to circulate around the cargo.

The Camber Design

Even though platform trailers must be very strong, they must also be very light. Use of aluminum in the construction has helped trailers meet these two requirements.

However, **aluminum is** one of the **lightest,** most **flexible** metals. It is so flexible that the trailer will flex as it goes down the road.

Some of the lightweight platform trailers will twist, bend and flex to an amazing degree. To compensate for this flexing, **some trailers have a built-in arch. This** is what's **known as "camber."** The camber is very easy to see when the trailer is empty. When the trailer is loaded, its weight will flatten the camber.

fig. 12-3
A cambered platform trailer is not truly flat, but rather has a slight arch to it. It will flatten out under the weight of the load.

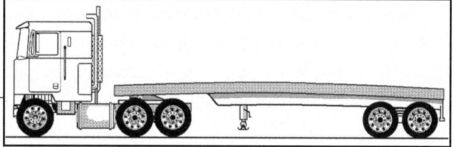

Walls

The interior of a van **may be smooth or ribbed,** depending on what it was meant to haul. Interior lining may be made in panels or all in one piece.

The walls of a trailer begin with studs that go from the floor to the ceiling. This develops the basic frame of the trailer. The studs are covered by plywood or heavy plastic. Plastic can take more of a beating from forklifts or cargo, but it is generally more expensive than plywood.

The inside lining of a refrigerated van is usually of pre-painted aluminum sheets which may be smooth or ribbed. The ribbed sheets are known to allow better circulation around the cargo. Note that whatever the material used for the inside walls, it must meet health standards to qualify for hauling food products. Fiber glass is popular for just that reason. It is nonporous and very easy to keep clean.

Reefer walls are of the interior post design. As you might expect, refrigerated vans must be well insulated, with several inches of foam insulation poured into the space between the inside panels and outside sheets.

Ceiling

A trailer's **ceiling is** very much **like** its **walls.** That is, outside studs are covered by sheet metal or aluminum while inside studs are covered by plywood or plastic.

The basic **construction of vans and refrigerated trailers** is very **similar.** However, a van has no wall or ceiling insulation unless it is an insulated van. As mentioned earlier, the refrigerated trailer is heavily enveloped with a high-quality insulation.

Exterior Skin

The side wall design of the common van is often the exterior post design. This design has side posts with pre-painted **aluminum sheets attached to the inside of the post.** This makes a simple, lightweight wall but **leaves the side posts exposed to create wind drag.**

Why not put the **posts inside the van?** Well, then they **are at the mercy of forklifts and cargo.** Sometimes they are left exposed but often a liner is added for protection.

Roof

The roof of most trailers is made of large aluminum sheets. Leaks are then not such a problem as with roofs that have many seams. In some trailers the sheets are stretched across roof bows. The bows are then fastened on both sides to the trailer's upper frame rails.

The roof is bonded to the roof bows with an adhesive material. A stronger type of trailer roof uses roof carlins. The sheets are riveted to the carlins, which are then riveted to the upper frame rails.

Doors

Swinging doors are the most popular doors for trailers. Such doors are hinged on the rear outside edges of the trailer. Refrigerated and moving vans often have a small door on the side of the trailer, which comes in handy when unloading in narrow streets or alleyways. At any rate, a side swinging door works in the same way a rear door works. A lever holds it tight against the trailer frame. A rubber seal around the door keeps out dust, rain or snow. With insulated and refrigerated trailers, the seal also keeps the inside temperature steady.

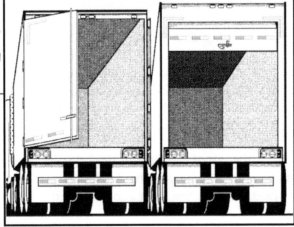

fig. 12-4
Swinging doors provide a better seal than roll-up doors, but roll-up doors don't have to be opened before the truck reaches the dock.

Another popular type of **door is the roll-up.** Like a garage door, it is built with tracks on runners. You open it by pulling up on the handle and sliding it up to lie along the ceiling. When closed, a lever on the door hooks to the floor to keep it shut.

A **roll-up doesn't seal as well as a swinging door,** so it is rarely used on a refrigerated trailer when a steady temperature must be maintained. The **roll-up is used mostly on trailers that deliver in the city.**

One advantage of a roll-up door over a swinging door is that drivers can back up to the dock before the roll-up door is opened. That's handy for trucks that load or unload many times a day. Swinging doors must be opened before the trailer gets to the dock.

Fasteners and Hardware

For the most part, **securing cargo on platform trailers is done with ropes, chains or nylon straps. Tarps** are used to **cover** the **loads** when required. Once again, it depends on the cargo. At any rate, the fasteners and hardware used in or on a trailer are accessory equipment.

Lights, Wiring and Air System

LIGHTS AND WIRING

All of the **lights on a trailer** are **connected to** the **tractor's electrical system.** They include clearance lights, turn signals, parking lights and brake lights. When you turn on any of these lights in the tractor, the same trailer lights will go on. The wires that control these lights are in the **tractor electrical cord,** commonly **called the pigtail.** The pigtail **attaches to** the trailer at an outlet in **the front of the trailer.**

Picture the electrical wiring system. One wire runs up from the outlet to the top of the trailer to power the front clearance lights. Several wires grouped into a cable run the length of the trailer to power the rear lights. Halfway down the trailer is a junction in the cable where two wires reach to the sides to power the side marker lamps. Finally, the cable separates at the rear of the trailer where it branches out to the various rear lights. This cable also powers the anti-lock braking system.

Light bulbs and wiring connections are in some ways rather delicate. As a trailer gets along in years, these **will loosen and corrode.** There really isn't much you can do to avoid the problem other than being aware of it and fixing whatever you have to as it occurs.

AIR SYSTEM

The **tractor** also **furnishes air pressure** to operate **the trailer brakes.** Next to the electrical outlet **at the front of the trailer are two air couplings.** These are commonly **known as "glad hands."**

One glad hand **provides air to the service brakes,** which use air pressure only when the brakes are being applied. **The other** glad hand **provides air to the emergency brake,** which is pressurized at all times.

Seals in the glad hands keep air from escaping when the system is pressurized. The glad hands are color coded to prevent mistakes when connecting the air lines from the tractor to the two glad hands on the trailer. The service line is colored blue and the control or emergency line is colored red.

The trailer's air lines begin in front and move underneath the floor to the rear where they are connected to all the valves and tanks that make up the trailer air brake system.

Chapter 12 Quiz

1. Of the following, _____ are NOT standard equipment on every trailer.
   A. suspensions
   B. frames
   C. axles
   D. side doors

2. Most commonly, trailers have _____ tires on each drum.
   A. studded
   B. super single
   C. dual
   D. recapped

3. The crank on the landing gear has more than one gear.
   A. True
   B. False

4. The trailer's _____ must carry the weight of the cargo and be able to flex under the weight of the load.
   A. dual tires
   B. spring system
   C. disc or spoke wheels
   D. axles

5. In terms of support, outside rails are _____ inside rails.
   A. stronger than
   B. about the same as
   C. not as good as
   D. more flexible than

6. In the middle of the bed plate is the _____ .
    A. kingpin
    B. air ride suspension system
    C. front axle
    D. leaf suspension system

7. The purpose of the bulkhead is to _____ .
    A. maintain good air circulation to the cargo
    B. insulate the trailer
    C. keep the cargo from sliding into the tractor
    D. make unloading easier

8. With the exterior post design, _____ .
    A. exposed side posts create wind drag
    B. the posts may be damaged by cargo and forklifts
    C. the side posts are connected to the roof bows
    D. an adhesive material seals the fiber glass rivets to the exterior skin

9. When the driver turns on the tractor's clearance lights, _____ .
    A. the pigtail disconnects from the glad hands
    B. the glad hands disconnect from the pigtail
    C. the trailer's clearance lights go on
    D. the trailer's clearance lights go off

10. The service air line glad hand on the front of the trailer is colored blue.
    A. True
    B. False

COUPLING AND UNCOUPLING

Connecting the Tractor and the Trailer

It is obvious that before you can pull a trailer, the trailer must be joined to the tractor. This is the process known as coupling. How is this done? What parts of the tractor and trailer are involved in this process? How do you separate them again?

Coupling and uncoupling aren't hard procedures, but for safety's sake they must be done right. You'll have to show you have both knowledge of and skill in coupling and uncoupling to get a CDL for combination vehicles. In this chapter we'll outline a procedure that will ensure a safe couple every time.

Pre-coupling Procedures

Connecting the tractor to the trailer begins with two simple "get ready" steps. First, make sure you have picked up the right tractor and trailer. This may sound a little silly now, but wait until the first time you confront a large terminal yard packed with equipment. You'll see rows and rows of vehicles that look much the same except for their vehicle numbers. Double-check the numbers given to you to make sure you have the equipment you are meant to have. Don't wait until you get to the right service area with the wrong vehicle to find out!

Next, inspect that equipment. Chapter 17 describes pre-trip inspection procedures drivers must make in detail so we won't cover those here. Before coupling, though, take a few extra minutes to check the fifth wheel and kingpin. Look for damaged or missing parts on the fifth wheel. See that the mounting to the tractor is secure. Make sure the trailer kingpin isn't bent or broken. Double-check that cargo is secure and won't shift.

Before you begin any coupling procedure, get out of the tractor and walk the area around the trailer and tractor. **Look for anything in your path that could damage the tractor or trailer.** Boards lying on the ground can fly dangerously about when popped from the ground by a tire. Nails, glass or other objects can do severe damage to a tire. Make sure the way is clear before you begin the first stages of alignment.

Work on the most level ground you can find if you have a choice about it. Uneven ground will make your task just that much harder. Then put chocks at the rear of the trailer tires. When you **chock the trailer tires at the rear** you're making sure the trailer won't roll backward from the pressure applied by the tractor as it moves under the trailer. If the trailer has spring brakes you may not need chocks. Refer to your company policy when in doubt.

Aligning the Tractor

What's involved in coupling? To put it very simply, you're going to **back the tractor up to the trailer so the coupling assemblies connect without moving the trailer backwards.** When joining the trailer to the tractor you will be concerned mainly with just two vehicle parts, the fifth wheel on the tractor and the kingpin on the trailer. This makes it sound just a little easier than it is. A proper coupling requires you to center the kingpin in the fifth wheel within a small margin of error. So in your backing, you have to be pretty precise about how you align the tractor and trailer.

The V-shaped slot in the fifth wheel allows for about six to eight inches error margin to either side of center on most models. This means that the fifth wheel must come into contact with the trailer kingpin at a point six to eight inches to either the left or right of center to complete the coupling without having to realign the tractor. It is up to you to **place the tractor so the trailer kingpin is as near to center of the fifth wheel V-slot as possible.**

Slow and steady really wins the race here. If you **follow the procedures step by step every time,** you should have few problems. This procedure involves the proper use of the rear view mirrors. As you back,

fig. 13-1
There's only about six inches leeway to the left or right of center on the fifth wheel.

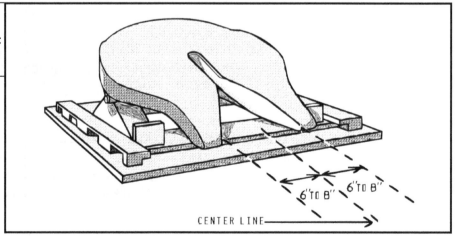

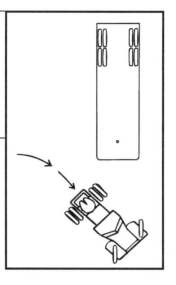

fig. 13-2
Approach the trailer, preferably from the right, and start to turn away from the trailer when the front of the tractor comes near the right corner of the trailer.

watch both mirrors. If your view of the trailer is the same in both rear view mirrors, you're centered. **Know the width of the tractor as compared to the width of the trailer.** Remember that the center of the fifth wheel is always in the center of the tractor frame and the kingpin is always in the center of the front of the trailer.

Before you attempt to align the tractor and trailer, learn about the physical characteristics of both. How wide is the tractor? If you service the same tractors day after day you should know their width, fifth wheel height, wheelbase and other important measurements. If a tractor is new to you, ask! It is not a sign of ignorance or inexperience to ask questions about the equipment that you will be servicing. It is a sign of a conscientious, careful mechanic.

What about the trailer? Is it 96 inches wide or 102 inches wide? How does this compare to the width of the tractor? How does it compare to the span of the mirrors on the tractor? This is all very important for determining the approach to the trailer.

To align the units properly you must be able to locate the center of the trailer by using its sides as a gauge in the rear view mirrors. We'll discuss how in detail later.

HORIZONTAL ALIGNMENT
The first step in aligning the tractor with the trailer is approaching the trailer. To illustrate this we will imagine that there is enough room in front of the trailer to maneuver the tractor easily. Approach the front of the trailer from either side (right or left). Experienced drivers prefer to **approach the trailer from the right** side (the trailer will be at your left). This gives the driver full view of the trailer from the window at all times during the first stage of alignment. This, of course, will become a choice you will have to make as you experience the different methods of approach.

As you approach the trailer, **steer away from the front** into the area in front of the trailer (see Figure 13-2). Taking it slow and easy, watch the mirrors as you start to straighten out in front of the trailer. Some novices assume that they should begin the turn away from the trailer after they are directly in front of it. Because each tractor has its own wheelbase and turning radius, this is a wrong assumption. Often, this would place the tractor far to the side of the trailer after the tractor is straightened out. It is wise to start the turn as the front of the tractor approaches the near corner of the trailer. This will place the fifth wheel in a closer alignment with the kingpin and less adjustment of position will be necessary.

As you pull away from the trailer, keep an eye on the mirrors. As you straighten the tractor in front of the trailer, **the corners of the trailer will appear evenly in the mirrors.** If there is an unequal amount of the trailer in one mirror, you are too far to the other side. For instance, if the right mirror shows a large portion of the trailer, and the left side very little, you will have to adjust the tractor further to the right. Do this by pulling forward while steering to the right. When you think you might be positioned more evenly, straighten the tractor.

It may be in your best interest to pull the tractor far in front of the trailer when beginning alignment. That will give you more room in which to **adjust your position as you back** toward the trailer. If you back slowly you can steer the tractor in the desired direction **to align the fifth wheel with the kingpin.** It is not unusual for the novice driver, or even the experienced driver for that matter, to adjust the tractor more than once before proper alignment is achieved. Never back under the trailer at an angle. You might push the trailer sideways and break the landing gear.

When an equal amount of the front of the trailer shows in each mirror, you are aligned with the trailer kingpin. You can stop working on position and start to back slowly.

Do not back completely under the trailer at this point. **Stop when the rear of the tractor is about five feet from the front of the trailer.** To gauge the stopping distance look at the tractor's drive tires in the mirror and judge their distance from the nose of the trailer. This is not to say that five feet from the trailer is the exact distance that should be left between the tractor and trailer. It should be the minimum left, though. Allow yourself enough room to walk safely and comfortably between the tractor and trailer as you inspect both. Set the tractor brakes, put the transmission in neutral and get out of the tractor. **Inspect the area around the trailer and tractor,** making sure it is safe to back the rest of the way.

From a vantage point under the trailer, **check the alignment of the fifth wheel with the kingpin.** It is much easier to notice any extreme offset from the ground than it is from the tractor. If they are aligned properly, proceed with the inspection and coupling. If they are not, return to the tractor and make any necessary adjustments in your position.

VERTICAL ALIGNMENT

As you walk around the area compare the level of the fifth wheel with the height of the kingpin. The coupling surface of the trailer should be just below the middle of the fifth wheel skid ramps. If the trailer is too

fig. 13-3
The levels of the kingpin and the fifth wheel must be matched so they connect properly.

WRONG   RIGHT   WRONG

far below the fifth wheel level, the kingpin will hit the tractor frame. If the trailer is too high, the kingpin could slide right over the top of the fifth wheel when you try to back under it. You could damage the rear of the tractor that way.

If you are either too high or two low, you will have to use the landing gear to **raise or lower the trailer to the fifth wheel level.** We'll be the first to admit that it is not at all easy to crank a loaded trailer up. It is hard on the landing gear and physically demanding of the person at the crank.

On most trailers, you turn the landing gear crank at the left side of the trailer clockwise to raise the trailer and counterclockwise to lower it. The main gear housing is under the trailer. As the crank is turned the gears spin to lower or raise the trailer landing legs. Most trailer gear boxes have two speeds. Use low gear while the landing legs are supporting most of the trailer's weight. High gear can be used when the trailer is empty or its loaded weight rests on the fifth wheel.

Although they are built of hardened steel the gears can become damaged if you aren't careful.

The landing gear crank is hinged and swings under the trailer to a latch which secures it to the frame while the trailer is in motion. If the crank handle were allowed to swing freely while the trailer is moving it could hit a nearby vehicle or passing pedestrian. Always **secure the crank handle** when you're done using it.

While you are right there at the landing gear, check the distance between the landing gear and the kingpin. Compare that with the distance from the center of the fifth wheel to the rear of the tractor's frame and mud flap brackets. A short, 28-foot pup trailer or other type of short trailer may not have the distance that could handle the rear end length of some tractors without damaging the mud flap brackets. In some cases sliding the fifth wheel rearward may provide the needed distance.

Now **inspect the fifth wheel.** Make sure that the locking mechanism (jaws) is opened. If it is closed the kingpin cannot slide into the jaws and complete the coupling. If it is even partly closed it could slam shut when the tractor comes into contact with the trailer. This would also prevent the kingpin from becoming locked in the fifth wheel. Be sure the fifth wheel is tilted down in the back, so the trailer can slide up when you couple.

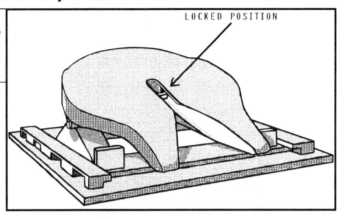

fig. 13-4
Note the position of the fifth wheel locking mechanism before you complete the coupling.

LOCKED POSITION

Also check to see that the surface of the fifth wheel has been properly greased. A fifth wheel that is poorly lubricated will not let the trailer rotate freely and smoothly when turning or backing. If it's dry apply a liberal amount of grease to the fifth wheel. You should always grease the fifth wheel when you service it.

If the truck has a sliding fifth wheel, make sure it's locked. (You'll read more about sliding fifth wheels in Chapter 15.)

Now you are ready to back the tractor closer to the trailer so you can start making the connection. If the trailer is not equipped with spring brakes, back the tractor until the skid ramps of the fifth wheel just toubh the apron of the upper coupler of the trailer. As they touch you should feel a light bump. Stop, set the parking brakes, put the transmission in neutral and shut off the engine. Now you are ready to start making the connections.

MAKING THE CONNECTION

The first step of actually coupling the tractor and trailer is to **connect the red air supply line.** There are two air lines, the service brake line and the emergency or supply line. These are almost always colored red for supply or emergency and blue for service. The connections at the front of the trailer will usually be painted the color of the air hose that should be connected to them, or labeled "service" and "emergency." Check the glad hand seals and secure the supply air line to the corresponding colored or labeled trailer connection.

fig. 13-5
Air control knobs. Trailer Supply (red) and Parking Brake (yellow).

(RED)   (YELLOW)

The supply air line should be supported so there's no chance it will be crushed or caught while the tractor is backing under the trailer.

After you return to the tractor, **charge the trailer air supply** by pushing the red trailer air supply knob. Wait until the air pressure is normal. Turn off the engine and listen for air leaks. Apply and release the trailer brakes and listen for the sound of the trailer brakes being applied and released. (If you don't hear the brakes being applied and released, you may have hooked up your air lines incorrectly.) Apply the trailer parking brakes by pulling the red trailer air supply knob back out. This activates the trailer spring brakes to keep the trailer from moving. Restart the engine and release the tractor brakes by pushing in the yellow tractor parking brake knob. Put the transmission in reverse and back slowly.

You will feel the weight of the trailer being transferred to the tractor as the apron of the upper coupler slides up the skid ramps of the fifth wheel. Continue backing slowly until progress is stopped by the kingpin locking into the jaws of the fifth wheel.

If the trailer is fairly light, you'll be able to get the tractor under it without much effort. If the trailer is heavily loaded, you will feel some resistance. If the trailer is a little too low and you can't get the tractor under it without a lot of effort, don't force it. Get out and jack that trailer up a little more. This isn't all that easy with a loaded trailer, but it's still the best solution. If the drive wheels start spinning when you meet that resistance, use the inter-axle differential lock to get more traction. for trailer equipped with spring brakes it's not necessary to connect the air lines prior to backing under the trailer. Remember, the spring brakes were set when the air pressure was released from the spring brake chamber which occurred when the trailer was parked. So, without hooking up the air lines or electrical cable, slowly back under the trailer.

To **check the connection,** try pulling forward very slowly. If the tractor will not move, the connection is complete. If it does move, stop immediately and back again.

Do not attempt to back under the trailer at high speed. This could damage the fifth wheel, the kingpin or the rear axle differential.

Put the transmission in neutral, shut off the engine and pocket the key. Get out of the tractor and check to **see that the fifth wheel locking jaw is closed around the shank of the kingpin.** To do this you must be under the front of the trailer and behind the fifth wheel. If the jaw is closed you will see it locked securely around the back of the kingpin and the kingpin will not be visible. There should be no space between the upper and lower fifth wheel. If the kingpin is clearly visible in the fifth wheel opening and the locking jaw is positioned to the side of the fifth wheel opening you do not have a good connection. The locking lever should be in the locked position. The safety catch must be in position over the locking lever (you may have to put it in place by hand). If the locking jaw is not secured around the kingpin, lower the landing jacks, pull the tractor forward and start the backing procedure again.

Determine that the kingpin is secured. for a trailer equipped with spring brakes, **connect both air lines and connect the single electrical supply cable (pigtail) to the trailer.** Return to the tractor and turn on the emergency flashers and trailer lights. Walk around the trailer to **make sure the lights are working.** Check the clearance lights and side marker lights. Walk to the back of the trailer and check the turn signals (turning on the emergency flashers at the tractor will activate the turn signals).

If none are working, there is possibly a bad connection at the trailer supply plug. Disconnect, then reconnect the pigtail securely into the trailer connection. If the lights still don't work, you will have to determine the cause and make the necessary repairs.

If only one light is not working its bulb may be out and need to be replaced.

While you're checking out the trailer tires, take the time to **gauge tire inflation.** Also **check for worn hoses or loose connections** on the trailer's brake system. The hiss of escaping air may be heard coming from these areas. Inspect rusty connections closely for cracks. Should any leaks exist, repair them immediately. A ruptured air hose or broken connection is sure trouble while the vehicle is moving.

The trailer can finally be considered connected and ready to roll. But you must first **remove any wheel chocks.** Never simply leave the chocks lying on the ground as you pull away, unless that is what is requested. Be courteous and place them where they belong.

Double-check the clearances between the rear of the truck frame and mud flap brackets and landing gear. Is there enough distance to allow for turning? Also check that there is enough clearance between the top of the tractor's tires and the underside of the nose of the trailer.

Now you should crank up the landing gear as high as it will go and secure the crank handle. Optimum ground clearance is available with the gear in its uppermost position. Never drive with the landing gear part way up. This should be the last thing you do before moving the tractor-trailer.

You are ready to return to the tractor and prepare to pull away. Do not simply disengage the trailer and tractor brakes and drive off. Perform one more test to assure yourself that the trailer is secured to the tractor.

Try pulling forward slowly. If the coupling is not secure and the tractor begins to pull out from under the trailer, stop immediately and back under the trailer. Engage all brakes, get out and crank the trailer landing gear down, and begin the coupling procedure again.

If the coupling is secure, the tractor will not move. You can then release the trailer brakes and begin a safe trip. A word to the wise: When you're pulling the tractor forward to check the firmness of your connection, do it slowly! Let's say your coupling isn't secure. If you were to drive the tractor out from under the trailer while the landing gear is up the trailer nose would lose its support and land on the tractor frame or, worse, on the ground. To correct this, heavy duty wreckers would have to lift the front of the trailer so the landing gear could be lowered. The landing gear alone isn't strong enough to raise a trailer, especially a loaded one, from this position.

COUPLING DOUBLES AND TRIPLES

You now know how to couple a tractor to a trailer. But how do you couple a trailer to a trailer? Double and triple rigs are becoming more and more popular with trucking fleets.

A double rig consists of a tractor, two trailers and a converter gear. A triple rig consists of a tractor, three trailers and two converter gears. The converter gear is needed to couple a trailer to a trailer. It is also called a con gear or a dolly. We'll call it a dolly.

Basically, a dolly is a fifth wheel on an axle. Except for the use of the dolly, coupling and uncoupling doubles and triples is basically the same as coupling and uncoupling the tractor and the first semitrailer.

Uncoupling Procedures

Once you have checked for hazards and obstacles and have parked the trailer in the desired location, set the parking brakes by pulling out both the red and yellow knobs. This evacuates the air from the spring brake chambers of the trailer and sets the brakes.

You may then **lower the landing gear.** Unhook the crank from its travel position, shift to high gear and turn it counterclockwise. This will lower the landing gear. Turning the crank will be fairly easy until the dolly plates come into contact with the ground. Then shift to low gear and crank until most of the trailer weight is on the dollies and not on the tractor. Don't lift the trailer off the fifth wheel.

Be aware of the dolly plates as you lower the landing gear. Some landing gear assemblies have plates which sit flat on the ground in their lowered position. These plates are connected to the dolly leg by heavy duty swivels. These swivels allow the dolly to sit evenly on uneven or rough surfaces. If the plate has swung into a position which would keep it from sitting flat on the ground it could be damaged and become useless. If it is in such a position, reposition it so it will sit flat when lowered.

fig. 13-6
Some landing gear assemblies have pads for dolly plates, as shown here. Others have wheels and still others have plates that swivel.

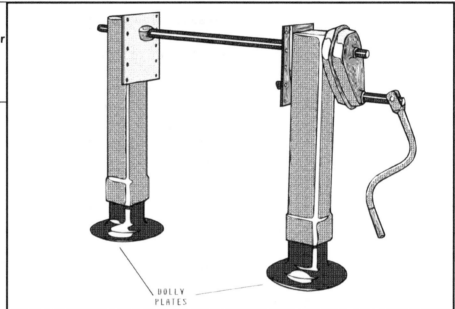

DOLLY PLATES

It is also wise to check the surface that the dollies will be sitting on when lowered. A heavily loaded trailer can sink into hot asphalt or loose dirt. On such surfaces you should always place something, a wide plank or dolly pad, under the landing gear plate. Cement is virtually the only surface which is likely to support a loaded trailer without allowing it to sink.

As you crank the gear watch and listen to the springs of the tractor. You will hear the springs relax as some of the weight is removed. When some of the weight is off the tractor, stop cranking. For an empty trailer, stop cranking when the pads or plates just barely touch the surface. After the landing gear is lowered replace the crank handle in its travel position. More than one person walking past a trailer has been injured by a free-swinging or projecting handle.

Next you should **disconnect the air supply lines and electrical cable from the trailer**. Stow each in its proper position at the rear of the trailer. Lines should be secured so they won't be damaged while driving the tractor. Hang the electrical cable with the plug down to keep water from getting in.

Now you can **disengage the fifth wheel locking mechanism.** This is done by using the release lever. The release lever may be permanently attached to the locking mechanism and can be accessed from the side of the fifth wheel. Reach under the trailer, grab the release lever and pull. This will disengage the locking mechanism. Keep your legs and feet clear of the rear tractor wheel to avoid being injured.

Other types of release levers are removable. When not in use this type should be kept in its proper place in the tractor side compartment. The removable release handle has a hook which fits into a slot on the fifth wheel jaw release. Simply place the hook in the slot and pull. If you are assigned to service a tractor with a removable release lever handle, make doubly sure the handle is in its place before driving the vehicle. A driver will not be happy to find the handle missing when attempting to release the fifth wheel far from home.

Once the tractor is completely uncoupled from the trailer you can safely pull away. **Pull away from the trailer** slowly. Stop with the tractor frame under the trailer. That way, if the landing gear collapses, the tractor will keep the trailer from falling to the ground. Apply the parking brake and leave the cab. Check one last time that the ground and the landing gear support the trailer. Then get back in the tractor, release the parking brakes and drive the tractor clear.

Be considerate of the next driver to pull the trailer. Don't leave the trailer cranked to a position lower than the fifth wheel level of the tractor.

Safety Precautions

In the interest of safety, we'll remind you that any time you plan to back the tractor to a trailer for coupling you should **fully inspect the area for safety hazards** like boards, nails, curbs or people. Correct any dangerous conditions before going any further.

Follow the procedures outlined, step for step. Don't take shortcuts, rush the job or force anything into place. Do it the hard way, that's usually the best and safest way to proceed.
The final piece of advice is: **GO SLOWLY.**

Chapter 13 Quiz

1. Under slippery conditions, keep the inter-axle differential un-
   locked to get more traction.
   A. True
   B. False

2. A poorly lubricated fifth wheel should be _____ .
   A. salted down
   B. greased
   C. dried off
   D. sanded down

3. If a single light on the trailer is not working, the _____ should be
   checked.
   A. entire electrical system
   B. electrical connection to the trailer
   C. electrical connection to the tractor
   D. light bulb

**Refer to this sketch of a tractor and trailer to answer Ques-
tions 4 through 9. Complete the sentence by inserting the
number of the component that makes the statement true.**

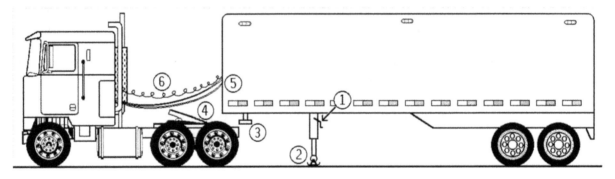

4. The _____ should be the first connection you make from the
   tractor to the trailer.

5. The jaws of the tractor fifth wheel lock onto the _____ of the
   trailer.

6. The _____ must be connected to check the trailer lights.

7. Always secure the _____ when you are done using it.

8. When coupling, the _____ should be the last trailer component moved from its original position.

9. Check the alignment of the _____ before backing the tractor under the trailer.

10. Only when there's ice or snow does a driver have to inspect the area around the trailer before backing.
    A. True
    B. False

BACKING A TRACTOR-TRAILER

Backing is Easy, Isn't It?

No, it isn't, but backing is something you'll have to learn to do. **You will have to show that you can back a tractor and trailer in order to get a Commercial Driver's License.** Backing a tractor-trailer may sound like a simple task, but it isn't, not even for the experienced driver. In fact, **most accidents involving tractor-trailers happen during backing.** It takes patience and practice to develop the ability to back a tractor-trailer skillfully and safely.

In this chapter, you'll learn the backing procedures used by experienced drivers. You'll learn pre-positioning, and steering procedures for backing. We'll also cover another not-so-easy procedure: parallel parking. But first, let's look at where and why backing accidents occur and how you can prevent them.

Backing Accidents

A good driving record is important to you, even as a mechanic. You don't want even one minor accident in the shop, yard or on the road. So, prepare yourself well to avoid backing accidents by knowing where and why they happen and how to prevent them.

WHERE THEY HAPPEN
The three most frequent types of backing accidents are those that occur

- **on the right side**
- **at the rear**
- **on the top**

of the vehicle.

Yes, backing into something at the top of the vehicle is a common backing accident! Low hanging wires and eaves can damage the overhead area of the vehicle. This type of accident is easily avoided. In fact, it should never happen. Simply make sure the area above is clear of anything that might tear off an exhaust stack or otherwise damage the top of the cab.

Backing accidents often occur at the rear of the trailer. You may think you are backing up to something only to find out at the last minute you have backed into something. The main reason for this type of backing accident is carelessness. However, something can move behind you after you think you've made sure the area is clear. That's one reason it's good to check, and then check again.

Many **backing accidents** occur **on the right side of the rig.** These **are the most difficult to avoid.** Many times when backing the tractor will be at an angle with the trailer and you will not be able to see the right side at all. Allow yourself more room on this side.

WHY THEY HAPPEN
Most accidents happen when the driver is in too much of a hurry. A **lack of attention** on the part of the driver **causes** many backing **accidents.** Backing takes a lot of concentration. Turn off the radio and the CB. The less noise there is to distract you, the less likely you will lose concentration and get into an accident.

However, carelessness causes **most backing accidents.** They most often **happen when drivers don't take the time to:**

- get out of the truck and check the area they are backing into
- use mirrors properly
- be prepared to stop immediately
- back slowly

So, right away you can see four procedures that will greatly reduce the likelihood of your having a backing accident.

HOW TO PREVENT BACKING ACCIDENTS
First, always **check the area you're backing into before you begin backing.** Get out of the truck, walk behind it and visually check the area. Even if you're just backing up in a straight line, get out and take a good look at the area. Never make the mistake that you can catch everything with your mirrors. Look up and down and all around. And, don't forget to look under your rig to make sure a stray animal hasn't turned up out of nowhere. Always check just before you begin backing. If any time at all has passed since the last time you checked, check again just before you begin backing. In other words, you should check the area, get into the truck and begin backing without further delay.

Whenever you can't clearly see what's next to you or behind you, you should stop, **get out and check the area you're backing into during the procedure.** This will be the case when you back from a blind side pre-position. You'll learn about blind side backing later in this chapter.

For now, you need to know that sometimes you'll need to stop, get out and check the area after each few feet of backing.

Second, **use the mirrors properly.** Once you're sure nothing is in the way on either side of the rig, behind the rig, over the rig or under the rig, you can begin to back using your mirrors. You may need to adjust the mirrors. Take time to do this. In some cases, it may be necessary to roll down the window and look back out of it while you back the rig. Be careful, though. If you hit something, you could slam your head into the door jamb. In any case, don't use just this or just one mirror. Watch both sides of the rig. And don't open the door and lean out of it. That makes it impossible to use the right side mirror, and increases the risk of being injured.

Third, **keep your right foot off the throttle.** You'll rarely need to use it to start the rig backing up anyway (if you do, use the lowest reverse gear possible). Move very slowly, and keep your right foot **poised over the brake pedal.** This prepares you to stop immediately to avoid hitting anything. Also, you'll eliminate the response time it would otherwise take to move your foot from the throttle to the brake. This response time is just as crucial to stopping in time when you're going backward as it is when going forward.

So, you can go a long way toward preventing backing accidents if you take the time to:

- always check the area you're backing into just before you begin to back
- stop, get out and check the area you're backing into during the procedure
- use both mirrors the entire time you're backing
- keep your right foot poised over the brake

Many traffic problems and accidents result from drivers backing tractor-trailers across city and suburban streets. Big as the rig is, cross-traffic may fail to recognize it as an obstacle. Some delivery areas are hard to get to other than by backing up to them. If you must back across a city street, you may have to find someone to stop traffic while you back.

You can't control the actions of others. However, you can often make up for the actions of others, if you see them coming. And, you can always make sure you are not the cause of a backing accident.

How to Steer in Reverse

There are three steps to any backing maneuver: jacking, following and straightening. **Jacking is turning the tractor so it is out of line with the trailer.** As you move backwards **this starts the trailer going back**

in a curve. To do this you start by turning the top of the steering wheel opposite the direction you want the rear of the trailer to go. Or, try this: Place your hand on the bottom of the steering wheel. Then move your hand (and therefore the wheel) in the same direction you want to the trailer to go first.

After you jack the tractor, you will need to **follow the trailer** around the curve. To do this, **reverse the steering angle. As the trailer moves backwards, the tractor will follow it.** Some people refer to this procedure as chasing the trailer.

Once the trailer has curved far enough you **straighten the tractor** by bringing it back into line with the trailer. To do this you increase the steering angle and continue backing until the tractor is straight with the trailer, then straighten the steering axle.

Steering backwards should always be slow and deliberate. Use the idle speed only. If the trailer should happen to get off course, stop and move forward so you can start over once again. As you back, always pay special attention to the front of the tractor, the front of the trailer, the angle of the tractor and trailer and the rear of the trailer.

Steering in Reverse
(refer to Figure 14-1)

Jacking (1): Turn the steering wheel to the right. The front of the tractor will point to the left. The rear of the tractor will point to the right, putting the tractor at an angle with the trailer.

Following (chasing) (2): Turn the steering wheel to the left. This maintains the angle between the tractor and the trailer. Follow the trailer around.

Straighten (3): Turn even more to the left to straighten the tractor with the trailer. When the tractor is in line with the trailer, straighten the wheels.

fig. 14-1
Steering in reverse.

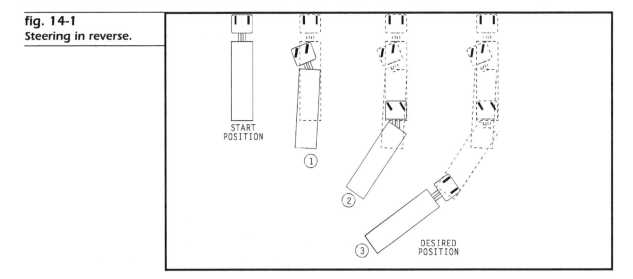

START POSITION

① ② ③

DESIRED POSITION

Your ability to jack and chase the trailer is put to the greatest test by a maneuver called the backward serpentine. This is difficult because you must make a series of jacking and chasing moves, one right after the other. You must be able to turn in one direction, then change directions, and then change directions again.

You may have to do a backward serpentine as part of your CDL skills test, and you'll have to do it with few if any stops for repositioning your vehicle.

Pre-Positioning

Now that you know where and why backing accidents occur and how to prevent them, you're ready to begin learning backing procedures. The first and perhaps the most critical is **pre-positioning. This is the position into which you place the rig before you begin backing.** These are the **three common pre-positions:**

- straight back
- clear side
- blind side

As we discuss the three pre-positions, let's assume you're driving a conventional pulling a 53-foot trailer. This is a popular rig on the road today and will serve as a good example of what is involved in the skill of backing. In our examples, you are backing the rig into a service bay to be serviced.

The distances which we will be dealing with apply to this type of rig. As you become a more experienced driver, you will learn that different sized rigs call for different distances and turning angles.

THE STRAIGHT BACK PRE-POSITION
Straight back backing is the easiest and safest to perform. So, whenever you can back straight in, you should. From this pre-position, **you have a clear view in both mirrors of the space you are backing into.** (You'll sometimes hear this space referred to as the hole, as we will in the following discussion.) Straight backing is the basis for all other kinds of backing. Get straight backing down good before you try the more complicated maneuvers.

THE CLEAR SIDE PRE-POSITION
Clear side is a term used to describe **backing** from a position which **lets you have a clear view in the left rear view mirror of the space you back into.** This is the type of backing you'll do most often. Remember that if you can back straight in, you should. If you can't back straight in, the second best choice is to back from the clear side pre-position.

Pre-Positioning for a Straight Back
(refer to Figure 14-2)

1. Stop, get out and inspect the area.

2. Pull ahead and as tractor passes the hole, steer hard away from the hole.

3. Steer back into line with the hole.

4. Pull ahead until tractor and trailer are straight and line up with the hole. If you do this right, as soon as the tractor and trailer straighten out you'll be directly in front of the hole. You'll be able to see it in both mirrors. You can now stop going forward and start going backward.

5. Back straight into the hole, adjusting as necessary to keep centered in the hole.

fig. 14-2
Pre-positioning the rig for a straight back involves these steps.

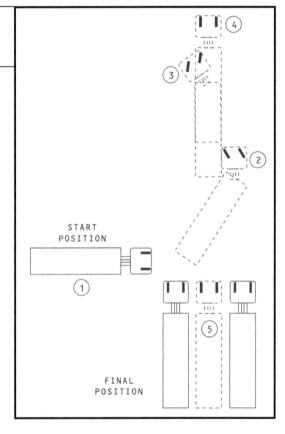

THE BLIND SIDE PRE-POSITION

With **a blind side position,** it is harder to see the area you're backing the rig into. The rear view mirrors are less useful. The left mirror will help you when turning and pulling forward. Once you start back, you can see with the right mirror and the spot mirror, although you may have to move around in the seat to do so. If the truck has motorized mirrors, adjust them to give you the best view.

This **is the most difficult and the most dangerous pre-position.** Avoid it, if you can. You won't always be able to avoid it, so you must know how to back from this position.

Backing in from the blind side uses the same steps as clear side backing. The only difference is it's harder to see what you are doing. The right side mirror will help you. At those times when you can't see, you should stop often and get out of the rig to check your position. It is a lot easier to stop, get out and check where you are a few extra times than it is to explain to the shop foreman why you backed into the wall of the shop.

Pre-Positioning for a Clear Side Back
(refer to Figure 14-3)

1. Stop, get out and inspect the area.

2. Pull ahead and steer away from the space.

3. When the tractor is at a 45-degree angle to the space, straighten the wheels and pull ahead until the tractor and trailer are in line and the trailer is pointing at the space. You will be able to see the space in your left mirror.

4. Start backing. Turn the steering wheel to the right to jack the tractor. Once the trailer is curving towards the space, turn the steering wheel to the left and let the tractor follow the trailer into the space.

5. When the trailer is in line with the space, turn the steering wheel even more to the left to straighten the tractor with the trailer. Continue backing.

fig. 14-3
Pre-positioning on the clear side to back a rig involves these steps.

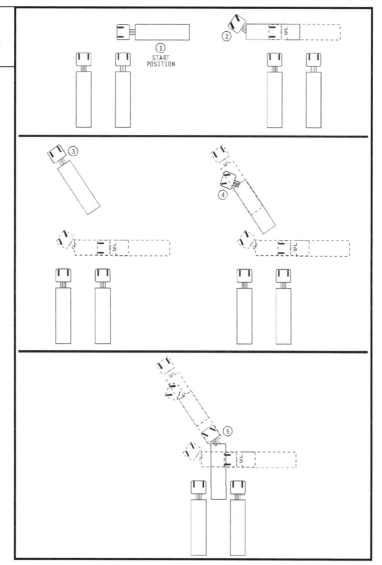

Remember, what you can see depends on your pre-position:

PRE-POSITION	WHAT YOU CAN SEE
Straight Back	You have a clear view in both mirrors of the space you are backing into.
Clear Side	You have a clear view in the left rear view mirror of the space you are backing into.
Blind Side	You are unable to see the area you are backing the rig into.

Docking and Backing into the Service Bay

When testing for your CDL, you may also be asked to perform a docking procedure. While you will not likely be backing a tractor-trailer into a dock at work, a routine part of your job might include backing a rig into a service bay. These procedures are basically the same. To be able to do this, **you must understand how to pre-position and how to steer backwards.** You have, however, just learned all about that. So, now you're ready for practicing!

If you must back from a blind side pre-position, **have someone help you from the ground.** Ask someone in the shop to help you. Most drivers and mechanics know what a chore it is to back up blind. You won't find it hard to get someone to help. Keep in mind, though, that it's still your responsibility to get it right.

Parallel Parking

Another maneuver you may be required to make to get your CDL is parallel parking. Like backing, **parallel parking is difficult.** In terms of difficulty, it comes close to blind side backing. The exact procedure differs

Docking

1. Inspect the area.

2. Pre-position the rig.

3. Operate at idle speed only.

4. Back up close to the dock.

5. Inspect the area behind the trailer and estimate the remaining distance.

with each tractor-trailer. Each rig will back and turn differently. One reason for this is that different rigs have different wheelbases.

Pre-Positioning for a Blind Side Back
(refer to Figure 14-4)

1. Stop, get out and inspect the area.

2. Pull ahead and steer away from the space.

3. When the tractor is at a 45-degree angle to the space, straighten the wheels and pull ahead until the tractor and trailer are in line and the trailer is pointing at the space. You will be able to see the space in your right mirror.

4. Start backing. Turn the steering wheel to the left to jack the tractor. Once the trailer is curving towards the space turn the steering wheel to the right and let the tractor follow the trailer into the space.

5. When the trailer is in line with the space turn the steering wheel more to the right to straighten the tractor with the trailer and continue backing.

fig. 14-4
Pre-positioning on the blind side to back a rig involves these steps.

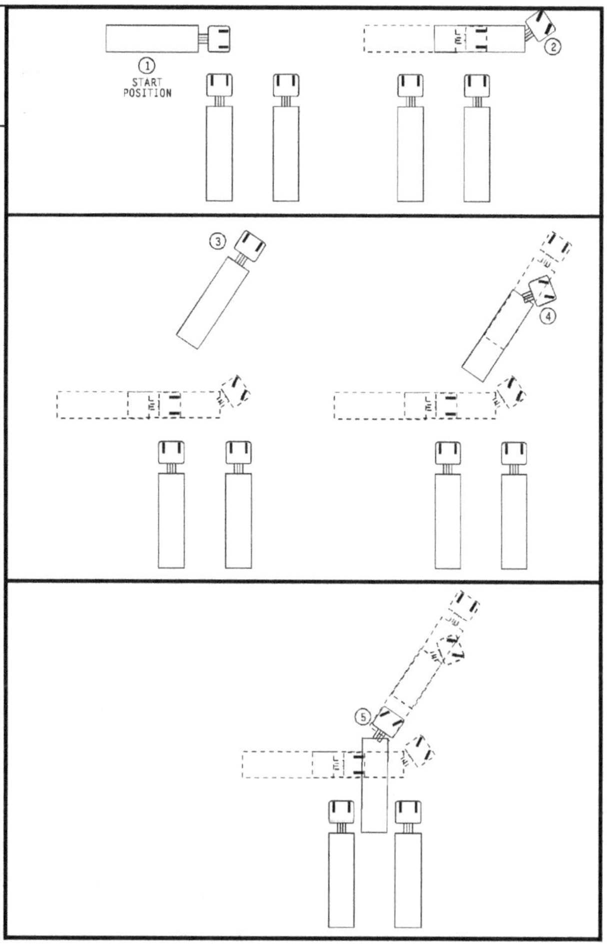

You should avoid parallel parking whenever you can, and you usually can. However, you may find yourself somewhere, sometime with no choice but to parallel park. Figure 14-5 illustrates how.

Parallel Parking
(refer to Figure 14-5)

1. Pull forward until the trailer is halfway past Vehicle A.

2. Turn the steering wheel to the left so your tractor directs the trailer to the right and the trailer starts heading toward the space.

3. When the trailer is pointing into the space, straighten the tractor by turning the steering wheel to the right and continue backing.

4. When the middle of your tractor is at the rear of Vehicle A, your right rear trailer wheels should be about three feet from the curb. Now turn right so the tractor directs the trailer to the left. This will start the front of the trailer into the space.

5. When your tractor will clear Vehicle A turn the steering wheel to the left so the tractor aligns with the trailer.

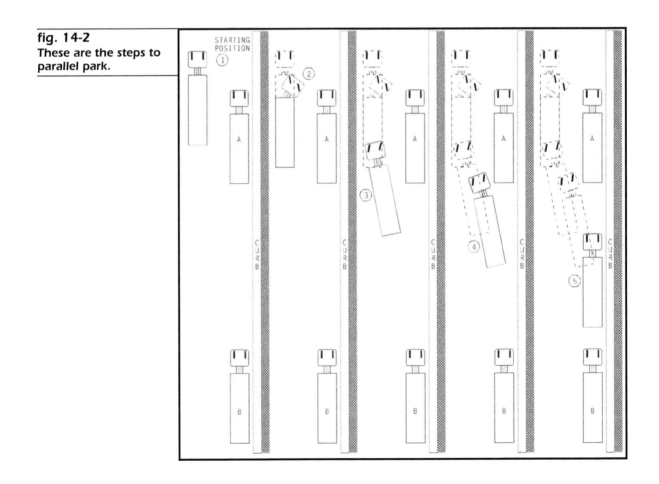

fig. 14-2
These are the steps to parallel park.

This procedure should bring you within inches of the curb. The sides of the front and rear tires must be within 12 inches of the curb for you to be legally parked. Remember, however, that rigs are wide vehicles. So, 12 inches from the curb may not keep the left side of the rig out of the traffic lane. Remember you have a long rig so you will need a long space to be able to parallel park successfully. Never try to parallel park unless you're sure you have enough room.

Parallel parking is quite a tricky maneuver. You will very likely have to pull forward and adjust your position a time or two before you can back neatly into the space.

Chapter 14 Quiz

1. The three most frequent types of backing accidents are those that occur on the right side, at the rear and _____ of the vehicle.
    A. at the fifth wheel
    B. on the left side
    C. on the top
    D. at the front

2. The most difficult backing accidents to avoid are _____ accidents.
    A. overhead
    B. right side
    C. left side
    D. rear of the trailer

3. Backing accidents most often happen when drivers fail to get out of the truck and check the area they are backing into or _____ .
    A. use mirrors properly
    B. turn on the radio or CB
    C. chase the trailer properly
    D. chock the wheels at the dock

4. When backing, your right foot should be _____ .
    A. poised over the clutch pedal
    B. positioned between the brake and the throttle
    C. resting lightly on the throttle
    D. poised over the brake pedal

5. Straight back, clear side and blind side are all examples of _____ .
   A. pre-positions
   B. chasing the trailer
   C. steering procedures
   D. jacking procedures

6. When you can see your parking space in both rear view mirrors, you're in a _____ pre-position.
   A. straight back
   B. proper
   C. clear side
   D. blind side

7. When you can see your parking space in your left rear view mirror, you're in a _____ pre-position.
   A. straight back
   B. proper
   C. clear side
   D. blind side

8. The procedure that creates an angle between the tractor and the trailer is known as _____ .
   A. jacking
   B. following
   C. chasing
   D. pre-positioning

9. Backing from the straight back position is the hardest position from which to back.
   A. True
   B. False

10. Parallel parking is a backing maneuver that you _____ .
    A. will never have to perform
    B. should choose over straight backing
    C. may need several tries to accomplish
    D. should be able to perform easily

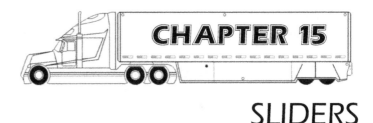

CHAPTER 15

SLIDERS

The Purpose of Sliders

For safety's sake and to prevent vehicle breakdown, cargo weight must be distributed to all of a tractor-trailer's axles. **Federal law limits the total weight that can rest on the tractor-trailer's axles to 34,000 pounds on tandems and 20,000 pounds on a single axle.**

To compensate for these weight restrictions, some tractors have a fifth wheel that can be slid forward or backward. This shifts and balances the weight of the trailer resting on the tractor's axles. This weight is called kingpin weight because it is the portion of the trailer's weight that rests on the trailer's kingpin. The kingpin is the pin on the trailer which connects to the tractor's fifth wheel. The adjustable fifth wheel that shifts this weight is called a **sliding fifth wheel or a "slider."**

Trailer weight rests on the kingpin and on the trailer's axle or axles. Some trailers also are built to help distribute weight between the kingpin and the axles evenly. They have a **sliding tandem axle,** also called a slider, that **moves forward and backward. Sliding tandems help balance the weight between the trailer's axles and the trailer's kingpin.**

The chief purpose, then, of sliders is simple. **Sliding fifth wheels and tandems, when used correctly, help distribute the weight of a heavily loaded trailer evenly to all of the tractor-trailer's axles.**

Not only are there certain maximum weights per axle but state bridge laws say those axles must be certain distances apart. This distance is known as the wheelbase and there is one for the tractor's axles and one for the trailer's axles. **The sliding fifth wheel of the tractor and the sliding tandem of the trailer let drivers adjust the wheelbase of the tractor-trailer and the trailer** in order to be in compliance with state bridge laws.

Another purpose the **sliding fifth wheel** serves is to **make it possible for a tractor to pull trailers with various kingpin settings.** Not all trailers have the same kingpin settings. Some kingpins are set further forward or backward on the trailer than others. A trailer with a kingpin set back more than 36 inches might put the trailer's landing gear too close to the tractor's rear wheels. If the landing gear and the wheels are

fig. 15-1
A sliding fifth wheel.

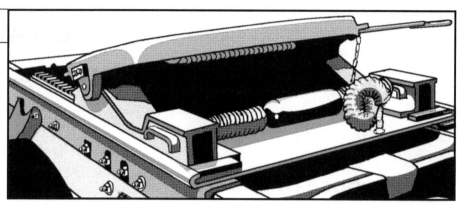

too close, they will come into contact with each other when the driver makes a turn. Sliding the sliding fifth wheel back toward the rear axle would keep this from happening.

A sliding fifth wheel can also improve mobility. When a fifth wheel is slid forward, the driver will have a shorter vehicle for tighter spaces.

Driver comfort is greater when the fifth wheel is located closer to the center line of the rear axle. When the rear axles are not overloaded, moving the fifth wheel rearward will give the driver maximum comfort.

fig. 15-2
A sliding tandem axle.

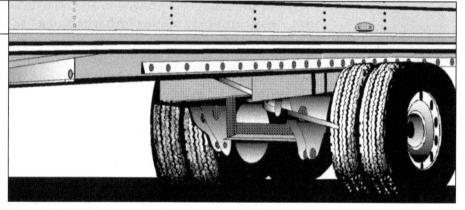

What You Should Know About Sliders

The most important thing for you to know is **how sliding** the tractor's fifth wheel or changing the location of the trailer's axles **will affect weight distribution** to all of the axles.

HOW SLIDERS WORK
When you **slide the fifth wheel forward** or toward the tractor's cab, more **weight is shifted to the** tractor's **steering axle.** When you **slide the fifth wheel back** or away from the cab toward the trailer's nose, **the tractor's rear axles will carry more** of the load.

The same principle applies to sliding the trailer's tandem axle. If the trailer's **tandem is slid forward,** closer to the tractor, **the tractor's** axles will carry less of the trailer's weight. The further to the rear you slide the trailer's tandem, the more trailer weight the tractor's axles will carry. (See Figure 15-3.)

fig. 15-3
Sliding the fifth wheel forward or backward affects the tractor's steering axle and drive axle weight.

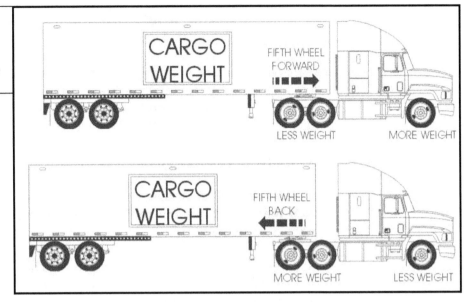

COMPONENTS

A sliding fifth wheel has three main components. They are:

- the slide baseplate
- the bracket
- the lock pins

The **slide baseplate is attached to the tractor**'s frame. Then **the bracket fits over the slide baseplate.** The **fifth wheel** is then **mounted on** top of the **bracket.** Lock pins on the mechanism keep the fifth wheel from sliding. Most tractors have an **"air powered" switch** on the tractor's dash that **locks and unlocks** the lock pins. When the **lock pins and locking mechanism are disengaged,** you can **slide the fifth wheel forward or back.** (Usually notches are about two to three inches apart.)

The trailer sliding tandem's main components are:

- the subframe (the sliding axle)
- the slide rails
- the lock pins
- the stop bar (on some sliding tandems)

The **subframe** of the sliding tandem **slides on** the **slide rails** to shorten and lengthen the wheelbase. **Sliding tandems** also have lock pins but you will usually **unlock** these **manually with** a lever called **a locking bar.** Some trailers have a safety feature called a "stop bar" that fits at the end of the rails upon which the tandem slides.

SWING RADIUS

Before you adjust a sliding fifth wheel you need to **make sure the tractor has plenty of room to pivot** and move. The tractor's ability to pivot on the fifth wheel without striking the trailer is **called** its **swing radius.** Generally, **a tractor should have room to make a 90-degree turn** without touching the trailer.

If the trailer's nose is too close to the rear of the tractor's cab, a sharp turn might be a sharp turn into disaster. Other tractor and trailer equipment might interfere when the rig makes a sharp turn. This equipment might include sleeper boxes, exhausts, refrigeration units and aerodynamic devices. Some trailers have **rounded front corners.** This **allows the trailer to be adjusted closer to the tractor.**

You also should make sure there is enough **room between** the **tractor's rearmost tires and the trailer's landing gear** for the tractor **to make a 90-degree turn.**

Be careful to take exact measurements. Do not just guess or take a visual estimate. Owner's manuals should include formulas to help you figure how far back or forward the fifth wheel should be placed. If you prefer, get some help from someone experienced in working with sliding fifth wheels.

Sliders and the Tractor-Trailer

Two dimensions on a tractor-trailer that are affected by the adjustment of sliders are **the trailer's wheelbase and** the trailer's **"A" dimension.**

HOW ADJUSTING SLIDERS AFFECTS A TRACTOR-TRAILER'S DIMENSIONS

The distance from the steering axle to the tractor tandem center point is the tractor's wheelbase. The distance the fifth wheel is set ahead of

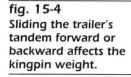
fig. 15-4
Sliding the trailer's tandem forward or backward affects the kingpin weight.

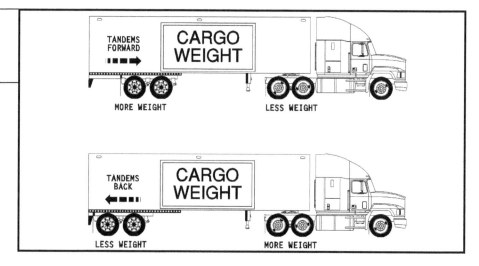

the tractor tandem center point is the tractor's "A" dimension. The tractor's wheelbase is not affected by sliders but the "A" dimension is. **As you slide the fifth wheel forward, the tractor's "A" dimension will increase.**

The distance from the trailer tandem center point to the kingpin is the trailer's wheelbase. The distance from the trailer tandem center point to the center of the trailer is the trailer's "A" dimension. **As you slide the trailer's rear axle forward, BOTH the wheelbase and "A" dimension of the trailer will decrease. As you slide the trailer's rear axle backward, BOTH the wheelbase and "A" dimension of the trailer will increase.** (See Figure 15-5 for these dimensions.)

fig. 15-5
Find the tractor, trailer and cargo weight, as well as the trailer and tractor's wheelbases and "A" dimensions.

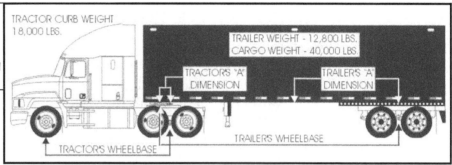

WHEN TO ADJUST SLIDERS
Although drivers are usually the ones responsible for the distribution of weight on their tractor-trailers, you may also occasionally need to make weight adjustments. Therefore, you should know a little about when to make these adjustments and what you should do.

For the most part, manufacturers' designs allow for 12,000 pounds of weight on the tractor's front axle (or steering axle). **If a tractor's steering axle is too heavy, slide the tractor's fifth wheel back.** This will move some of the tractor's front axle weight to the tractor's rear axles. Generally, **sliding the fifth wheel two inches represents anywhere from 150 to 300 pounds of weight being shifted.**

If the tractor's tandem is too heavy, you have two choices. You can **slide the fifth wheel forward.** This will take away some of the weight on the tractor's rear axles and move it to the steering axle. **Or you can slide the trailer's tandem forward** toward the tractor. This changes the kingpin weight because you changed the "A" dimension of the trailer along with its wheelbase. This will take some of the tractor's rear axle weight away and shift it to the trailer's axles.

On the other hand, **if the trailer's tandem is too heavy,** you can **slide the trailer's tandem back** toward the rear of the trailer. This will put more weight on the trailer's kingpin which will be taken by the tractor's axles. **Sliding the trailer's tandem one notch could represent between 400 and 600 pounds being shifted.**

How to Adjust a Sliding Fifth Wheel

When you are required to **adjust a sliding fifth wheel:**

- Make sure the tractor-trailer is in a straight line on level ground. The slightest pivot of the fifth wheel will cause the sliders to bind.
- Engage the differential lock.
- Set the trailer brakes only.
- Place chocks in front of the trailer's tires. Lower the trailer's landing gear.
- Release the lock pins. For vehicles with a power air slide release, flip the air slide release valve on the dash to the "unlock" position. (On vehicles with a manual release, pull the operating lever located near the fifth wheel.)
- Check to see that both lock pins have released. If lock pins are not released, try to lower the trailer landing gear a few more inches. This will release pressure on the lock pins and will allow the fifth wheel to slide more freely. Mark the notch the fifth wheel is currently using for reference.
- The tractor's fifth wheel should now be able to slide. Very slowly, move the tractor forward or backward to the desired fifth wheel position.
- Engage or set the slide lock pins. With the air slide release, put the control valve in the "locked" position. With a manual slide release, trip the operating lever to allow the lock pins to engage.
- Check both lock pins. Make sure they are fully engaged. If they are not, keep the trailer brakes locked and drive the tractor forward slightly. This will engage the lock pins in the lock pockets.
- Raise the landing gear, remove the chocks, unlock the differential lock and release the trailer brakes.

Do not try to slide the fifth wheel while the vehicle is in motion. Doing so puts the tractor and trailer in danger of breakaway or rollover.

How to Adjust a Sliding Tandem Axle

When you are required **to adjust a sliding tandem,** do the following:

- Make sure the rig is in a straight line on level ground.
- Engage the differential lock.
- Set the brakes on the tractor and the trailer.
- Chock the trailer's tires.
- Remove the stop bar from behind the slider.
- Pull the operating handle all the way out and place it in its unlocking position. This will release the lock pins. Mark the notch the tandem is in or place the stop bar in the desired location.

- Release the tractor brakes only and slowly drive forward or backward until the tandem is in the desired location.
- Release the operating handle and visually check to make sure the lock pins have locked. (Each lock pin should visibly extend through the holes in the track rails.) Make sure the axles are not out of line. Misaligned axles will cause their tires to "scrub" or scrape the road rather than roll with it.
- Remove the chocks.
- Lock the stop bar in both body rails immediately behind the slider.
- With the trailer brakes applied, gently rock the trailer backward and forward to make sure the sliding axle is locked.
- Unlock the differential lock.

Do not try to slide the trailer's tandem while the vehicle is in motion. Doing so puts the tractor and trailer in danger of breaking away.

When Sliders Bind

Sometimes, sliders will stick or "bind" and will not slide easily. When this happens, **do not keep trying to release the bind with tractor power.** One slow steady tug forward and backward is all the stress you should put on the tractor's driveline and rear end. **If the sliders are still bound, restraighten the tractor-trailer.** Most binding, particularly with sliding tandems, is caused when the trailer sits on uneven ground. **A little water on the trailer's sliding tandem rails can loosen even particularly stubborn binds.** Never use oil or grease. Occasionally, on the air-powered sliding fifth wheel, the **lock pins** will lock up or **get stuck.** When this happens, **try tapping on the lock pins with a hammer.**

Chapter 15 Quiz

1. Usually, when the trailer's sliding tandem binds, _____ .
    A. the load is too heavy
    B. the tractor-trailer combination is not parked level and straight
    C. the slide rails need greasing
    D. the tractor needs to be serviced

2. Most five axle tractor-trailer combinations are limited to _____ .
    A. 12,000 pounds of weight on the steering axle and 34,000 pounds of weight per tandem axle
    B. half the kingpin weight on the steering axle and 34,000 pounds of weight per tandem axle
    C. equal amounts of weight up to 34,000 pounds, on every axle
    D. 80,000 pounds of kingpin weight

3. Sliding the fifth wheel forward _____ .
   A. increases the tractor's "A" dimension number
   B. reduces the tractor's "A" dimension number
   C. increases the trailer's "A" dimension number
   D. reduces the trailer's "A" dimension number

4. A sliding fifth wheel adjusts the weight placed on the trailer's tandem.
   A. True
   B. False

5. The position of the _____ can affect the swing radius of the tractor.
   A. sliding tandem
   B. sliding fifth wheel
   C. steering axle
   D. payload

6. Each notch on a fifth wheel represents roughly 150 to 300 pounds of kingpin weight being shifted.
   A. True
   B. False

7. Before sliding the fifth wheel you should _____ .
   A. set the landing gear
   B. unplug the electrical connection to the trailer
   C. chock the tractor's wheels
   D. make sure the differential lock is not engaged

8. To lose weight from the steering axle slide the fifth wheel backward.
   A. True
   B. False

9. To lose weight from the tractor's tandem, slide the fifth wheel backward or the trailer's tandem backward.
   A. True
   B. False

10. To increase the trailer's kingpin weight _____ .
    A. slide the trailer's tandem forward
    B. slide the tandem backward
    C. slide the fifth wheel backward
    D. slide the fifth wheel forward

CHAPTER 16

AUXILIARY BRAKES

What They Are

If you've just heard the term "auxiliary brakes," you might think they must be devices that attach to the service brake system. Actually, auxiliary brakes are **separate from the service brake system.** It is true, though, that auxiliary brakes **help the service brake system,** at least in the sense that they assist in:

- slowing the vehicle
- controlling the vehicle when slowing or descending a grade
- saving wear and tear on the service brakes

It's important to remember that **auxiliary brakes are not used to stop a vehicle, only to slow it.** They can provide almost all the slowing power needed in any ordinary driving situation that calls for reduced speed. They are **often called vehicle retarders.**

THE ADVANTAGES
Auxiliary brakes provide increased savings and increased safety to today's truck driver.

Increased Savings
Studies from the Highway Research Institute show that auxiliary brakes save thousands of dollars a year per truck. These savings are found mainly in **reduced service brake maintenance** costs and in **reduced trip time.**

Not only is maintenance on the service brakes decreased, but the life of the service brakes is increased. In fact, one manufacturer claims that if drivers use auxiliary brakes, their **service brakes will last** up to three times **longer.** How does an auxiliary brake accomplish this? Using the auxiliary brake to reduce speed, rather than or in addition to the service brakes, cuts down on the use of the service brakes.

Auxiliary brakes also **reduce tire wear.** Nothing wears tires out faster than pounding down on the brakes. With a retarder helping to slow the truck down, flat spots and other types of tire wear are reduced.

Increased Safety

A report from the Insurance Institute of Highway Safety shows that a Class 8, heavy duty over-the-road vehicle without an auxiliary brake is almost three times more likely to get into a runaway situation on a downhill grade than a Class 8 vehicle with an auxiliary brake.

An auxiliary brake:

- gives the driver better control of the vehicle
- reduces service brake overheating and brake fade
- reduces brake lining and drum wear by providing another means of slowing
- slows the vehicle more smoothly without shifting
- reduces driver fatigue
- provides better control on downgrades

To sum up, auxiliary brakes share the job of slowing the vehicle down with the service brakes. The use of an auxiliary brake makes the truck easier to control, safer to drive and more economical to operate.

WHY THEY'RE NEEDED

Auxiliary brakes are becoming more popular and more necessary due to many factors, such as:

- aerodynamic designs of modern rigs
- the trend toward heavier payloads
- the lifting of weight restrictions
- increased popularity of pulling combination trailers

Aerodynamic designs increase fuel savings, but also **make a vehicle harder to stop.** Because the air drag that holds the truck back is reduced, the brakes have to work harder to slow or stop the truck. This increases the chance of brake fade and wears the brakes out faster. Heavier payloads, the lifting of weight restrictions and pulling more than one trailer all add to the weight the brakes must stop.

Types of Auxiliary Brakes

Some auxiliary brakes work by slowing the engine. So, they are also called engine retarders or engine brakes. Other auxiliary brakes work differently. No matter how they work, though, the purpose is still the same. They assist the service brakes in slowing the truck. That's why they're also called retarders.

THE ENGINE RETARDER

Engine retarders **work by changing the timing** in the valves. As usual, the engine compresses air on the compression stroke. Then when the piston is near top dead center, fuel is injected. It ignites and the piston is pushed back down in the power stroke. However, when the engine retarder is switched on, just before the piston reaches top dead center, the exhaust valve opens and releases the compressed air before fuel is injected. The energy used to compress the air goes up the exhaust stack and out into the atmosphere. No energy is transmitted to the drive train. Thus, the engine is slowed, and so is the rig.

As you can see, an engine retarder **changes the power-producing diesel engine into a power-absorbing air compressor.** There are many types of engine retarders, but the most popular is the Jacobs, or Jake, Brake.

The Jake Brake

The **four major components** of any Jake Brake are **the solenoid valve, the control valve, the master piston and the slave piston.**

The solenoid valve activates the movement of pressurized engine oil to the brake housing and the control valve regulates it. The master piston senses engine timing and transmits it to the slave piston. At the proper time the slave piston moves and opens the engine exhaust valves.

fig. 16-1
(A) A piston and cylinder operating with the Jake Brake not activated.
(B) What happens when you turn the Jake Brake on.

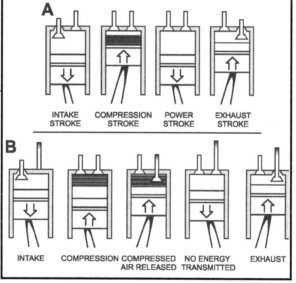

Let's step back now and see how the Jake Brake retards the engine. When the truck is in operation, simply the force of its moving makes the engine turn. It takes energy to make the pistons rise during the compression stroke. Under normal operation, the engine creates more energy than it uses when the fuel is injected and burned. But the Jake Brake opens the exhaust valve and releases the compressed air before the fuel is injected. This means the engine can't produce any power. In fact, as the pistons rise, they absorb power from the force of the moving truck and thus slow it.

The Jake Brake is **activated by controls located in the cab.** Once the system has been turned on, the operation is usually automatic. It comes into play whenever you take your foot off the throttle. The switch that turns the Jake Brake on and off is located on the dash. On many engines the Jake Brake can be progressively applied. This means **the driver can control how many cylinders are affected** and used to provide braking. **The more cylinders used, the more braking force** is provided.

Progressive application can be controlled in several different ways. One way is that the on-off switch will have three positions: off, low and high. Another way is to have two switches, one to turn the system on and off and the other to control the application.

The Mack Dynatard system operates on the same principle as the Jake Brake system.

THE EXHAUST BRAKE

The exhaust brake slows the rig by **partly closing the engine's exhaust system** and putting back pressure on it. This makes the pistons work against the pressure that builds up in the exhaust manifold. **Instead of sending energy to the driveline, the engine works hard to force the exhaust buildup out of the stack.** This is how the exhaust brake retards the engine. Exhaust brakes are also referred to as **"compression brakes" or "butterfly type"** exhaust brakes.

The Williams Blue Ox Exhaust Brake

The Williams Blue Ox is one example of an exhaust brake. The **main components** of this brake system are **the brake housing, the air cylinder and the baffle plate.** When this retarder is activated, the air cylinder moves the baffle plate. The baffle plate nearly closes off the exhaust pipe. This creates back pressure in the exhaust system. Instead of the exhaust flowing freely out the exhaust pipe, the piston has to work hard to force it out. As the pressure builds up, the engine has to work harder to try to push more exhaust out of the stack.

In other words, on the exhaust stroke, the exhaust valve is open. With the exhaust brake on, that exhaust air is partly prevented from escaping into the exhaust manifold. With the exhaust buildup, it will take more effort to turn the engine. Because **the engine has to use more energy to fight** this **back pressure,** its energy output is reduced. This causes the truck to slow.

When the retarder is turned off, the baffle plate returns to the "open" position and the engine returns to normal operation.

THE HYDRAULIC RETARDER

The hydraulic retarder is either built into the transmission or added to its side. It works by **causing the engine to work against the pressure of a fluid,** usually transmission or engine oil.

Hydraulic retarders use the same principles as an automatic transmission. In the transmission there is a rotor that is attached to the crankshaft of the engine and a stator that is attached to the input shaft of the transmission. These are mounted close together and oil fills the space between. As the engine spins, the vanes on the rotor cause the oil to spin with it. The spinning oil makes the stator turn the transmission. See Figure 16-2(A).

The hydraulic retarder **has a** similar **rotor and stator.** But the stator is not attached to the transmission input shaft and cannot turn.

Once the hydraulic retarder unit is activated, engine oil is pumped into the unit through a valve. The vanes of the turning rotor pick up the oil and force it against the stator. Since **the oil cannot turn the stator it acts as a drag on the engine, thus slowing the truck.** See Figure 16-2(B).

You can control the amount of oil allowed to enter the unit. In this way, **you control the retarding effect.** To get a greater retarding effect, you allow more oil to be pumped into the unit.

fig. 16-2
The principle of (A) automatic transmissions and (B) hydraulic retarders.

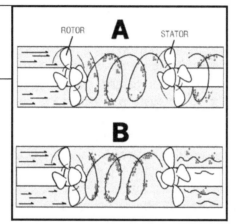

When the hydraulic retarder is turned off, the hydraulic retarder control valve shuts off the oil supply. The rotor pushes out the remaining oil from the hydraulic retarder unit. This permits the engine to run freely again.

Hydraulic retarders use an oil cooler because the friction built up inside the unit is extremely high, causing high heat. Hot oil flows through the cooler which is usually mounted on the side of the engine.

This retarder **can be set to work automatically** whenever you take your foot off the throttle, just like a Jake Brake. Or it **can be operated manually.**

Let's look at some examples of the hydraulic retarder.

The Cat BrakeSaver
The Caterpillar, or Cat, BrakeSaver is usually mounted between the engine and the flywheel. Its major components are the brake housing, stator and rotor. This manufacturer uses engine oil.

Allison Retarders
Detroit Allison has two types of hydraulic retarder, one an add-on, the other a built-in part of the transmission. This manufacturer uses transmission oil.

The Allison MTB is an add-on retarder mounted on the back of the transmission. An **add-on hydraulic retarder is also called an output retarder.** In addition to hydraulic fluid, this retarder also uses a friction clutch that continues retarding at low speeds, making this retarder **more versatile.**

The Allison Brake Preserver is a part of the transmission. **A built-in hydraulic retarder is also called an input retarder.** Its operation is very similar to that of the Cat BrakeSaver, but it's located between the automatic lockup clutch and the gears.

Allison retarders are air-activated and have the following controls:

- throttle apply interlock
- service brake protection
- system control valve
- retarder on light

The throttle apply interlock prevents you from activating the retarder while the accelerator is depressed.

The service brake protection system protects against a leak in the retarder apply system. Both the retarder and the air brakes are fed by the same system. A leak in the retarder apply system would bleed the air out of the service brake system. If this happened you'd be left without the primary brake system—the service brakes—and without the retarder. The protection system senses a leak in the retarder and shuts off the air supply to the retarder. This protects the air supply for the brakes.

The system control valve allows the retarder apply system to be turned off. The retarder on light indicates when the retarder apply system is on.

The Hale Retarder
This hydraulic auxiliary brake is mounted on the power take-off part of the transmission. It can be mounted on almost any type of vehicle. It works at low rpm and you can control the amount of retardation.

THE ELECTRIC RETARDER
Electric retarders are driveline devices, actually large alternators that are usually installed between the transmission and the axle. They'll be attached to the vehicle's frame or to the transmission itself. They work by creating **powerful electromagnetic fields** that **pull on the driveline or on the trailer axle** and thus **slow the vehicle.**

The Jacobs ER
This electric retarder is mounted on the drive shaft. It has four retarding positions and works off a hand control and/or a foot control. Its powerful alternator can put enough drag on the driveline to stop the vehicle. Its greatest advantage is that it can be used on any type of heavy duty vehicle.

The Ilasa
This electric retarder is similar to the Jacobs ER. It can be mounted on a tractor axle, but it's intended to be mounted on a trailer axle. It consists of two rotors, one on each side of a very powerful electromagnet. It's more powerful than the Jacobs ER, but it's also a lot heavier.

When to Use the Auxiliary Brakes

How the auxiliary brakes will be used depends in part on the type of system that is installed in a truck. However, no matter what type of vehicle retarder a truck uses, it should be activated in the following situations.

BOBTAILING
Do not use the retarder when you bobtail. Do not use it when you're pulling an empty trailer, either. If the retarder is on and the service brakes are applied in these circumstances, **the wheels may lock up.**

CITY DRIVING
Although **most auxiliary brakes will stall the engine at low rpm,** some still function very well. For instance, the following retarders all continue to operate very efficiently at low rpm. If the truck has one of these retarders, leave it on in the city as long as the road surface is dry:

- Jacobs ER
- Allison MTB
- Ilasa
- Hale

The other retarders work best at high rpm and should be turned off during periods of low rpm driving. Also **the Jake Brake should rarely be used in town.** This is because **it makes a lot of noise.** It is not a good idea to drive through a residential area and have the Jake Brake on every time you approach a stop light. Some communities have noise ordinances so you can be ticketed for doing this.

When a hydraulic retarder is used with an automatic transmission, the transmission fluid can overheat. You may have to reduce the retarder power or turn it off.

HIGHWAY DRIVING
In normal weather conditions when the road surface is dry, **leave the auxiliary brakes on all the time.** They will help you maintain good control on the highway. Whenever you take your foot off the accelerator, the retarder will come into play and immediately begin to slow the vehicle.

DRIVING IN ADVERSE WEATHER CONDITIONS

If the road surface is wet or **slippery from rain,** snow or ice, the driving conditions are considered "adverse." If you leave the auxiliary brake on in these conditions, you can increase the risk of a skid or a jackknife. The reason for this is that all the braking force from the retarder is transmitted to the drive axles. Then, if you also apply the air brakes, even more braking force is on the driving axles. If the road surface is slippery this can cause the drive axles to slide. When that happens you are headed for an accident.

If the road is covered with ice or snow, **turn the retarder off.**

If the road is clear, but the weather is generally wet and the temperature is below freezing, turn the retarder off whenever you approach a bridge or a freeway ramp.

If it begins to rain, turn the retarder off for the first 15 minutes. These are the most dangerous minutes of a rainstorm because as the water mixes with the oil buildup on the road, the surface becomes very slippery.

If it's raining or **the road is wet, reduce retarder power.** If the retarder doesn't have more than one setting, turn it off.

DRIVING IN ROLLING TERRAIN

Service brakes don't cool much between downgrades in rolling terrain. This is one time when you'll appreciate the auxiliary brake. Instead of relying on the service brakes, **turn on the retarder** and select a gear that lets you go down those hills at a safe and controlled speed. **Gear down, keep the engine speed near its rated rpm** and let the retarder do the work.

DRIVING DOWN HILLS

This is when the retarder will come in most handy. In fact, it could save your life. It will certainly save the service brakes, a lot of money and a lot of fatigue.

As always, before you start down a hill, **choose a gear that will let you descend at a constant, controlled speed with almost no use of the service brakes.**

The old rule was that to descend a hill you should use whatever gear you used, or would use, to climb the hill. With the new trucks and engines though, you can ascend a grade much faster than you should descend it. With some retarders, however, the old rule of thumb applies.

What follows is a list of general rules that may help you choose the gear **depending on the type of auxiliary brake installed** in the truck, the type of engine installed in the truck, the load and the hill.

ENGINE RETARDERS. Use the same gear you used, or would use, to climb the hill.

EXHAUST RETARDERS. Use one gear lower than the gear you used, or would use, to climb the hill.

HYDRAULIC RETARDERS. If the retarder is a built-in part of the transmission, use the same gear you used, or would use, to climb the hill. If the retarder is an add-on, use one gear higher than the one you used, or would use to climb the hill.

ELECTRIC RETARDERS. Use one gear higher than the one you used, or would use to climb the hill.

As you descend a grade, **use the service brakes only if the rpm or vehicle speed gets too high.** Retarders can make you over-confident about your ability to stop the truck quickly. Drivers have been known to drive too fast, depending on the retarders and service brakes to stop the truck quickly. This is a dangerous practice. It also puts more strain on both the retarder and the service brakes. **Don't rely on the retarder to do all the work of stopping** the truck. Always **drive** the truck at a **safe speed.**

Chapter 16 Quiz

1. Auxiliary brakes _____ .
   A. attach to the service brake system and are used to stop the vehicle
   B. are separate from the service brake system and are used to stop the vehicle
   C. attach to the service brake system and are used to help slow the vehicle
   D. are separate from the service brake system and are used to help slow the vehicle

2. Using auxiliary brakes increases the life of _____ .
   A. the engine
   B. the transmission
   C. the service brakes
   D. the drive train

For Questions 3, 4, 5 and 6, match the description in Column A with the type of retarder in Column B.

Column A Description   Column B Retarder Type

3. The _____ changes the   A. electric retarder
    timing in the valves.

4. The _____ partly closes   B. engine retarder
    the engine's exhaust
    system.

5. The _____ causes the   C. exhaust brake
    engine to work against
    the pressure of a fluid.

6. The _____ slows the   D. hydraulic retarder
    vehicle with a magnet.

7. The illustration below shows the Jake Brake in operation.
    A. True.
    B. False

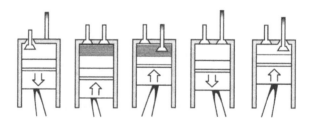

8. An input retarder is an add-on device, while an output retarder
    is built-in.
    A. True
    B. False

9. When you bobtail, you should put your retarder on the lowest
    setting possible.
    A. True
    B. False

10. If the road is covered with ice or snow, turn off the retarder.
    A. True
    B. False

VEHICLE INSPECTION

Need for Inspections

Inspections are just part of the responsibilities drivers must deal with every day that they drive. You should be aware of exactly what drivers do to inspect their trucks throughout their journey. You will be required to make some of these same inspections when you test for your Commercial Driver's License. You must make these inspections of heavy vehicles you yourself will be driving.

Part 396 of the Federal Motor Carrier Safety Regulations covers the vehicle inspections required by the Department of Transportation. You may wonder why the government makes such an issue of inspections. When you take a truck out, even for a short distance, you have a responsibility to uphold. You are sharing the road with others, in vehicles large and small. You want to be sure that the truck will respond to your control so you can drive it safely.

A truck must be in top running order for this to take place. And the only way for drivers to be sure their vehicles are in good condition before they get behind the wheel is for them to make a personal inspection of all parts and accessories.

Don't you think it makes sense to make sure everything is in order before taking off down the road with a large and very expensive piece of equipment? Certainly you would check your car before taking off on a cross-country trip. You would want to **make sure everything is in good running order** so you can avoid any unnecessary trouble on your trip.

Personal Safety

No one is more important to you than yourself. Therefore, **whenever you must go on the road ensuring your personal safety should be your first concern.** When you comply with the laws and regulations set down by the Federal Motor Carrier Safety Regulations, you ensure your safety while driving.

After you inspect the vehicle, you gain a **feeling of confidence.** You are free from worry that something might break down and lead to further complications. This feeling alone can make a difference in how you drive. If you are not worrying about whether the brakes will hold or the lights will work, your mind is free to focus on the traffic. This simply **allows you to drive better and safer.**

Required by Law

Why are there laws requiring the inspection of vehicles you plan to operate? Laws are **guidelines** which have been set up **to protect everyone:** the carrier, the client, the public and the driver. They set standards and provide some assurance that these standards will be met. If there were no regulations, what would stop a less professional driver from jumping in an unsafe truck and heading down the road? The fact that you completed a full inspection on a vehicle would be small comfort if the other driver plowed into you because the brakes failed.

Regulations also serve as a constant reminder of the steps which should be taken for the safe operation of the vehicle. Without a set of guidelines, it is too easy to forget all the steps that must be taken each and every time a driver heads out on a trip.

CARRIER'S REQUIRED RECORDS
According to the regulations, it's actually **the carrier** who **is charged with seeing that vehicles are inspected and that records are kept** of these inspections. In practice, though, it's **the driver** who usually **does the actual inspection** and **fills out the reports.** In doing so, the driver is acting as the carrier's agent. And, if the vehicle you're driving is found to be unsafe, you are most likely to be fined.

Regulations call for carriers to **maintain a regular system of inspection** covering all their vehicles. Also, they must **keep a maintenance record** on each of the vehicles.

DRIVER'S RESPONSIBILITIES
Drivers will **inspect their vehicle before and after they go on a run.** Specifically, the regulations require all drivers to inspect their vehicle at the end of their run and report any repairs that should be made. Then, in their pre-trip inspection, they verify those repairs have been made.

But here's where practice differs slightly from policy. What usually happens is that the pre-trip inspection is more thorough than the post-trip. In the pre-trip, the driver not only checks that repairs were made, but also make sure that various systems and components are in good working order. This makes sense when you consider that drivers may not always have the same truck today that they had yesterday. We'll look at how the pre-trip and post-trip inspections work together later in this chapter.

Types of Inspections

There are several types of inspections. They each have a slightly different purpose.

PRE-TRIP INSPECTION
The **pre-trip inspection involves a complete circle check** of the vehicle that will be driven. The driver checks a number of sites along the **inside and outside of the tractor and trailer,** making a full circle around the vehicle. By following the same steps every time the driver will not overlook any part of the inspection duties.

You, the mechanic, like the driver, have to show you can perform a pre-trip inspection to get your CDL.

IN-TRANSIT INSPECTION
The responsibility to make inspections doesn't stop once the driver moves out on the road. In-transit checks are something drivers should include as part of proper road operations. Being aware of the condition of the vehicle while they drive can prevent a major problem from taking place.

The law does not require that the driver **inspect the vehicle while it is in transit.** However, it is good practice to do so. The vehicle may have passed the pre-trip inspection, but **problems can develop while drivers are out on the road.** It is suggested drivers make a quick check at every meal stop.

---

fig. 17-1
The post-trip inspection form requires drivers to identify with an "X" any needed repairs and mechanics to certify repairs were made.

DRIVER VEHICLE INSPECTION REPORT
(TO BE COMPLETED DAILY IN ACCORDANCE WITH RULE 396.11 OF SAFETY REGULATIONS AS PRESCRIBED BY THE D.O.T.)

OWNER'S NAME *Beck Trucking Co.* VEHICLE NUMBER M·420 D·608

DRIVER *Frances Sanchez* DATE 2-22

ITEMS TO CHECK	DRIVER'S REPORT	MECHANIC'S REPORT	ITEMS TO CHECK	DRIVER'S REPORT	MECHANIC' REPORT
BEFORE STARTING ENGINE			**AFTER STARTING ENGINE**		
OIL - IF ADDED INSERT # GALS.	✓		FUEL SYSTEM	✓	
FUEL - IF ADDED INSERT # GALS.	✓		COOLING SYSTEM	✓	
COOLANT	✓		ENGINE	✓	
BRAKE LINES TO TRAILER	X		LEAKS	✓	
ELECTRICAL LINES TO TRAILER	✓		HEADLIGHTS	✓	
DRIVE LINE	✓		TAILLIGHTS	✓	
COUPLING DEVICES	✓		STOP & TURN LIGHTS	✓	

There are circumstances which even warrant a stop at a safe place off the road to make a check of certain conditions. A load of hazardous materials demands a tire check at the beginning and end of each trip and every time the truck is parked. Driving a reefer means a driver will want to stop and check the temperature periodically. This is the time to make an in-transit inspection just to remain on the safe side.

POST-TRIP INSPECTION

According to Section 396.11, **a report of the vehicle's condition must be made at the end of each day's work.** Section 396.3 and Part 393 detail the parts and accessories which must be checked. Any defects must be reported and repaired. Whoever makes the repairs, be it you the mechanic or the driver, must **sign the report to certify repairs have been made.**

This driver's vehicle inspection report (DVIR) then forms the basis of the next pre-trip inspection. The driver will verify that needed repairs were made and that nothing else is wrong with the vehicle.

OFFICIAL ROADSIDE INSPECTIONS

Section 396.9 of the DOT safety regulations authorizes **a special agent of the Federal Motor Carrier Safety Administration (FMCSA) to stop and inspect the vehicle.** This agent could be a federal or state DOT representative, highway patrol officer, weigh master or other government official. This inspection could take place alongside the road, or at a port of entry station.

This is an inspection drivers definitely want to pass. If they don't, **their vehicle can be declared "out of service"** by the special agent. The inspection takes only about 15 or 20 minutes. If there are no problems found with the vehicle, drivers can be on their way once again knowing that they are behind the wheel of a safe vehicle. If the vehicle is declared out of service by the inspector, the driver cannot drive it until the repair has been made and the vehicle has been reinspected. If the vehicle cannot be repaired right where it is, it will have to be towed to a repair shop.

The roadside inspection is concerned with the most common violations that can take place as a result of the driver's failure to make the pre-trip inspection. **The driver is also subject to inspection.** The agent will check **to see if the driver's logs are up to date.** The driver's condition is also observed to make sure the driver is truly able to operate the vehicle safely.

If a vehicle does not pass the roadside inspection, the driver must deliver the report to the driver's carrier within 24 hours. Once the motor carrier has received the inspection report, the carrier has 15 days to take care of the problems stated on the report.

To make the business of official roadside inspections more efficient, 48 states, Canada and soon, Mexico will have joined an organization called the **Commercial Vehicle Safety Alliance.** The CVSA **developed a standard inspection** that can be conducted quickly by a mobile unit. That's the Critical Item Inspection, which involves checking the brakes and steering, tires and wheels, the fifth wheels, drawbars and suspension.

Once the driver and vehicle pass the inspection, the vehicle will receive a sticker. The sticker is good for three months. It shows concerned officials that the vehicle has been inspected recently and passed. In CVSA-member states, **if a truck passes the Critical Item Inspection, the truck is not likely to be subject to another roadside inspection for 90 days** unless the official notices something clearly wrong.

fig. 17-2
This is one procedure to use when inspecting a truck.

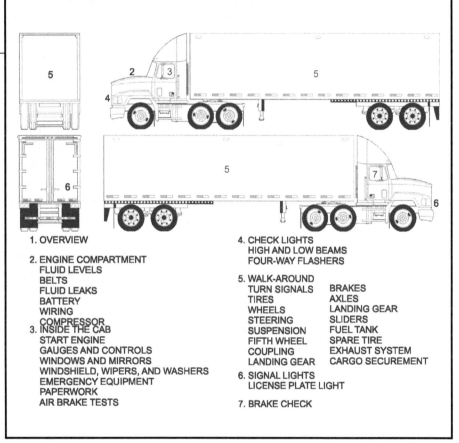

1. OVERVIEW

2. ENGINE COMPARTMENT
   FLUID LEVELS
   BELTS
   FLUID LEAKS
   BATTERY
   WIRING
   COMPRESSOR
3. INSIDE THE CAB
   START ENGINE
   GAUGES AND CONTROLS
   WINDOWS AND MIRRORS
   WINDSHIELD, WIPERS, AND WASHERS
   EMERGENCY EQUIPMENT
   PAPERWORK
   AIR BRAKE TESTS

4. CHECK LIGHTS
   HIGH AND LOW BEAMS
   FOUR-WAY FLASHERS

5. WALK-AROUND
   TURN SIGNALS   BRAKES
   TIRES   AXLES
   WHEELS   LANDING GEAR
   STEERING   SLIDERS
   SUSPENSION   FUEL TANK
   FIFTH WHEEL   SPARE TIRE
   COUPLING   EXHAUST SYSTEM
   LANDING GEAR   CARGO SECUREMENT

6. SIGNAL LIGHTS
   LICENSE PLATE LIGHT

7. BRAKE CHECK

Making Inspections

When making inspections, it helps to **follow a routine.** That way nothing is forgotten. One routine you might use has seven steps:

- Note the vehicle's condition in general. Review the most recent vehicle inspection report looking for problems that require special attention.

- Check the engine compartment.
- Start the engine and inspect inside the cab.
- Turn off the engine and check all the lights.
- Walk all around the vehicle checking critical parts.
- Check the signal lights.
- Start the engine and check the brakes.

Here are some other specific things the CDL examiner might expect you to do.

OVERVIEW

Make sure the vehicle is level, **not leaning to one side** or the other. Unevenness might be caused by flat tires, broken springs or defective air bags. Check the ground under the truck for puddles or **wet spots,** which **mean something is leaking.** Search until the leaks are found. Any black streaks of oil on the inside sidewall of a tire mean a wheel seal is leaking. Review the most recent Daily Vehicle Inspection Report (DVIR) for the truck you're inspecting. You'll learn more about the DVIR later in this chapter.

IN THE ENGINE COMPARTMENT

Make sure the parking brakes are set or chock the wheels. **Check fluid levels.** Look for the radiator coolant level just below the neck of the filler cap. Use the dipstick to check the oil. **Check** the tension and condition of **belts** by pressing down on them. There should be no more than ¾ inch of slack. **Look for** small **oil leaks. Check the battery connections, the battery box** and holddowns. Look for corrosion around the battery posts, and **check the battery fluid level.** Make sure all the **vent caps** are **in place.** Look for cracked or **worn wiring insulation and broken** or disconnected **wires. Check the compressor oil supply** and the supply of alcohol in the alcohol evaporator, if you have one.

INSIDE THE CAB

Put the gearshift in neutral ("park" if it is an automatic). **Start the engine** and listen for strange noises. **Check all the gauges.** Make sure they work and give normal readings. (Chapter 2 has details on what normal readings to expect.) **Test all switches and controls** to make sure they work.

Check the air brake system. The air brake system checks are described in Chapter 4. You will get an air brake restriction on your CDL if you cannot show the examiner you can perform these tests. Do them during the engine start part of the pre-trip inspection.

Clean and **adjust the mirrors. Check** the windows **for cracks.** If the glass is dirty clean it. **Check the supply of windshield washer fluid.** Make sure the wiper blades are in good condition, and that the wipers work. If there is anything (stickers, signs) that will obstruct your view while driving, remove it. **Only stickers and decals required by law** are permitted.

Make sure the **fire extinguisher is properly charged and rated.** It must be rated at least 5 B:C. If haz mat is being hauled, the fire extinguisher must be rated at least 10 B:C. The truck must also **have three reflective triangles.** Unless the truck has circuit breakers, it must also **have spare fuses.**

CHECK THE LIGHTS

Turn off the engine. Turn on the headlights and the four-way flashers. Leave the cab (take the key with you) and **make sure the headlights and four-ways are working.** Make sure **both high and low beams** work. Turn these lights off. **Turn on** the **parking, clearance, side marker and identification lights and right turn signal** before starting the walk-around inspection. The license plate light should be lit when the headlights are on.

WALK-AROUND INSPECTION

Start at the **left front side.** Walk toward the **front** of the truck, inspecting as you go. Inspect the front of the truck. See that all the lights there are clean and working. They should be amber in color.

Walk down the **right side,** inspecting critical areas there. Note that the right turn signal is working. It should be amber or white in color. If the tractor is a cabover, see that the cab lock is engaged.

Go on to inspect the **back** of the truck. Check all the lights and reflectors there. They should be red. If the truck has mud flaps, make sure they're not torn, dragging or rubbing on the tires. Make sure the license plate is securely in place and clean.

Walk back to the cab, inspecting the **left side** of the truck. Check that all the lights and reflectors are clean and free of damage, amber color in front, red at the rear. If the battery is here instead of the engine compartment, inspect it now.

During the walk-around, closely inspect the following parts and systems:

TIRES. **Check the tread depth.** Remember, $4/32$ of an inch of tread are needed on the steering axle and $2/32$ of an inch are needed on the rest of the tires. Are there any cuts in the rubber? Do any of the plies show? Are duals touching? Are tire sizes, or radials and bias types mixed on the same axle? Check for cut or cracked valve stems. **Check the tire pressure** with a gauge.

WHEELS. **Check the lug nuts** for tightness. Look for any cracks starting to form around the lug nuts. Rust or bright metal are signs the nuts are loose and the wheel is not mounted tightly. Look for damaged rims and missing parts. Check for welding repairs, which are prohibited. **Check the hub oil level.**

SUSPENSION. **Check for cracked or broken leaves.** Check for deflated or hissing air bags. Note spring hangers that allow the axle to move out of position. Look for damaged or missing torque rods or arms, U-bolts or spring hangers. Check the condition of the shock absorber.

BRAKES. Check for loose or missing parts and **check the push rod travel**. Refer to Chapter 4 for more details on adjusting the slack adjuster. See that brake linings have not worn thinner than $\frac{1}{4}$ inch. Brake shoes and linings should not have oil, grease or brake fluid on them.

AXLES. Powered axles should not leak oil. Check the condition of the lift mechanism on retractable axles. If they're air-powered, **check for leaks.**

SLIDERS. Make sure **locking pins** are firmly in their holes **and locking devices** are **in place.**

AIR SYSTEM. Look for hoses that are kinked, rubbing or worn. Listen carefully for hissing noises. **Search for the source of the leak.** Drain water from the air tanks.

COUPLING. **Make sure** the trailer air and electrical **connections are made properly** and that lines are not dragging. Be sure to check all air and electrical connections throughout a double or triple combination.

FUEL TANKS. **Double-check the fuel level** in all tanks. See that the tanks are mounted securely, that fuel crossover lines aren't hanging dangerously low, that capt are secure and that there are no leaks.

FIFTH WHEEL. **See that the coupling is secure.** Make sure the fifth wheel release lever is locked. There should be no space between the upper and lower fifth wheel. Don't forget to **check** the fifth wheel, locking lever and safety chains on **the dolly** in a double or triple rig.

LANDING GEAR. If the trailer is coupled to the tractor, the **landing gear should be up and the handle stowed away.**

SPARE TIRE. **Make sure there is** a spare tire, that **it's in good condition** and that it's **mounted securely** in the rack.

EXHAUST SYSTEM. Look for loose, broken or missing pipes, mufflers or stacks. See that **exhaust system parts aren't rubbing against** fuel system parts, tires or **other** moving vehicle **parts. Check for** exhaust system **leaks.**

STEERING SYSTEM. Look for bent, broken or missing parts. If the truck has power steering, make sure you **check** the hoses, pumps and the **level of power steering fluid. Check for leaks. Steering wheel free play should be no more than two inches** to either side of a 20-inch steering wheel. **Shake the steering arm, tie rod and drag link at each wheel to see they are not loose.**

CARGO SECUREMENT. Make sure there are the **minimum number of tiedowns** according to FMCSR Part 393.100, and that **all bindings and chains are in good condition** and secure. **Check blocking and bracing** to assure yourself that the load won't shift once the truck is in motion. **Check the seals** on sealed cargo. Check locks and latches on trailer doors. Check the tailboard or endgate, if there is one. Any canvas or **tarp must be tied down** so it won't flap or billow out. If the vehicle is hauling an oversized load, make sure you have the required signs, lights and flags. If the vehicle has side boards or stakes, make sure they are free of damage and securely in place. Check the headerboard, if there is one. Make sure that it's in good condition.

CHECK THE SIGNAL LIGHTS

When the vehicle has been thoroughly inspected, get back in the cab. Turn off the lights. Pull down the trailer brake hand valve. Next, turn on the front turn signal. Go out and **make sure the stop lights** are on and that **front and rear signals are working.** The front signal should be amber or white, the rear signal red, amber or yellow.

CHECK THE BRAKES

Checking the brakes means checking the service and parking brakes, as well as the air brake system. Put on the trailer brakes, then try to move forward in the lowest gear. **If the trailer brakes are working and the coupling is secure, they should hold the truck back.** Use a similar method to check the service brake. Release the parking and trailer brakes. Then **test the service brake's power to stop the truck while moving forward in low gear. Test the parking brake** by applying it while stopped. Then **see if it holds while trying to move forward.**

Daily Vehicle Inspection Report Form

Just as drivers make an inspection each day before going out on the road, so too will they need to fill out the daily vehicle inspection report form. This is a checklist of all the items which must be inspected and which must be in safe operating condition before the vehicle may be driven.

Figure 17-3 is one example of a vehicle inspection report form. With this type of form the person inspecting the vehicle would make a check mark for every component of the inspection that needed attention. You

fig. 17-3
On this driver's inspection report, drivers would check off only those items that need attention. If there are not defects, the driver would mark the "NO DEFECTS" box.

DRIVER'S INSPECTION REPORT
(SEE INSTRUCTIONS ON REVERSE SIDE)
CHECK DEFECTS ONLY, Explain under REMARKS
COMPLETION OF THIS REPORT REQUIRED BY FEDERAL LAW, 396.11 & 396.13.

Truck or Tractor No. _____ Mileage (No Tenths) | | | | | | Trailer No. _____

Dolly No. _____ Trailer No. _____ Location: _____

POWER UNIT

GENERAL CONDITION
- ☐ Cab/Doors/Windows
- ☐ Body/Doors
- ☐ Oil Leak _____
- ☐ Grease Leak _____
- ☐ Coolant Leak
- ☐ Fuel Leak
- ☐ Other _____

_____ (IDENTIFY)

ENGINE COMPARTMENT
- ☐ Oil Level
- ☐ Coolant Level
- ☐ Belts _____
- ☐ Other _____

_____ (IDENTIFY)

IN-CAB
- ☐ Gauges/Warning Indicators
- ☐ Windshield Wipers/Washers
- ☐ Horn(s)
- ☐ Heater/Defroster
- ☐ Mirrors
- ☐ Steering
- ☐ Clutch
- ☐ Service Brakes
- ☐ Parking Brake / Emergency Brake
- ☐ Triangles
- ☐ Fire Extinguisher
- ☐ Other Safety Equipment
- ☐ Spare Fuses
- ☐ Seat Belts
- ☐ Other _____

_____ (IDENTIFY)

EXTERIOR
- ☐ Lights
- ☐ Reflectors
- ☐ Suspension
- ☐ Tires
- ☐ Wheels/Rims/Lugs
- ☐ Battery
- ☐ Exhaust
- ☐ Brakes
- ☐ Light Line
- ☐ Fifth-Wheel
- ☐ Other Coupling
- ☐ Tie-Downs
- ☐ Rear-End Protection
- ☐ Other _____

_____ (IDENTIFY)

☐ NO DEFECTS

TOWED UNIT(S)

- ☐ Body/Doors
- ☐ Tie-Downs
- ☐ Lights
- ☐ Reflectors

- ☐ Suspension
- ☐ Tires
- ☐ Wheels/Rims/Lugs
- ☐ Brakes

- ☐ Landing Gear
- ☐ Kingpin/Upper Plate
- ☐ Fifth-Wheel (Dolly)
- ☐ Other Coupling Devices

- ☐ Rear-End Protection
- ☐ Other _____

_____ (IDENTIFY)

☐ NO DEFECTS

REMARKS: _____
_____
_____
_____
_____ ☐ _____

REPORTING DRIVER: Date_____
Name _____ Emp. No. _____

REVIEWING DRIVER: Date_____
Name _____ Emp. No. _____

MAINTENANCE ACTION: Date_____
Repairs Made   No Repairs Needed ☐
R.O. #'s. _____
Certified By: _____
Location: _____

SHOP REMARKS: _____

may have the truck brought to you for repairs along with the form you'll be signing and dating after repairs are made. The vehicle inspection report form is often combined with the driver's daily log, printed on the back.

Actually, the inspection report form serves two functions. It helps to remind drivers of all the things which must undergo keen examination each day. And it is written proof that the inspection did take place. The law requires that this report be filled out, and it must be turned in at the end of each day's completed work assignment.

FILLING OUT THE REPORT

Drivers must make sure that they do not overlook any part of the checklist. They can't rush through it. Their report must list any and all problems that could hamper the safe operation of the vehicle in question. If the inspection fails to turn up any defects, this too should be stated in the driver's report.

The report must identify the motor vehicle and it must be signed by the driver. In the case of team operations, only one driver need sign the report. If the driver operates more than one vehicle in one day, that driver must fill out a vehicle inspection report on each vehicle.

REPAIR DEFECTS PROMPTLY

A defect can affect the safe operation of the vehicle. No matter what it is, the problem should be taken care of promptly.

In fact, the regulations require the **carrier to see to it that any defect is taken care of** to return the vehicle to a safe condition of operation.

If repairs are not made to correct the defect, it is against the law to take the vehicle out onto the road. Don't forget, the safety of the public is threatened by the presence of an unsafe truck on the public roadway.

Chapter 17 Quiz

In questions 1 through 3, match the section or part of the FMCSR in Column A with the area of inspections it regulates in Column B.

Column A	Column B
1. Section 396.11	A. vehicle inspection
2. Part 396	B. official roadside inspections
3. Section 396.9	C. the driver vehicle inspection report

4. There is only one official vehicle inspection report form.
   A. True
   B. False

5. If a vehicle bears a CVSA inspection sticker, a pre-trip inspection is not necessary.
    A. True
    B. False

6. Drivers must fill out a vehicle inspection report form _____ .
    A. only on the first vehicle they take out each day
    B. only if the vehicle they take out is different than the one they had the day before
    C. only if they're owner-operators
    D. on each vehicle they operate during the day

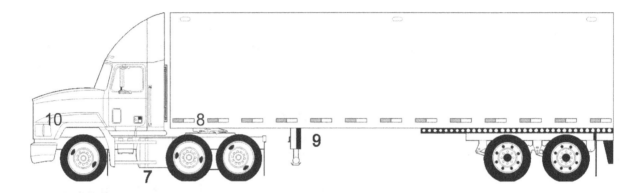

Refer to the illustration above to answer questions 7 through 10. The numbers in this illustration indicate some of the sites to be checked in the required inspection. Match the inspection activities listed in Column B with the numbered sites in Column A.

Column A Inspection Sites   Column B Inspection Activities

7. _____   A. Landing gear is up and the handle is stowed away.

8. _____   B. Coupling is secure and the release lever is locked.

9. _____   C. Turn signals and emergency flashers work properly.

10. _____   D. Fuel level is correct.

PREVENTIVE MAINTENANCE

The Importance of Preventive Maintenance

Even though, as a mechanic, you are not driving full time for your employer, you should be concerned with preventive maintenance for motor vehicles. Preventive maintenance is important in terms of overall safety and economy. The point of a preventive maintenance program is to **spot a minor problem before it turns into a major problem.** By fixing small problems instead of large ones, expensive repair bills can be prevented.

A preventive maintenance program is going to cost the truck owner or trucking company some money. However, in terms of overall expenses, it's like buying insurance. The company is making sure that expensive towing is rarely needed to rescue a vehicle that's broken down on a run. Plus, it's better to spend a little bit of money in the company's own Maintenance shop than a lot on roadside or outside repair bills.

The idea of saving a lot of money for major repairs by spending a little on a preventive maintenance program must certainly make sense to you. If you've ever owned a car, you've probably put out a little money and effort for upkeep in order to save yourself a lot of hard work and major repair bills later. Spending a few dollars to top up the oil now and then is certainly smarter than spending thousands on a new engine because yours seized up for lack of proper lubrication.

Preventive maintenance helps **ensure that drivers will be driving safe vehicles.** It's against regulations to allow an unsafe vehicle out on the road. You, as well as drivers, inspect that vehicle routinely to make sure it's safe. Of course you don't stop with merely inspecting the truck. You have to see that any defects which threaten the safety of the vehicle are repaired. A good preventive maintenance program takes care of minor defects before they become safety hazards.

There are different levels of service checks that help to make a motor vehicle safe for the open road. The checks range from the very basic to the more involved levels which include extensive maintenance work, engine and brake work. Some of these levels involve work that the driver can do. Others are jobs for you, the mechanic.

Driver's Daily Checks

By now you're probably convinced of the wisdom of fixing small problems before they become big ones. So how do you discover these problems? As you might have guessed, you **inspect every vehicle in the fleet often,** and listen intently to the reports of the drivers of those vehicles.

Of course, **as required by regulations, you must inspect a vehicle every time you take it out,** even if you are just going up the road to exchange a roadworthy tractor for one needing repairs. And, if these inspections disclose any defects that could threaten the safety of the vehicle, those should be repaired promptly. Plus, on your report, you'll have a chance to note any other defects you find. Chapter 17 covers these required inspections in more detail.

It may be part of your job to **inspect more thoroughly than regulations require.** You could be responsible for making **daily service checks** on the vehicles that will be driven out on the road. There is no need to wonder just what the daily service check should include. Your supervisor will provide you with a schedule of all the items you're expected to check. Often, you'll find this **includes the driver's daily inspection required by regulations.**

It may be part of your responsibility to **make minor repairs,** or full-time drivers may do them. They may be required to top up fluid levels, replace blown bulbs, tighten down fittings and the like. This is no big chore when the truck is in the yard. But say a driver is making a check somewhere out on the road, miles from a truck stop? What if that driver is low on coolant, or has a light burned out? For this reason, the drivers may have an emergency repair supply kit in the truck with a few spare bulbs and perhaps a grease gun in it.

Remember, helping the driver out is only part of your vehicle inspection responsibilities. Occasionally, you will still have to perform a daily service check. The driver's daily service check instructions might read something like the following. This example procedure is listed in one carrier's driver's manual.

Power Unit
- Check fuel, oil and coolant levels.
- Check ammeter for proper alternator operation.
- Check all gauges. Oil pressure at operating temperature and rpm must be 30 psi or above. Oil temperature must be between 140 and 250 degrees F. Coolant temperature must be between 165 and 210 degrees F.
- Parking brake should hold vehicle on any grade likely to be operated.

- Low air pressure warning devices should operate at all pressures at and below 60 psi.
- Speedometer should work accurately.
- Make sure horns work.
- Clean windshield. There should be no cracks over $\frac{1}{4}$ inch wide or damaged areas larger than $\frac{3}{4}$ inch.
- Make sure windshield wipers and washers work and add washer fluid if needed.
- Adjust rear view mirrors to show highway along both sides of vehicle.
- Trailer air supply control should stay in when pushed.
- Cab should be equipped with seat belts.
- Emergency equipment should be within ready reach. The fire extinguisher shall have been inspected within the last 12 months. The cab should be equipped with spare fuses and three red emergency reflectors or triangles.
- If snowy or icy conditions are expected, there should be tire chains for at least one driving wheel on each side.
- Make sure both high and low beams on headlights work.
- Make sure brakes are adjusted properly.
- Check for proper operation of front clearance lights, identification lamps and turn signals as required by Sec. 393 Part B, FMCSR.
- Check exhaust system for leaks, charring or damage to electrical wiring, fuel supply or other combustible part of the vehicle.
- Service and emergency air hoses and connections must be secured against chafing, kinking or other damage and must not drag on the frame, fuel tank or deck plate. Tape must not be used to secure these components.
- No tire shall have fabric exposed through the tread or sidewall, nor less than $\frac{2}{32}$ inch tread depth. Front tractor tires must have at least $\frac{4}{32}$ inch tread depth.
- Check wheels for cracks, or missing or loose studs or nuts.
- Secure brake tubing against chafing, kinking or other mechanical damage. Check for leaks.
- Brakes must have adequate brake lining on all wheels.
- Check for cracked or broken brake drums, diaphragms or other chamber leaks. Have missing, broken or disconnected parts repaired before vehicle is operated.
- Check steering for loose or missing nuts or bolts. Check for excessive play. Excessive play is present when too much movement is required at steering wheel before front wheels move from straight-ahead position. For trucks with manual steering, free play should not exceed $2\frac{1}{2}$ inches on a 20-inch steering wheel ($5\frac{1}{4}$ inches of free play is acceptable if you have power steering). For 22-inch steering wheels, the maximum free play is $2\frac{3}{4}$ inches with manual steering, $5\frac{3}{4}$ inches with power steering. Hard steering must be repaired before vehicle is operated.

- Fuel tank must be free of leaks, and have a securely attached cap with gasket.
- Check side marker lamps and reflectors for proper operation as required by Sec. 393 Part B, FMCSR.
- Battery must be covered unless located in engine compartment or covered by a fixed part of the vehicle. Cable ends should be clean and fit tightly on clean terminal posts.
- Check rear tractor lamps and reflectors as required by Sec. 393 Part B, FMCSR.
- Check suspension for broken leaves and missing or loose U-bolts. Defects likely to cause an axle shift must be repaired before vehicle is operated.
- Lower half of fifth wheel must be secured and must not shift on frame. Cracks, breaks, loose or missing mounting brackets or locking devices must be repaired before vehicle is operated.

fig. 18-1
Check to see that the vehicle has the required lamps and reflectors, and that they are all operating.

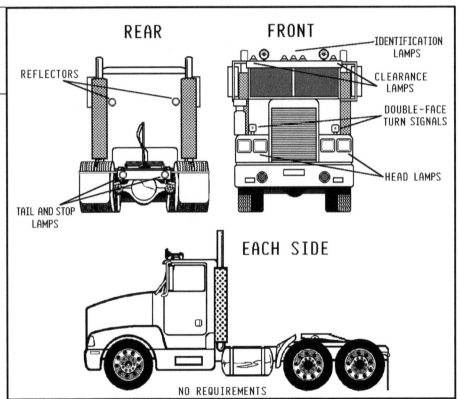

Towed Unit

- Check lamps and reflectors at rear of towed unit for proper operation as required by Sec. 393 Part B, FMCSR.
- Check tires. No tire shall have fabric exposed through the tread or sidewall, nor less than $\frac{2}{32}$ inch tread depth.
- Check wheels for cracks, or missing or loose studs or nuts.

- Secure brake tubing against chafing, kinking or other mechanical damage. Check for leaks.
- Brakes must have adequate brake lining on all wheels and be properly adjusted.
- Check for cracked or broken brake drums, diaphragms or other chamber leaks. Have missing, broken or disconnected parts repaired before vehicle is operated.
- Check side trailer marker lamps and reflectors for proper operation as required by Sec. 393 Part B, FMCSR.
- There must be no bare, loose, dangling, chafing or poorly connected electrical wires.

As you can see, this company's program of checks includes the inspection required by DOT regulations, and then some.

fig. 18-2
Required lamps and reflectors for towed units.

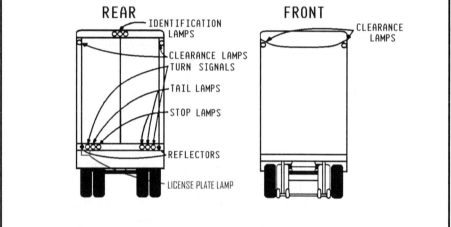

Types of Service Checks

We've talked about your role in finding small problems and getting them repaired before they become big, expensive ones. But that's not all there is to preventive maintenance. There's another aspect to PM. That is when you **give the vehicle service, before it needs repair.** It's **replacing parts before they wear out, or give out.** Here's where the Maintenance Department, and scheduled service, comes in.

There are **different levels of service** for the vehicle being driven. They range from taking care of the very basic needs to doing a major overhaul. The most basic is the A level of service. Next is the B level, then the C level.

A vehicle is scheduled for service on the basis of time, or miles, or a combination.

Often, vehicles may come due for service while drivers are out on the road. Their employer will have given them instructions about what to do in such a case. They may be told to wait until they return to the terminal, or to get it done en route. They may be directed to a particular garage, or told to get the service at a truck stop on their route.

The following will give you a clear idea of what takes place in the different levels of service provided in a good program of preventive maintenance.

PRE-SERVICE CHECK

Before a truck is brought in for service, there are some checks and minor repairs you should (or could be required to) make. Many will be covered by the driver's daily service check we outlined in the last section. Here are some others.

Check the starter and charging systems. If the dashboard has a voltmeter, it will read around 11 to 15 volts all the time. If it has an ammeter, it should show a charge right after starting, and when lights and other electrically-powered accessories are in use. Once the engine is started, the alternator should be putting power back into the batteries. The maximum amount of charge should be around 75 amps and no more than 15 volts. You're not likely to see even these maximums unless it's really cold outside or the truck has been sitting for some time. If you do, something's wrong, which calls for further checks.

Inspect the batteries and cables for corrosion. This is probably the most overlooked part of the truck. Starting with the negative side, pull the cable end off the posts. Check for corrosion inside and out, and up inside the insulation cover. Bad cables should be replaced. The insulation will be swollen if there is corrosion under it. Then check the water level in the battery. Even "maintenance free" batteries can run dry. Fill batteries with distilled water. Use tap water only in an emergency. Put the cables back in place tightly, starting with the positive one. These simple steps just might solve the problem, and save some vehicle down-time.

If the batteries and cables are in good shape, and you still have a problem, it could be the regulator or the alternator. The voltage could be set too low. Adjust the voltage regulator as necessary.

Next, with the engine running, **check the air compressor and governor.** If you listen carefully to the engine, you can hear when the compressor is working, and when the governor cuts out. Your first check is to see that the air pressure builds from zero to 120 psi within five minutes at the most. The governor should cut out with a range of 115 to 130 psi. Stab and release the brakes until the compressor comes on. The governor should cut in again at 100 psi. Faulty operation calls for further attention.

Check the clutch for free play. Move the clutch pedal with your hand or foot. It should start moving easily, then get harder and harder to move. The distance from the pedal's normal position to where it resists movement is the amount of free play, and it should be between one inch and $1\frac{3}{4}$ inch. The company you work for may want all the clutch adjustments to be made by the mechanics only, rather than the drivers.

The driver's daily service check may have turned up problems with wander in the steering. This could be due simply to a low front tire. You may be able to air up the tire and fix the steering problem with no need for further service.

With the engine stopped, check the engine compartment. **Look for cracked or worn belts.** Pull on them to see if they're too loose. Look for exhaust leaks around the exhaust manifold and turbocharger. A black streak is a sign of a leak. You'll want to see that this gets fixed for sure. Exhaust fumes leaking into the cab could make the driver sleepy or sick, and lead to an accident.

A-LEVEL SERVICE

The A-level service is the **most basic** type of service that can be done. It includes checks and adjustments which a driver could take care of without any trouble. However, a large carrier company is likely to have the A-level service done on a regular basis in the company shop.

The three primary tasks that are taken care of at this level of service check are:

- the tire inspection
- brake inspection
- fluid level checks

The fluid levels which should be checked are the oil, water, power steering, windshield washer and battery.

Brakes are inspected to ensure both the proper application and release. During a brake adjustment, wheel seals can be checked to see that they are not starting to leak or seep. Brake drums can also be checked to make sure that they are not cracked.

An air pressure check is also included in the A-level check. Under DOT regulations, a tractor-trailer is not to lose more than 3 to 4 pounds of air pressure in one minute when the engine is turned off and the service and spring brakes are released and the foot (service) brakes are applied to 90 psi. If there is an air leak, repairs can be made at this time.

Tires are checked for proper inflation, and also for tread depth and any uneven or unusual wear patterns. Tread depth must comply with federal safety regulations. Dual tires should also be equal in height to prevent one tire from doing all the work.

Other tasks which are a part of the A-level service include a check of the boxes: transmission and differentials. The vehicle is also checked for any leaks which may be present. The U-joints are checked and so is the safety equipment: flares, the triangle reflectors and the fire extinguisher.

B-LEVEL SERVICE

Now, let us take a look at the B-level service. To start with, **everything that takes place in the A-level service also takes place at the B level.** This **additional service includes changing the oil, oil filter and fuel filter.**

Today's engines are for the most part equipped with two oil filters. One is the primary filter which is commonly called the full flow filter. The second filter is known as the "by-pass" filter. The full flow filter collects all of the larger pieces of debris that collect in the oil. The "by-pass filter" is a finer filter than the full flow filter and filters out even finer bits and pieces of debris trapped in the oil system.

When the oil is being changed, a sample of the old oil may be sent to a laboratory for testing. The tests show the amounts of coolant, iron, aluminum, dirt and other forms of debris found in the oil. This debris is scrapings from the engine, the result of wear and tear on various parts. Such tests can reveal much about the condition of the inside of the engine. Your employer may have a schedule as to when oil should be sampled and tested or its condition simply monitored.

Fuel filters are changed one at a time and they should be changed on a regular basis. Their function is to filter out any water or other foreign matter which may be present in the fuel. Clean fuel helps protect the engine.

HIGHER LEVELS OF SERVICE

Other levels of service for the motor vehicle **begin with** the services included in the **A and B levels,** and go on from there. Advanced service levels **include engine tuning, brake change and changing or rebuilding other components** when called for by wear or failure.

Tuning the engine calls for running the overhead. When this should be done varies, depending on the manufacturer. It involves adjusting valves and injectors. This service is necessary because of the wear and tear placed on the valve stems of the valves and rocker arms. If this adjustment is not made on a regular basis, the result will be a drop in fuel efficiency and possible damage to the engine.

A brake change must be taken care of whenever the lining on the brake shoes reaches $\frac{5}{16}$ or $\frac{1}{4}$ inch in thickness. In the case of trucks that do the same kind of runs day in and day out, the brakes are sometimes changed on a routine basis based on a predetermined amount of miles traveled.

With today's trucks, engines will run strong for a distance of anywhere between 300,000 to 500,000 miles or more. Transmissions and rear ends will generally hold up for a distance of over a million highway miles.

When an engine is being rebuilt or when engine components are being changed, the radiator is removed and sent to a radiator shop where it will be cleaned both inside and out. This will insure maximum cooling power for the new engine. This is vital to the life of an engine as overheating a new engine can shorten the length of time it could be expected to operate by one half or more.

There are some parts which will go unchanged during this program of regular maintenance. These items include the alternator, starter and water pump, just to name a few. This is because these components are not subject to much wear. An alternator could last the lifetime of the truck. It would only be changed if it were faulty.

Winterizing and Summerizing

Every vehicle should get special attention for adverse weather conditions. If you'll be driving in very cold weather, you should make sure the tire chains are in good condition. Know how to put them on. Also:

- check the antifreeze level
- make sure the heaters and defrosters work
- use windshield washer antifreeze

For very hot weather:

- double-check the engine oil supply
- check the antifreeze level
- double-check the condition and tightness of the drive belts
- double-check the condition of the coolant hoses

Cleaning the Truck

A clean truck can be a big help to you in doing inspections and preventive maintenance. It's easier to see early signs of wear on a clean truck.

Keep the engine clean as well. Before the cleaning, note any fluid leaks or spots. A steam-cleaned engine will clearly reveal bright spots and rust on the metal parts, signs of premature wear or poor adjustment. Steam-cleaning isn't cheap, but it's cheaper than an engine overhaul. And that's the point of preventive maintenance.

Chapter 18 Quiz

For Questions 1 through 5, study the tractor sketched below. The arrows point to sites you would inspect as part of the driver's daily service checks. Match those sites, listed in Column A, with the checks you would be making at those points, listed in Column B.

Column A
Service Check Sites

1. _____

2. _____

3. _____

4. _____

5. _____

Column B
Service Checks

A. Check the coolant level in the radiator and add fluid if need be.

B. Check tread depth on tire.

C. Check steering wheel free play.

D. Check windshield wipers for proper operation and top up washer fluid if needed.

E. Check high and low beams on the headlights for proper operation.

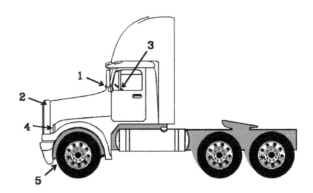

The Maintenance Supervisor for a large carrier is making out a service schedule for the company's trucks. His shop performs three levels of service, A, B and C, the highest level of service. Five different services are listed on the schedule below. Our Supervisor has put Xs in the boxes to show which services are to be performed at which level, but he hasn't finished the schedule. Complete it by answering Questions 6 though 10.

	A	B	C
brake inspection	X	?	X
check rear end for leaks	X	X	?
change fuel filter	?	X	
run the overhead	X	?	X
change the alternator			?

6. Should a brake adjustment be performed at level B?
   A. Yes
   B. No

7. Should the rear end be checked for leaks at level C, the highest level of service?
   A. Yes
   B. No

8. Should the fuel filter be changed at service level A?
   A. Yes
   B. No

9. Should service level B include running the overhead?
   A. Yes
   B. No

10. Should the alternator be automatically changed at level C, the highest level of service?
    A. Yes
    B. No

AIR CONDITIONING SYSTEMS

The Importance of Comfort Control

The cab of a truck is a driver's office – and home away from home. Of course drivers spend their working hours behind the wheel. When they're out on the road, they often spend their off hours in the cab's sleeper berth. You can see that they spend a lot of time in that truck. As you can imagine, they want to be comfortable. That means cool in hot weather, warm in cold weather and fresh air year-round. A failure in the cab's climate control systems can quickly ruin a driver's day, or night. **Drivers who are stressed by heat, cold or sleepless nights can't work effectively or safely.** They will greatly appreciate your attention to an air conditioning system that isn't working, or isn't working to capacity.

Going from the simple to complex, a cab's climate is controlled by:

- ventilation systems
- heating systems
- cooling systems

Ventilation Systems

Ventilation systems provide outside air to the cab. When the vehicle goes forward, it pushes against the outside air. **Vents** (when they're open) **allow** this **outside air to enter the cab.** This is **referred to as "ram air."** A heater/air conditioner blower can create this air movement when the truck isn't moving, or boost that air movement when the truck is moving. Some trucks have an electric motor-driven blower or ventilation fan. The **fan circulates the air around the inside of the cab.** You can reach this fan from the engine compartment or under the dashboard.

You may also find air-actuated cylinders that open or close vent gates and control how much air comes into the cab and how it's circulated.

Heating Systems

Heat is provided for the cab by the engine cooling system. The truck's heating system operates on the principle that heat always flows from a warm area to a cooler area.

Hot engine coolant passes through a heat exchanger. **A blower motor blows cool cab air into the exchanger.** In the heater core, **heat flows from the coolant to the cooler air,** much the same way that heat is transferred from the engine's radiator to the outside. A fan drives the warmed air into the cab. Control doors direct where the warmed air goes. A heater control (or coolant flow) valve controls the flow of coolant from the engine into the heater core. A thermostat regulates the coolant temperature.

You may find a heater in the cab on both the driver and passenger side, and in the sleeper. The sleeper unit may be separate from the cab heater.

A combination air conditioner/liquid-cooled heater provides heating, cooling, dehumidifying and defrosting functions in one unit.

The engine must be running, even if just at idle speed, **to power the heating system** just described. **Idling burns fuel and shortens engine life,** so truck owners aim to shorten idling time. Still, drivers want to be warm, even when the engine is shut down. One solution is a supplementary coolant heater. Controlled by a thermostat, it keeps engine coolant at a preset temperature, enough to keep the cab warm. These heaters work much like a common space heater but use diesel instead of kerosene.

Another option is an **auxiliary power unit** (APU). This consists of a separate onboard engine and power generator. An APU **uses a fraction of the fuel that the main engine uses when idling.** APUs willl not only run a heater but power an air conditioner and other onboard accessories like televisions and microwaves, too.

fig. 19-1
An auxiliary power unit uses only a small amount of fuel to power a heater, and other onboard accessories.
Photo courtesy of www.eere.energy.gov

Cooling Systems

Just as ventilation systems bring outside air into the cab, **truck cooling systems take heat from inside the cab and move it outside.** Refrigerants transfer heat away from inside the cab.

fig. 19-2
Latent heat causes a change of state without changing the temperature.

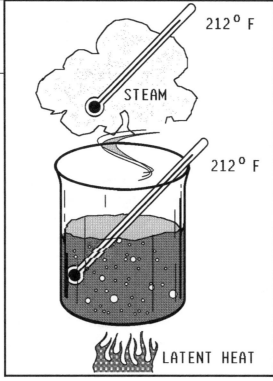

Cooling systems work on the principle of latent heat, and on changing matter from one state to another.

At any one time, **matter exists in one of three states: liquid, solid or vapor or gas.** Take water, for example. It can be ice (solid), water (liquid) or steam (gas), depending on its temperature.

When a substance changes from one state to another, it releases or uses heat energy. **Latent heat is the heat needed to change the state of a substance.**

When a fluid boils and changes from a liquid to a gas, it takes up heat without raising the temperature of the resulting gas. When a gas condenses and changes to a liquid, it gives up heat without lowering the temperature of the resulting liquid.

The heat described above is called latent (hidden) heat. Latent heat is the heat added to or taken from a substance which causes a change of state without causing a change of temperature.

At a certain point, **heat added to water** does not change the temperature of water. Instead, it changes the state of water. It **changes it from a liquid to steam or gas.** In the same way, at a certain point, **heat taken from water** does not change the temperature of the water. Instead, it **changes the state of water from liquid to ice (a solid).** Whenever a substance changes its state of matter, latent heat is involved. The heat seems "hidden" because it can't be measured by a thermometer.

Changing the state of a refrigerant in an air-conditioning system creates cooling because, as you've just read, **heat always moves from a warmer area to a cooler area.** Keep in mind that **cooling is** not a process of adding cold to something hot. It's **the process of removing heat.** Also,

- heat is absorbed when liquids are heated and become gas
- heat is released when gas condenses into a liquid.

The **temperature at which a liquid vaporizes or a gas condenses depends upon the pressure exerted on the liquid or the gas.**

The atmosphere, or air, around the earth presses down on the earth. At different elevations, air pressure differs. There is less air pressing down on Mount Everest than on Death Valley. If you've traveled much, you may have noticed that temperature at which water boils differs slightly in the mountains than at the shore.

The effect of **pressure is vital to the basics of cooling.** Liquid can vaporize, or become a gas, at high temperatures. A gas can condense, or become a liquid, at lower temperatures. The temperature at which a liquid becomes a gas or a gas becomes a liquid depends on pressure. In an open container (or vessel), water becomes a gas (steam) at 212 degrees Fahrenheit. But in a closed vessel, it can be heated two to three degrees hotter before it becomes a gas.

A closed container creates pressure because there is nowhere for the water to go as it turns to steam. As it turns to steam, the steam stays in the vessel and presses down on the remaining water. It will take longer for all of the water to turn to steam. The water will get hotter before it changes to steam.

That's how a pressure cooker works. A little water does a lot of cooking very quickly in a pressure cooker. That's also how a radiator cap works in engine cooling systems. It pressurizes the engine cooling system. Thus, the temperature at which the coolant will boil is raised.

Water under pressure gets hotter before it turns to steam. So, it can absorb more heat from other matter before it changes into a gas.

A cooling system is a closed system. Most cooling systems do not use water as a coolant. But the principle is the same. The coolant is in a closed vessel so it can absorb more heat from other matter before it changes into a gas. Then as it vaporizes, it takes more heat in the form of latent heat. It uses pressure and latent heat to create the cooling effect.

THE REFRIGERATION CYCLE

The cooling system cycles refrigerant through four stages. Refer to Figure 19-3, a diagram of the refrigeration cycle.

fig. 19-3
The refrigeration cycle.

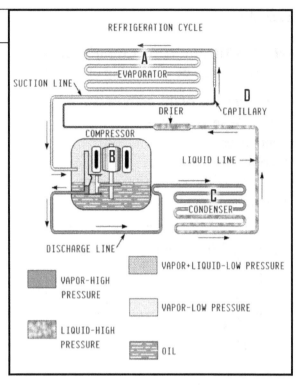

REFRIGERATION CYCLE

A
EVAPORATOR
SUCTION LINE
D
DRIER   CAPILLARY
COMPRESSOR
LIQUID LINE →
B
C
CONDENSER
DISCHARGE LINE

VAPOR-HIGH PRESSURE

LIQUID-HIGH PRESSURE

VAPOR+LIQUID-LOW PRESSURE

VAPOR-LOW PRESSURE

OIL

The arrows in Figure 19-3 show the direction of the coolant flow. A is the evaporator, B is the compressor, C is the condenser and D is the flow control device (an expansion valve, capillary tube or other metering device). Between the expansion valve and the evaporator the coolant is a low pressure liquid. The expansion valve allows the coolant to become a fine mist which can absorb heat better and vaporize (turn into a gas) more easily.

Between the evaporator and the compressor, the coolant is a low pressure gas. The evaporator changes the coolant from a liquid to a gas. The coolant absorbs heat from the cab air. The absorbed heat causes the coolant to boil. This point in the cycle creates the cooling in the cab.

At the compressor, the low pressure gas is changed to a high pressure gas. Some compressors operate similar to the air compressor in the air brake system. (Refer to Chapter 4.) You may find other types of pumps in use. The process of compressing the coolant creates heat.

This high pressure gas leaves the compressor for the condenser, which is a heat exchanger. Again, like the vehicle's radiator, the condenser is positioned in the vehicle's air flow and ram air cools the coolant. The engine cooling fan can also create this air movement. Heat moves from the coolant to the outside air. The coolant condenses from a gas to a liquid.

Between the condenser and the flow control device, it's a cooler, high pressure liquid.

So, to review the process, the compressor compresses the low pressure gas into high pressure gas. At the condenser, the coolant condenses from a gas to a liquid, releasing heat from the coolant gas to the outside air. Then the gas condenses to a liquid. The expansion valve changes the high pressure liquid into a low pressure liquid as it meters how much coolant goes into the evaporator. In the evaporator the heat inside the cab moves into the coolant. Removing heat from the cab creates the cooling effect. The coolant changes into a low pressure gas.

Pretty cool, huh?

REFRIGERATION CYCLE COMPONENTS

The high-pressure side is made up of the:

- discharge side of the compressor
- high-side service valve
- condenser
- receiver-dryer
- inlet side of the expansion valve
- hoses that connect the parts

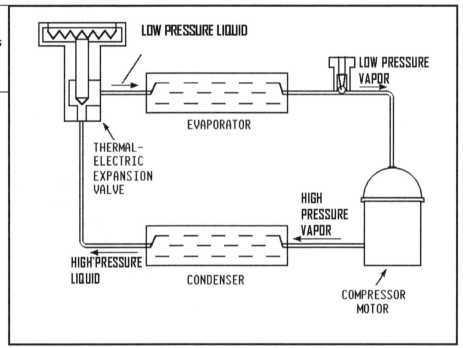

fig. 19-4
The thermostatic expansion valve divides the high pressure and low pressure sides of the refrigeration cycle.

LOW PRESSURE LIQUID

LOW PRESSURE VAPOR

EVAPORATOR

THERMAL-ELECTRIC EXPANSION VALVE

HIGH PRESSURE VAPOR

HIGH PRESSURE LIQUID

CONDENSER

COMPRESSOR MOTOR

The low-pressure side is made up of the:

- outlet side of the expansion valve
- evaporator
- suction side of the compressor
- low-side service valve
- hoses that connect the parts

REFRIGERANTS

The refrigerants in a cooling system are used because they

- boil at a low temperature
- change states easily.

Refrigerants are also required to have minimal impact on the environment.

The 1970 Clean Air Act gave the Environmental Protection Agency the authority to regulate **several substances determined to be toxic or hazardous to the environment.** The 1990 Clean Air Act added more substances to the list. This **included R-12, the refrigerant commonly used in truck air conditioning systems** and R-22, the refrigerant commonly used in trailer reefer systems.

R-12 was phased out and replaced by hydrofluorocarbon (HFC) R-134a.

R-22, the refrigerant used in reefer systems, is less harmful to the environment than R-12. It was therefore available for use in new equipment until 2005 and can be used in service and replacement until 2020. R-134a will not produce enough cooling for frozen cargo but will work for loads that simply must be kept cool.

Other alternative refrigerants and refrigerant blends continue to be developed and tested.

Propane is widely used as a reefer system refrigerant in Mexico, and is used in the refrigerators of recreational vehicles. It's not a threat to the environment if released into the air but it is highly flammable. Note that if propane is drawn into a recovery station, it will disable it.

The Clean Air Act greatly affects the work of mechanics servicing air conditioning systems. They must recover refrigerants like R-12 and not allow them to escape into the atmosphere. **Mechanics must observe practices that reduce refrigerant emissions.** By law, system leaks must be repaired according to the equipment's annual leak rate.

Perhaps most significant to you at this stage is that mechanics must be certified to work on refrigeration systems. Three organizations conduct recognized training programs leading to this certification:

- the Mobile Air Conditioning Society (MACS)
- the International Mobile Air Conditioning Association (IMACA)
- the National Institute of Automotive Service Excellence (ASE)

Though the systems look similar, R-134a is not a replacement for R-12. **Systems that used R-12 have to be retrofitted.** Different equipment must be used to service an R-134a system. Putting R-134a into a system meant to use R-12 will contaminate that system. (Besides, it's illegal to do so!) This would also damage service equipment. Contamination of an R-12 system with R-134a can mislead a troubleshooting mechanic.

Further, **mineral oil lubricants used with R-12 systems can't be used with R-134a.** The oil would drop out of circulation, reducing heat transfer and lessening the cooling. The compressor will lack for lubrication and moisture in the system will freeze. Instead, the lubricants polyalkylene glycol (PAG) and polyolester (POE or ester) are used.

COOLANT OIL

Coolant oil is used in a cooling system for two reasons. It lubricates the compressor and its motor. And, it cools the compressor.

Coolant oil is heated to extreme temperatures. So it must be able to stand extreme temperatures. The oil in a cooling system is also cooled to low temperatures. It must be able to stand that too. It must not damage the equipment. It must remain fluid in all parts of the system.

You can see that coolant oil must be a special kind of oil. First of all, it's dehydrated. That means as much water as possible has been removed from it. Water in a cooling system can cause more damage than any other substance.

Good coolant oil has:

- good miscibility
- low viscosity
- low wax content
- thermal stability
- low pour point

"Miscible" refers to how well coolant and oil mix. Some coolants mix well with oil. They **are miscible.** This is a plus. It means the parts that need oil will get oil. This protects the compressor. It means the evaporator will not get coated with oil.

Oil is more likely to separate from the coolant gas as the vaporizing temperature goes down. When the vaporizing temperature goes down, there is another effect. The viscosity of oil increases. **"Viscosity" is the ability of a fluid to resist flow or change of shape.** So as temperature decreases, oil tends not to flow. The **oil must have low viscosity.** That means it must flow even in the coldest part of the system. It must lubricate even in the hottest part of the system. The high miscibility of R-12 helps decrease problems with viscosity.

All oils contain some amount of wax. But a **good coolant oil has a low wax content.** If wax separates from the oil, it can cause problems. It can plug valves or flow control devices. The less wax in the oil, the less chance there is this will happen.

Coolant oil should remain stable as temperatures differ. This is called good thermal stability. The oil should not form hard carbon deposits at hot spots in the system. For instance, compressor valves are hot spots. Carbon deposits could plug the valves.

The **oil must remain in a fluid state.** It must remain in that state even in the coldest part of the system. This is called **a low pour point.**

As a service technician, you must be able to tell when oil is dirty. When you remove oil from a system, it should be clean. If it is discolored, it is impure. In that case, you may need to change the oil. Always use only oil that is suggested by the manufacturer. Always keep coolant oil tightly sealed. If it's exposed to the air, it will absorb moisture.

SAFETY

There are many safety rules to remember **when you work on truck cooling systems.** To be safe when working with coolants, follow your company's policies and guidelines for workplace safety.

One thing you **don't** want to **forget** is **that the engine is running.** It must be running to do some of the tests that are needed for proper service. Watch out for exhaust, moving belts, electrical shorts and other engine hazards.

Coolant isn't a danger if handled correctly. Even though it doesn't burn, when refrigerant contacts heat or flame, such as in an open flame leak detector, poisonous phosgene gas is created. Do not let the coolant container get hot. Temperatures at and above 125 degrees Fahrenheit can cause the coolant drum to explode. **Never heat a coolant drum.** Do not burn empty cans.

fig. 19-4
Wear safety goggles and gloves when working with coolants.

Wear safety goggles and gloves. Do not wear leather gloves as refrigerant can cause leather to stick to skin. If **liquid coolant** touches you, it **will freeze your skin.** The coolant boils and evaporates very quickly. That causes frostbite. Frostbite can be treated. Pour cool water on the area but don't rub the skin. Keep the skin warm with soft cloth.

Any contact with your eyes, however, is not so easy to treat. Serious eye damage or blindness can result. If coolant contacts your eyes, flush them immediately to raise the temperature above the freezing point.

Use large amounts of room-temperature water for at least 15 minutes. Go to the doctor without delay.

Always discharge coolant slowly and properly. If you discharge the coolant too quickly into the system, some of the coolant oil will be pushed out of the compressor. That will lead to compressor damage.

Under Clean Air Act regulations, **refrigerants must be recovered and recycled.** The service facility in which you work should have the equipment required for this. Note that when coolant is released into the air, it takes up space rapidly. That means it displaces the air. In a small, closed room you could suffocate. **Always keep the air moving when you work with coolants.**

Do not charge the system with liquid coolant when the compressor is running. In fact, never open a coolant drum to the high-pressure side of a cooling system when the unit is running. The drum can explode at pressures above 170 psi. The normal pressure for the high-pressure side is 250 to 270 psi.

Keep coolant drums right side up when you charge a system. If the drum is on its side or upside down, liquid coolant might enter the unit. If liquid coolant gets into the compressor, it will damage the compressor.

Do not bend or twist lines. Service technicians who are careless sometimes bend or twist the metal lines when they service a system. This can cause cracks, broken lines and loose connections. That leads to a loss of coolant which can cause injury or damage. Don't be a careless technician. Take care not to bend or twist the metal lines when you service a system.

Chapter 19 Quiz

1. A truck's ventilation system works only if the truck is moving.
   A. True
   B. False

2. The truck's heating system operates on the principle that _____.
   A. heat flows from a cooler area to a warmer area
   B. heat flows from a warmer area to a cooler area
   C. matter never changes its state
   D. latent heat causes a change in temperature

3. Heat is provided for the cab by _____ .
    A. air-actuated cylinders
    B. the engine heating system
    C. the engine cooling system
    D. a kerosene space heater

4. Auxiliary power units can _____ .
    A. warm the cab
    B. cool the cab
    C. run accessories like microwaves
    D. all of the above

5. Cooling systems work on the principle of latent heat.
    A. True
    B. False

6. The temperature at which a liquid vaporizes or a gas condenses depends on the_____ .
    A. atmospheric pressure
    B. ram air
    C. coolant
    D. heat source

7. Just before the coolant goes into the evaporator, it flows through the _____ .
    A. compressor
    B. receiver
    C. expansion valve
    D. condenser

8. Refrigerants used in cooling systems should _____ .
    A. boil at high temperatures
    B. do not change states easily
    C. have little impact on the environment
    D. conform to ASE regulations

9. Good coolant oil _____ .
    A. is not miscible
    B. has high viscosity
    C. has a high pour point
    D. none of the above

10. To be safe when working with coolants, _____ .
    A. wear leather gloves
    B. keep the area well-ventilated
    C. turn off the vehicle's engine
    D. release the coolants into the air

CHAPTER 20

EMISSIONS

The End of the Story

Black clouds of **smoke billowing from the exhaust stacks** may once have been a recognizable symbol of the heavy truck. Soon, that **may be a thing of the past.** With every passing year, the interest in having clean air grows stronger. As far back as 1955, the **federal government has acted to control air pollution.** Heavy trucks were found to be major contributors of **polluting gases** and **particulate matter**, the fine powder that turns exhaust into black smoke.

Particulate matter – PM – is a complex **mixture of dry solid** fragments, **solid cores with liquid coatings and small droplets of liquid.** These tiny particles can be made up of many different materials such as metals, soot, soil and dust. They not only dirty the air outside the truck. U.S. Environmental Protection Agency (EPA) studies have shown disturbing levels of particulate matter inside the cab.

fig. 20-1
Particulate matter is what turns a truck's exhaust into black smoke.

To limit or reduce pollutant emissions from diesel vehicles, the **EPA regulates** both the **quality of on-road diesel fuel** and the **pollutant emission levels from engines** under the authority of the Clean Air Act. In addition, many states test the smoke put out by trucks as part of inspection programs for control of PM emissions.

The pursuit of clean air addresses many factors. Three have had a noticeable impact on the equipment, the driver and of course, the diesel mechanic.

Nitrogen Oxides

In the chapter on engines, you learned about the **internal combustion** process. In brief, air is compressed inside the cylinder of a diesel engine. Diesel fuel is injected into the engine's cylinders. The piston compresses the air in the cylinder. This increases the air's temperature enough to ignite the fuel. **When** the diesel fuel ignites, the air gets hotter yet. It **expands and pushes the piston down, rotating the crankshaft. That's the power cycle** in a nutshell.

fig.20-2
Smog causes serious damage to the environment and the health of anyone who breathes it.

Higher temperatures mean a **more efficient engine** and **good fuel economy.** However, those high temperatures can **cause gases** to combine. Nitrogen and oxygen combine **to form nitrogen oxides**, or NOx. Those NOx compounds have become more of a concern. That's because when they leave the engine through the exhaust system, those gases combine with the atmosphere. **Too much NOx in the atmosphere creates smog. Smog** is not just an ugly nuisance. It **causes serious damage to the environment, and** to the **health** of anyone breathing the polluted air.

Since 1979, the EPA has regulated NOx emissions from diesel engines. Diesel engine manufacturers have had to come up with new technologies to meet the standards. In October of 2002, new NOx standards required the diesel engine industry to introduce additional technology.

As you have seen, high cylinder temperatures cause NOx. Therefore, **NOx** can be reduced by lowering cylinder temperatures. This can be done by limiting the amount of oxygen in the cylinder. That creates lower cylinder temperatures which in turn leads to less NOx being formed.

One way to do this is to **recirculate some exhaust gas into the cylinder** – EGR for short.

COOLED EGR SYSTEMS

In a cooled EGR system, exhaust gases flow through a transfer pipe to the EGR cooler. Water from the **truck's cooling system cools** the

exhaust gases. The **cooled exhaust gases** then **flow** through the EGR transfer pipe **into the intake manifold.** A cooled EGR system could require the use of costlier oils and might lead to shorter engine life.

INTERNAL EGR (NON-COOLED EGR)
Changes in valve timing allow exhaust gas to simply remain in the cylinder and mix with the incoming air. Internal EGR is inefficient and reduces fuel economy. It's used primarily in off-road vehicles.

VARIABLE GEOMETRY TURBOCHARGER
A variable geometry turbocharger has moveable vanes that allow the engine's electronic controls to adjust the exhaust pressure in the system. This ensures that there is always enough pressure for adequate EGR flow.

REED-VALVE TECHNOLOGY
This technology does not use a turbocharger. It relies instead on normal exhaust gas pulses in the exhaust manifold to push exhaust gases through the EGR cooler and into the intake manifold. A one-way valve in the EGR transfer pipe allows exhaust gases to enter the intake manifold, but keeps the incoming fresh air from entering the exit manifold.

These exhaust and cooling systems can add up to about 300 pounds to the weight of the truck.

fig. 20-3
Exhaust gases flow through a transfer pipe to the EGR cooler.

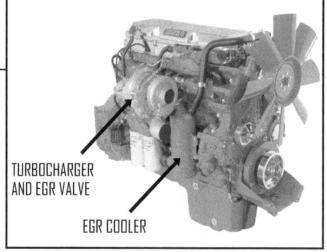

TURBOCHARGER AND EGR VALVE

EGR COOLER

Sulfur

In December 2000, **EPA** published additional standards for on-road heavy-duty diesel engines that would take effect beginning in 2007. These standards apply to diesel-powered vehicles with gross vehicle weight rating (GVWR) of 14,000 pounds or more. Heavy-duty diesel-engine trucks are required to put out greatly reduced emissions of NOx, particulate matter and hydrocarbons. The **standards** also **required** that the **sulfur content of transportation diesel fuel oil** produced by domestic refineries **be drastically reduced** by 2007.

Ultra-low sulfur diesel is crucial to the successful development of emission control equipment for heavy-duty diesel engines. **Sulfur can contaminate catalysts used in meeting the emission standards**. (A catalyst is a substance that changes another substance or process without being changed itself.) ULSD was to be completely phased in for both on-road and off-road U.S. vehicles by June, 2007. Model Year 2007 and newer diesel engines were required to use high-efficiency catalytic exhaust emission control devices or other approaches that would be just as effective. On-highway diesel fuel sulfur levels were required to be less than 15 parts per million (reduced from 500 ppm) starting in June 2006. The combination of the **new diesel engines and** the **lower sulfur diesel fuel** would **result in reduced emissions** to the atmosphere. This fuel can be used in all diesel engines with little or no modification to the engine or fuel system.

The primary benefit of using ULSD is emissions reduction. Using ULSD fuel without particulate filters or oxidation catalysts could provide up to a 13 percent reduction in PM, a 13 percent reduction in hydrocarbons (HC), a 6 percent reduction in carbon monoxide, and a 3 percent reduction in nitrogen oxide (NOx). If ULSD is used with particulate filters or oxidation catalysts, the reductions are 20 to 80 percent in PM, 90 percent in (HC), 90 percent in carbon monoxide (CO) and 15 to 20 percent in NOx.

Several diesel fuel properties other than the sulfur change as a result of moving to ULSD:

- lubricity
- energy content
- cetane number

LUBRICITY

Lubricity is a measure of the fuel's ability to lubricate and protect the various parts of the engine's fuel injection system from wear. The **processing** required **to reduce sulfur** to 15 ppm also **removes naturally-occurring lubricity** agents in diesel fuel. To manage this change the American Society for Testing and Materials (ASTM) adopted the lubricity specification defined in ASTM D975 for all diesel fuels and this standard went into effect January 1, 2005.

Additives or blending ULSD with biodiesel **increases** the **lubricity** of ULSD. Biodiesel itself is an alternative to conventional Number 2 diesel fuel. You'll read about biodiesel in greater detail later in this chapter.

Other potential issues with ULSD are the cold flow properties. In cold weather, **the cloud point of ULSD is higher** than conventional diesel. Therefore, ULSD may require added precautions, such as additives or heated storage tanks.

ENERGY CONTENT

The same **processing required to reduce sulfur** to 15 ppm also reduces the aromatics content and density of diesel fuel. (Aromatics are a characteristic of molecules.) This **results in** a **reduction in energy content.** The reduction is about a one percent and may affect fuel mileage.

CETANE NUMBER

This **same processing causes** an **increase to the cetane number.** The cetane number rates how quickly a fuel will ignite in a diesel engine. A fuel with a high cetane number will ignite quickly. This means better fuel economy and better engine performance.

EQUIPMENT CONCERNS

In some vehicles, using **ULSD causes fuel system leaks.** A leak in the fuel system can be dangerous. A fire could start if diesel fuel comes in contact with hot engine parts. The leaks seem result from the combination of the changed aromatics content, the material and age of the seals. **Seals may need to be inspected and replaced more often.**

Pre-2007 engines can use the same motor oil as before. However, Model Year 2007 engines and newer with an EGR engine, diesel particulate filter and running ULSD should use an API (American Petroleum Institute) CJ-4 heavy duty motor oil.

HYDROCARBONS

Clean air standards require stricter control of hydrocarbons (HC) as well as **NOx** *and **PM.** The NOx and HC standards began phase-in at 50 percent of new vehicle sales in model years 2007 through 2009. In 2010, all new on-road vehicles are required to meet the NOx and HC standards.

Particulate Matter

The biggest change in the 2007 **emission-compliant engines** is the addition of **filters** and systems **to trap PM.** These filters **must be cleaned,** or "regenerated," from time to time. Raising the exhaust temperature above 1,200 degrees F. will achieve this.

In most cases, this **will happen automatically** as the driver operates the vehicle. Driving conditions usually create exhaust temperatures that are hot enough. However, stop-and-go driving and cold weather could lead the filter to clog. These filters might need more than an occasional regeneration. A sensor or alert will warn the driver that the filter will have to be regenerated within the next 60 miles. If **drivers** can't get on the highway and raise the temperature and pressure enough to start the automatic regeneration, they **can force regeneration.** They can park the vehicle and increase the engine RPMs to create enough heat for regeneration. You may find that the drivers using the vehicles that you service need some help to understand the equipment's special demands.

The EPA mandates a minimum diesel particle filter service interval of 150,000 miles.

Alternative Fuels

ULSD is one alternative to conventional number 2 diesel fuel. **Four other alternatives** are:

- number 1 diesel fuel
- compressed natural gas (CNG)
- propane
- biodiesel (B20)

NUMBER 1 DIESEL FUEL
Number 1 diesel fuel has lower sulfur than conventional number 2 diesel and, therefore, provides some emissions benefits. In addition to lower sulfur, the fuel has better cold flow properties than conventional diesel. This makes it a good alternative for cold weather operations.

Some potential drawbacks of Number 1 diesel fuel include **reduced lubricity**, which can be helped with additives, and **reduced fuel economy.**

COMPRESSED NATURAL GAS (CNG)
Natural gas is one of the most common forms of energy used today. Compressed natural gas (CNG) is used in thousands of vehicles worldwide, including buses and some heavy trucks. This is mainly due to its lower cost and the fact it generates fewer exhaust and greenhouse gas emissions than gasoline- or diesel-powered vehicles.

Overall, **CNG offers lower fuel costs, increased performance** and **emissions reductions.** Generally, CNG **costs** 15 to 40 percent **less** than gasoline or diesel fuel. In conjunction with the increased performance experienced by CNG vehicles, operators get a longer lasting, lower-operating cost vehicle. Emissions reductions are significant for CNG fueled vehicles at approximately 90 percent for CO, 35 to 60 percent for NOx and 50 to 75 percent for HC.

Two drawbacks exist for CNG vehicles: vehicle cost and fuel economy. The **increased vehicle cost** of $3,500 to $6,000 is primarily due to the higher cost of fuel storage cylinders. Also, CNG vehicles have to be fueled more often. This is due to the **lower energy content** of CNG.

PROPANE

Propane, or liquefied petroleum gas (LPG), has been used as a transportation fuel since the 1940s. Transit buses and trolleys sometimes use LPG. A few makes of heavy trucks can use propane as a fuel. Most vehicles that use this fuel are dual-use vehicles. They can switch between gasoline or propane fuel. The benefits of propane-fueled vehicles include cost and emissions reductions. The **cost of propane**, depending on market factors, is usually **close to gasoline**. Propane **can provide carbon monoxide and hydrocarbon emissions reductions.**

The primary drawbacks with propane vehicles are the cost of the vehicle and reduced fuel economy. Overall, **propane-fueled vehicles cos**t $3,000 to $5,000 **more** than gasoline-fueled vehicles. Additionally, these vehicles **get reduced fuel economy** compared to gasoline-powered vehicles.

BIODIESEL (B20)

"Biodiesel" is a clean-burning fuel containing **no sulfur or aromatic compounds.** It is produced from a number of renewable sources including soybean oil, rapeseed (canola) oil and animal fats. This isn't a new idea. Back in the 1890's, Rudolph Diesel, the engine's inventor, considered vegetable oil as a possible fuel. Fats and oils for biodiesel can be obtained from agricultural supplies or by recycling used oil like cooking grease. The most common form of biodiesel found in the United States is derived from soybean oil.

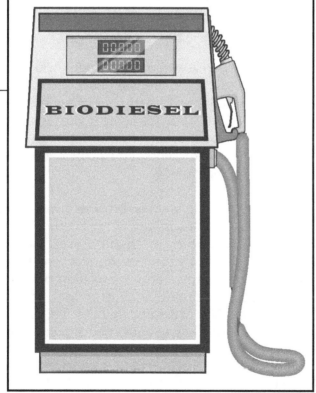

fig. 20-4 Biodiesel is a fuelt that is produced from renewable resources such as soybean oil.

Biodiesel can be used in its pure form, B100 ("neat biodiesel") or blended with conventional diesel. The most common blend is B20. It contains 20 percent biodiesel blended with 80 percent conventional diesel. The major advantage of B20 when compared to other alternative fuels is that it can be used in any diesel engine with little or no modification to the engine or fuel system.

Most Original Engine Manufacturers (OEM) have issued statements that support the use of biodiesel in certain percentages. However, **biodiesel could impact** certain **elastomers** (rubber-like materials) and natural rubber compounds in the fuel system. When biodiesel fuels are used, seals, hoses, gaskets and wire coatings should be inspected often. According to the National Biodiesel Board's experience, there is less impact on these components when using blends of 20 percent or lower. Currently, OEMs are switching to components suitable for use with low-sulfur and biodiesel fuel.

The benefits of B20 include **enhanced lubricity, fuel system cleaning properties and environmental benefits**. In addition to enhanced lubricity, biodiesel acts as a solvent and **cleans engine systems.** Note that this can cause fuel filter clogs when biodiesel is first used so fuel filters should be monitored.

A final advantage of using biodiesel is the environmental benefit. A 2002 EPA draft report indicated that soybean-based B20 **reduces particulate matter** by 10 percent, **hydrocarbons** by 21 percent and **carbon monoxide** by 11 percent. Nitrogen oxide is increased by 2 percent.

Potential **drawbacks of biodiesel** use **include cost, cold flow properties, fuel economy and shelf life.** The cost to add a percentage point of biodiesel to conventional diesel is one cent. Therefore, the additional cost to add up to 20 percent biodiesel, B20, to conventional diesel fuel is approximately twenty cents. As more refiners of this fuel enter the market, fuel prices should decrease.

Cold flow propblems arise when diesel fuel, including both biodiesel and conventional diesel fuels, are used in very cold temperatures. According to the United States Department of Agriculture, the cold filter plugging point of B20 is approximately 7 degrees warmer than with conventional diesel. However, this small increase in the temperature at which B20 starts to freeze compared to conventional diesel does not present problems for most users.

Another drawback of using biodiesel is **lower fuel economy.** Overall, conventional diesel contains more energy content, and therefore provides higher fuel economy than biodiesel. According to EPA, plant-based B20 contains more energy content than animal-based B20. This energy content has a direct relation on fuel economy with plant-based biodiesel providing better fuel economy than animal-based biodiesel. EPA estimates that the fuel economy penalty for B20 is between 1.6 percent (plant-based biodiesel) to 2.15 percent (animal-based biodiesel). However, B20 has a higher cetane number than conventional diesel and therefore has a shorter ignition delay period, resulting in less engine noise. It can be used without reducing engine reliability or durability.

A final potential issue with B20 is shelf life. The current industry standard is that biodiesel should be used within six months. Most fuel is used long before six months so this should not present a problem unless an operator is storing fuel for a long period of time. If this is the case, the fuel should be tested prior to use.

Emissions Programs

Cleaner air for all would seem to be a good enough reason to cut polluting emissions. If not, heavy penalties for not doing so provide another incentive to comply with the new standards.

The State of California charges fines for excessive smoke. They are:

- Notice of Violation: For pre-1991 vehicles that have smoke opacities greater than 55 percent but less than 70 percent and have not received a citation in the past 12 months, a Notice of Violation is issued. Similar to a "fix-it ticket," the Notice of Violation has no penalty if repairs are made to the engine and a Demonstration of Correction form is submitted to the Air Review Board within 45 days. Only one Notice of Violation may be issued to a vehicle within a 12 month period.
- If repairs are not made and a Demonstration of Correction form is not submitted within 45 days, a First Level citation will be issued. For pre-1991 engines with 70 percent or greater smoke opacity and 1991 and newer engines with greater than 40 percent opacity, that have not received any citations in the past 12 months a First Level Citation is issued. The penalty for a First Level Citation is $300 if engine repairs are made and a Demonstration of Correction form is submitted to the ARB within 45 days.
- The penalty is increased to $800 if repairs are not made and a Demonstration of Correction form is not submitted with the ARB within 45 days.
- Any further violations within a 12 month period earn a Second Level citation of $1,800. In addition, a Demonstration of Correction form must be submitted and the vehicle must be retested by the ARB in order to clear the citation.
- In extreme cases, the CHP may take a vehicle out of service for an outstanding citation if the penalty has not been paid, or if the vehicle has not been repaired.

In Connecticut, if a vehicle does not pass the minimum exhaust emissions as set forth by the Diesel Emissions Program, the vehicle operator will be fined $300 for the first offense and $500 for the second and any subsequent offenses. In addition to the fines, the owner of the vehicle will have to submit to the DMV documentation that the vehicle has been repaired within 45 days of the test date. Failure to repair the vehicle within the required 45 day period will lead to the suspension of the vehicle's registration.

Other states and cities have similar programs.

Chapter 20 Quiz

1. Heavy truck emissions add _____ to the air.
   A. NOx
   B. PM
   C. HC
   D. All of the above

2. To reduce pollutant emissions from diesel vehicles, the EPA regulates the _____ of diesel fuel.
   A. quantity
   B. quality
   C. price
   D. importation

3. Nitrogen oxide production can be reduced by _____.
   A. lowering engine cylinder temperatures
   B. limiting the amount of oxygen in the cylinders
   C. recirculating exhaust gas into the cylinders
   D. all of the above

4. An advantage of ULSD over Number 2 diesel is USLD's _____.
   A. higher lubricity
   B. higher energy content
   C. higher cloud point
   D. reduced pollutant emissions

5. Sulfur can contaminate catalysts used in heavy-duty diesel engine emission control equipment.
   A. True
   B. False

6. Particulate matter _____.
   A. can pollute the air in the truck cab
   B. is a liquid pollutant
   C. can regenerate a filter
   D. cannot be reduced by using ULSD

For questions 7, 8, 9 and 10, match the alternative fuel in the column on the right with the characteristic in the column on the left.

Fuel Characteristics	Alternative Fuel
7. requires costly fuel cylinders	A. Number 1 diesel
8. is comparable to gasoline in cost	B. compressed natural gas
9. has a lower sulfur content than conventional number 2 diesel	C. propane
10. acts as a solvent and cleans engine systems	D. biodiesel (B20)

Index

C

D

E

F

G

U

V

W

CPSIA information can be obtained
at www.ICGtesting.com
Printed in the USA
LVHW061022140922
728359LV00011B/231